INTERMEDIATE ACCOUNTING

VOLUME TWO

THIRD EDITION

THOMAS H. BEECHY
SCHULICH SCHOOL OF BUSINESS, YORK UNIVERSITY

JOAN E.D. CONROD
FACULTY OF MANAGEMENT, DALHOUSIE UNIVERSITY

PREPARED BY
ELIZABETH FARRELL
SCHULICH SCHOOL OF BUSINESS, YORK UNIVERSITY

SUSAN COHLMEYER
MEMORIAL UNIVERSITY OF NEWFOUNDLAND

McGraw-Hill
Ryerson

Toronto   Montréal   Boston   Burr Ridge, IL   Dubuque, IA   Madison, WI   New York   San Francisco   St. Louis
Bangkok   Bogotá   Caracas   Kuala Lumpur   Lisbon   London   Madrid   Mexico City   Milan   New Delhi   Santiago
Seoul   Singapore   Sydney   Taipei

Study Guide for use with
Intermediate Accounting
Volume 2
Third Edition

ISBN: 0-07-094397-4

1 2 3 4 5 6 7 8 9 10 CP 0 9 8 7 6 5

Printed and bound in Canada.

Care has been taken to trace ownership of copyright material contained in this text; however, the publisher will welcome any information that enables them to rectify any reference or credit for subsequent editions.

Executive Sponsoring Editor: Nicole Lukach
Developmental Editor: Suzanne Simpson Millar
Production Coordinator: Paula Brown
Supervising Editor: Anne Nellis
Printer: Canadian Printco, Ltd.

The authors gratefully acknowledge the permissions granted by the CICA, Atlantic School of CAs, Ontario Institute of CAs, CGAA, and CMA Canada to reprint selected material and cases.

Extracts from CGA-Canada Examinations Suggested Solutions/Examiner's Comments, published by the Certified General Accountants Association of Canada © CGA-Canada, 2005. Reprinted with permission.

STUDY GUIDE *for use with*
INTERMEDIATE ACCOUNTING, 3rd edition

VOLUME 2
TABLE OF CONTENTS

Chapter 12 Liabilities.. 1

Chapter 13 Shareholders' Equity... 29

Chapter 14 Complex Debt and Equity Instruments 59

Chapter 15 Accounting for Corporate Income Tax 86

Chapter 16 Accounting for Tax Losses 114

Chapter 17 Accounting for Leases... 136

Chapter 18 Pensions and Other Post-Retirement Benefits........ 181

Chapter 19 Earnings per Share 209

Chapter 20 Restatements 230

Chapter 21 Financial Statement Analysis.................................... 258

VOLUME 2
STUDY GUIDE *for use with*
INTERMEDIATE ACCOUNTING, 3rd edition

Thomas H. Beechy & Joan E. D. Conrod

Study Guide
prepared by

Elizabeth Farrell
Schulich School of Business, York University

Susan Cohlmeyer,
Memorial University of Newfoundland

EXCERPTS FROM TEXTBOOK PREFACE

What is intermediate accounting all about? There is a vast body of knowledge that must be mastered before you can account for the activities of an enterprise. Intermediate accounting is the nuts-and-bolts course where it all happens. Although a few topics are covered in greater depth in advanced accounting courses, virtually every important topic is included in an intermediate accounting course. Mastery of the content of intermediate accounting is crucial for anyone who hopes to either use or prepare accounting information.

Accounting in general involves a blend of technical know-how and professional judgement. So that's what *Intermediate Accounting* appropriately dwells on: technical knowledge and professional judgement, covering the range of corporate reporting topics.

In selecting material to include in this book, we have taken a fresh look at the realities of Canadian business practice. Accounting practices and policies have been in the public eye as never before, with both fraud and judgement issues causing material restatements. It's the perfect time to focus on judgement in accounting policy choice. In addition, there has been a tremendous explosion in accounting standards recently, and this text reflects many new standards. It also has a uniquely Canadian agenda.

Here's what this book reflects:

Introduction Each chapter has an introduction that explains the objectives of the chapter in narrative form.

Concept Review Throughout each chapter, there are periodic pauses for the student to stop and think through the answers to basic questions covering the previously explained material. This helps comprehension and focus! If you have trouble determining the correct response to the concept review questions, the answers can be found in the Study Guide and on the book's website.

Summary of Key Points At the end of each chapter, a summary of key points lists the key ideas explained in the chapter. This is meant to reinforce the chapter material.

International Perspective Most chapters include a review of international accounting policies, and differences that are found both internationally and in different countries. While the U.S. position is very important to us here in Canada, and is discussed when appropriate, there are many other countries around the world worth watching!

Integration of Cash Flow Material throughout the Text The cash flow statement (CFS) is reviewed in Chapter 5, following coverage of the income statement and balance sheet. Students can thus learn how to do the statement early in the course. Following this chapter, though, the cash flow implications of various complex transactions are reviewed in each relevant chapter. There is cash flow assignment material in most chapters of the book. For those instructors who like to emphasize cash flow material at the end of the course, an appendix has been added to the final chapter that summarizes cash flow statement issues and provides a comprehensive example. This is reinforced with assignment material in the last chapter.

Cases More than 80 cases are included in *Intermediate Accounting,* and there is at least one new case in every chapter in the third edition. The cases typically are not single-subject, paragraph-long "think pieces," but rather are meant to portray circumstances evocative of real life. Students have to put themselves into the situation and grapple with the facts and real users and uses to arrive at appropriate accounting policies for the circumstances. A blend of professional judgement and technical skills is needed to respond to a case. Case coverage is not limited to "one chapter" bites, but integrates material learned to date. For those trying to build a base of professionalism, the use of cases consistently over the term is highly recommended. Cases can be assigned for class debriefing, class presentations, or written assignments.

Assignment Material There is an extensive range of assignment material at the end of each chapter. The assignments give students the opportunity to learn by doing.
We have selected a few assignments from each chapter and put their solutions in the Study Guide and on the book's website; students can practise on their own. These selected assignments are highlighted by an icon in the margin. Excel templates for selected assignments have been developed; these assignments are marked with an icon in the margin.

Stars in the margins at the end of each chapter indicate length, with one star being the shortest assignment, and three stars being the longest assignment.

Integrative Problems From time to time in the book, there are integrative problems that formally deal with accounting topics covered in five or six chapters. These problems are a great pre-test review!

Ethics Material Ethics material has been incorporated into case material. Essentially, when an accountant makes a recommendation on a contentious choice of accounting policy, ethics are tested. We decided against putting in smaller ethics "vignettes," as it is always painfully obvious that the accountant is meant to take the high path and demonstrate good ethics. We feel that our students exercise more true-to-life ethical judgement when they have to make a tough judgement call and recommend an accounting policy that is "good" for one group but "bad" for another. Ethical overtones are highlighted in the case solutions to help instructors draw them out in discussion and evaluation.

The Accounting Cycle The basic debit and credit of the accounting world is hardly a topic for an intermediate accounting course. It represents the baby steps, and we're trying to learn how to run, or at least jog. For many students, this material was covered in a high school course or an introductory accounting course. Others, who avoided the course in high school and/or who took a conceptually oriented introductory course in college or university, may need grounding in this area. Therefore, we have included the accounting cycle as an appendix to Volume I, to allow maximum flexibility to instructors. Some courses may formally devote time to this appendix, and others may use it as a reference only.

TOPICAL HIGHLIGHTS OF THE TEXT

Chapters 12 and 13
These chapters deal with straightforward debt and shareholders' equity issues. The debt chapter looks at the always-challenging long-term debt issues, including material on effective and straight-line interest calculations. The financial instrument rules are integrated into these chapters. The new requirement for reporting other comprehensive income, including certain types of unrealized foreign currency gains/losses, is fully explained.

Chapter 14
Classification of debt versus equity, and appropriate treatment of hybrid financial instruments, are the topics in this chapter. Students learn how to determine the substance of a financial instrument, rather than its legal form, and account for it accordingly. Revised accounting standards for convertible debt are fully reflected in the material. Students also learn the nature of derivative instruments and why they are reported at fair value. The chapter then turns to accounting for stock options and provides an overview of the various circumstances in which options are granted. The two basic accounting paths, recognition and disclosure, are established. The chapter has complete coverage of the AcSB rules for employee stock options.

Chapters 15 and 16
Accounting for income tax remains two separate chapters, to acknowledge that many instructors prefer to spend two blocks of time on this most challenging area. The Chapter 15 material has been extensively rewritten to establish a three-step process for typical situations. The focus of Chapter 16 remains accounting for the tax effect of losses — carrybacks and carryforwards. This is difficult material for students, but the Chapter 16 problems incorporate the prior chapter material, and allow solid reinforcement of the steps associated with tax accounting.

Chapter 17
The leases material has been consolidated into one chapter, with appropriate focus on the lessee. Most companies lease something as a lessee, and thus lessee accounting is very commonly encountered in practice. Both the judgemental issues of lease classification and the complex calculations are extensively reviewed in this chapter, with examples.

Lessors, on the other hand, are rare. They tend to be quite specialized entities — financial intermediaries. Since lessors comprise a specialized industry, accounting by lessors is presented in a chapter appendix. The appendix includes an overview of the major aspects of lessor accounting and how it contrasts with lessee accounting. The appendix may be omitted if the instructor does not wish to deal with this specialized industry.

Chapter 18

Pensions and other post-retirement benefits are complex, long-term arrangements with employees. Accounting issues are also complex and have been structured in a worksheet format to improve clarity and comprehension. The worksheet has been carefully explained to help students — and instructors — get comfortable with this topic.

Chapter 19

Earnings per share material includes explanation of basic and diluted EPS. The procedural steps associated with organizing a complex EPS question are emphasized, to provide more comfort and support in this complicated area.

Chapter 20

Accounting policy changes and error corrections require restatement of one or more prior years' financial statements. Restatement is surely a current topic, given the number of fraud-based restatements reported in the public press over the last few years. This chapter deals with the theory and mechanics related to such restatement, reflecting new AcSB standards.

Chapter 21

The text concludes with a review of financial statement analysis, and emphasizes the importance of accounting policy choice and disclosure in the analysis of published financial statements. There is an extensive case illustration, based on a real Canadian company, that demonstrates the importance of accounting policy choice. This chapter also includes an appendix on the cash flow statement. The appendix summarizes the impact on the CFS of various transactions, and includes a comprehensive example. This appendix is meant to reinforce the CFS for instructors who like to deal with the statement as a stand-alone topic that reviews many topics within Intermediate Accounting.

ACCURACY

The text has been extensively reviewed and proofread prior to publication. All assignment materials have been solved independently by individual "technical checkers" in addition to the authors. Nevertheless, it is inevitable that a few errors remain, for which we accept full responsibility. If you find errors, please e-mail the authors at *j.conrod@dal.ca* or *tbeechy@schulich.yorku.ca*. There are thousands of calculations in this text — it's a daunting task to bring them to the degree of accuracy we'd like to be famous for. Your help will be greatly appreciated.

CHAPTER 12

LIABILITIES

What is a liability? Answering this question may appear obvious but many complications exist. This chapter reviews the common forms of debt. Chapter 13 discusses accounting for share equity. Chapter 14 discusses debt arrangements that have some attributes of debt and some attributes of equity.

1. WHAT IS A LIABILITY?

The liabilities of a business are its obligations (debts). A liability is defined in the *CICA Handbook*, paragraph 1000.33:

> (a) *...embodies a duty or responsibility to others that entails settlement by future transfer or use of assets, provision of services or other yielding of economic benefits, at a specified or determinable date, on occurrence of a specified event, or on demand;*
> (b) *the duty or responsibility obligates the entity leaving it little or no discretion to avoid it; and*
> (c) *the transaction or event obligating the entity has already occurred.*

CICA

The characteristics of a liability are:
- a highly probable *future* sacrifice of assets or services,
- constituting a *present* obligation,
- the result of a *past* transaction or event.

Matching of expense to revenue leads to the recognition of a liability as an offset to the expense. The obligation may be a general one, not necessarily to a particular party.

2. TYPES OF LIABILITIES

There are two basic types of liabilities, financial and non-financial. **Financial liabilities** (payables) are debt instruments that require some form of cash payment. They give rise to corresponding financial assets for another individual or company. Financial liabilities are measured at the fair value of the consideration received. If payments are to be received far in the future the cash flows must be discounted using the borrower's interest rate for debts of similar term and risk. If a liability does not meet the definition of a financial liability it is a non-financial one. Deferred revenues, and costs expected to arise in the future related to current periods are the common examples of non-financial liabilities. Assets retirement obligations are an example of a non-financial liability required to be recognized by the handbook.

Contractual obligations do not become liabilities until the service specified has been received. Contractual obligations may required disclosure even though they are not liabilities. The handbook identifies the required disclosure for contractual obligations.

A **contractual obligation** is a commitment that will become a liability in the future, once the event has occurred. Examples of contractual obligations are executory contracts and purchase agreements.

Valuation of estimated liabilities (usually non-financial) can be an issue. The liability exists but the amount is not known with certainty. If an estimate is not possible the liability cannot be recognized. This is unusual. Warranty liabilities, an example of estimated liabilities, are explained in your text. When estimates change the change is made prospectively. Estimated liabilities are classified as current or long term depending on their nature.

A **contingent liability** is one that will become a *real* liability only if and when another event happens.

The *CICA Handbook,* paragraph 3290.04, states:

In the preparation of the financial statements of an enterprise, estimates are required for many on-going and recurring activities. However, the mere fact that an estimate is involved does not of itself constitute the type of uncertainty which characterizes a contingency.

There are three possibilities for reporting contingent liabilities:
1. Accrue the estimated cost as a liability on the balance sheet and as a loss on the income statement.
2. Disclose in the notes to the financial statements.
3. Neither report nor disclose in the notes.

The accounting treatment depends on two characteristics:
1. Likelihood of the contingency occurring.
2. Measurability of the resulting liability or loss.

The table in the textbook shows how to apply the characteristics.

Typical, loss contingencies include the following: threat of expropriation of assets; pending or threatened litigation; actual or possible claims and assessments; guarantees of indebtedness of others, obligations of commercial banks under "standby letters of credit"; and agreements to repurchase receivables (or the related property) that have been sold (all of the above may be accrued). A **recurring operating contingent loss exposure** is one that normally exists in the business's operations. It merits no special reporting treatment. Examples: the risk of loss or damage of enterprise property by fire, explosion, or other hazards, general or unspecified business risk: and risk of loss from catastrophe assumed by property and casualty insurance companies, including re-insurance companies (not accrued).

Guarantees are contingent liabilities but are covered by a separate handbook section that require an extensive list of disclosures, the essence of which is provided in your text.

3. CURRENT LIABILITIES

A **current liability** is an obligation that is due within the next operating cycle or the next fiscal year, whichever is longer (usually one year (Section 1510)). Current liabilities are normally listed in descending order according to the strength of the creditors' claims. A common sequence is:
- bank loans
- other notes payable
- current portion of long-term liabilities
- trade accounts payable
- other payables
- accrued liabilities
- unearned revenues
- miscellaneous deferred credits

4. SOURCES OF SHORT-TERM FINANCING

The most obvious source of short-term financing is through trade credit extended by suppliers. Some purchases are made by signing a **promissory note** which obligates the company to pay the supplier. Short-term bank loans to businesses are usually **operating lines of credit** which are typically secured by a **lien** or charge on accounts receivable and inventory. These are usually due on demand but in practice are often a permanent fixture on a company's balance sheet.

Remember if a company's account frequently changes from positive to negative the overdraft is part of the cash and cash equivalents. **WATCH!**

5. LONG-TERM LIABILITIES

A **long-term liability** is a liability with repayment terms extending beyond one year from the current balance sheet date or the operating cycle of the borrower—whichever is longer. Long-term debt may include:
- bank loans
- notes payable
- mortgages
- other asset-based loans
- publicly issued bonds, secured or unsecured
- long-term leases

Term loans and commercial mortgages are common forms of long term bank financing. Repayment can be through blended payments or principal plus interest. Rates may be fixed or float. The rate may be fixed for the term of the loan but the amortization period may be longer.

Long-term leases are covered in Chapter 17, and financial instruments in Chapter 14.

Accounting for bonds and debentures is not complex and becomes easier by doing as many problems as possible. **WATCH!**

Covenants are conditions placed on a company as a condition of maintaining the loan. They can be accounting-based (e.g. maximum debt-to-equity ratio), or restricted actions (e.g. restrictions on dividend payments).

Some debt agreements require the establishment of a **sinking fund**, cash restricted to retire the debt.

6. ACCOUNTING FOR LONG-TERM DEBT

A **long-term debt** is recorded at the present value of the future cash flows, dis-counted at the effective interest rate. Interest is accrued as time passes, and principal and interest payments are accounted for as cash is disbursed.

Bonds are long-term liabilities, as they generally require repayment along with interest on the principal. Bonds have a *face value* and a *stated interest* rate. If the market interest rates are lower than the stated interest rates, the bond will trade at a *premium*. If the market interest rates are higher, the bond will trade at a *discount*.

The selling (market) price of a bond is the present value of all fixed future cash flows discounted at the effective (yield or market) interest rate.

PV = Present value of the bond.
= Present value of the face value + Present value of the periodic interest payments.

WATCH! To calculate the present value of the face value, use Table 1–2 at the end of the Textbook (Present Value of 1:P/F). Locate the appropriate "effective interest" column then follow it down to "number of periods". This will give you the factor you multiply the face value by.

WATCH! To calculate the present value of the periodic interest payments use Table 1–4 at the end of the textbook (Present Value of an Ordinary Annuity: P/A). Locate the "effective interest" column, then follow it down to the "number of periods". This will give you the factor you multiply the periodic interest payments by.

Illustration

A company sold and issued $150,000 of 4-year, 8% (payable semi-annually) bonds payable. The bonds were sold when the effective interest rate was 10%.

Required

Compute the price of the bonds.

Present value = PV of face value + PV of periodic interest payments.

Face value = $150,000

Periodic interest payments = $150,000 × 4% = $6,000 (stated interest = 8%, paid semi-annually = 4%)

Effective interest rate = 5% (annual rate of 10% divided by 2)

Periods = 8 (4 years times 2) (semiannually)

$$
\begin{aligned}
PV &= (\$150,000, P/F, 5\%, n = 8) + (\$6,000, P/A, 5\%, n = 8) \\
&= (\$150,000 \times .67684) + (\$6,000 \times 6.46321) \\
&= \$101,526 + \$38,779 \\
&= \$140,305
\end{aligned}
$$

The bonds were sold at a *discount* = ($150,000 − $140,305) = $9,695.

It is rare that a bond's market value will be the same as its face value or carrying value: **Premium** or **discount** on bonds is the difference between the face value and the present value of bonds.

WATCH!

The premium or discount is amortized to income as an adjustment to the interest expense over the life of the bond. There are two methods of amortization:

1. *Straight-line method.* An equal dollar amount of discount or premium is amortized throughout the bond term. This method is only acceptable when it the results are not materially different from the effective interest method.
2. *Effective interest method.* A constant effective rate of interest is maintained.

Your text provides examples of bonds selling at face value, at a premium and at a discount. Exhibit 12–3 in the text presents a summary table: Accounting for Bonds.

Interest Dates Differing from Statement Dates

When the accounting period ends between interest dates, it is necessary to accrue interest since the last interest date to the end of the accounting period.

Balance Sheet Classification

Long term loans are classified as long term on the balance sheet but the portion due within one year (or the operating cycle) is separated and classified in current liabilities. Accrued interest is also classified as current.

Bonds Issued Between Interest Dates

Bonds sold between interest dates are sold at the appropriate market price plus accrued interest.

Debt Issue Costs

Debt issue costs are not recorded in the initial recording of the liability. They are treated as a deferred charge and amortized separately. The straight line amortization methods is normally used.

Up-Front Fees

Up-front or administrative fees are often charged by lenders when granting a loan. The up-front fee increases the loan's effective interest rate. At the inception of the loan debit up-front costs as a deferred financing cost. As interest is recognized using the effective interest credit the deferred financing cost.

Liabilities Held for Trading

Financial liabilities held-for-trading are reflected at their fair market value. Only financial institutions have this type of liability.

7. DEBT RETIREMENT

Removing debt from the balance sheet is derecognition. It can occur at or before maturity. Financial liabilities are normally retired when due. The debtor is thus relieved of all the obligations related to the debt. However debt can be extinguished before maturity for a variety of reasons.

Derecognition at maturity is straightforward. There are no gains or losses to be recorded. When debt is extinguished early there may be a gain or loss. When interest rates drop a loss would occur. Accounting for early debt retirement involves the following:

- Updating interest expense, discount or premium, and related issue costs to the retirement date.
- Removing the liability accounts.
- Recording the transfer of cash, other resources, or the issuance of new debt securities.
- Recording a gain or loss.

When one bond is replaced with another **refunding** takes place. The gain or loss must either be :

1. Included in income in the year of refunding.
2. Amortized over the life of the old bond.
3. Amortized over the life of the new bond.

The Handbook does not provide guidance in this area. The decision will be made based on financial reporting objectives.

Defeasance is accomplished by placing assets in an irrevocable trust sufficient to pay the debt and obtaining agreement from the creditor that the liability is extinguished when the debtor makes the payments into the trust. When this happens the liability is treated as having been extinguished and no longer appears on the balance sheet. The defeasance gain/loss is the difference between the book value of the liability and the payment required by the defeasance agreement.

In-substance defeasance, a corporation places assets in an irrevocable trust for exactly the same purpose as described above for defeasance, but the creditors do not agree to release the company from any further liability relating to the debt. This practice is no longer available as a means of removing debt from the balance sheet.

8. FOREIGN EXCHANGE ISSUES

Many long-term loans are from foreign lenders This adds an additional form of risk to the borrowing and causes gains or losses when exchange rates fluctuate. Some companies hedge the loans by arranging equal and offsetting cash flow. This can be done through operating hedges or forward contracts.

9. ACCOUNTING FOR FOREIGN CURRENCY-DENOMINATED DEBT

Foreign currency monetary liabilities are reported on the balance sheet at the spot rate on the balance sheet date The exchange gain or loss (unrealized) is reported in net income. If the debt is hedged this changes.

10. INTEREST RATE RISK MANAGEMENT

Interest rates are hard to predict. Firms with a large volume of debt try to reduce the risk relating to interest rates by having a balanced portfolio of fixed and floating interest arrangements. An **interest rate swap** happens when two companies agree to pay each other's interest cost. The terms and conditions must be properly recorded and disclosed.

11. DISCLOSURES FOR LONG-TERM LIABILITIES

In the *CICA Handbook,* Section 3210 deals with long-term debt and Section 3860 deals with financial instrument disclosure and presentation. The disclosures include details of terms and conditions, interest rate risk, and fair values.

12. CASH FLOW STATEMENT

The textbook provides an example of the impact of a bond payable on the cash flow statement where there is a discount and a premium.

13. INTERNATIONAL PERSPECTIVE

The IASB requires fair value accounting only for financial liabilities held for trading (by financial institutions). Disclosure of fair value is however required for all financial liabilities. CICA standards are in agreement with international standards in this area.

TRUE–FALSE QUESTIONS

T F 1. A liability may be recognized and reported even though the exact amount of the liability is not known.

T F 2. The existence of a legally enforceable claim is not a prerequisite for an obligation to qualify as a liability.

T F 3. Legal, accounting, underwriting, commission, engraving, printing, registration and promotion costs relating to the issue to debt are included in the initial recording of the bond liability.

T F 4. A warranty is an example of a contingent liability .

T F 5. Dividends in arrears on cumulative preferred shares should be accrued as a current liability.

T F 6. Footnote disclosure is required for a lawsuit where it is likely but the amount cannot be determined.

T F 7. A guarantee is a type of contingent liability but special disclosure of guarantees is required.

T F 8. The cash interest payment on bonds should be calculated using the effective interest rate.

T F 9. Although a long-term liability is recorded at its present value, the carrying value of the liability should not be adjusted for subsequent changes in the market rate of interest.

T F 10. A premium related to a bond issue should be recorded as a deferred charge and reported as an intangible asset.

T F 11. The carrying value of a bond increases over the term to maturity if the bond is sold at a discount.

T F 12. The amortization of a premium by the effective interest method creates successive increases in interest expense over the life of the bond.

MULTIPLE CHOICE QUESTIONS

____ **1.** Liabilities are:
   a. any accounts having credit balances on the balance sheet.
   b. obligations to transfer ownership shares to other entities in the future.
   c. obligations arising from past transactions and payable in assets or services in the future.
   d. a contractual obligation such as purchase order issued for a specific item of inventory or equipment to be delivered in the future.

____ **2.** Which of the following typically would **not** be classified as a current liability?
   a. Bonds payable maturing within one year.
   b. A guarantee of the indebtedness of another party.
   c. Non-trade notes payable.
   d. Rent revenue received in advance.

___ 3. Assuming a bond is sold at a discount and the effective interest method is used as maturity approaches
   a. the unamortized amount decreases and the annual interest increases.
   b. the unamortized amount decreases and the annual interest decreases.
   c. the unamortized amount increases and the annual interest increases.
   d. the unamortized amount increases and the annual interest decreases.

___ 4. Which of the following contingent losses generally requires an accrual?
   a. Lawsuits with likely positive income of $500,000.
   b. Lawsuits with likely negative outcome.
   c. Environmental spill.
   d. Company is guarantor of loan.

___ 5. A loss on a purchase contract should be recognized if:
   a. the contract is either cancelable or noncancelable.
   b. the contract is noncancelable and the market price remains stable.
   c. the contract is noncancelable and the market price is higher than the contract price.
   d. the contract is noncancelable and the market price is lower than the contract price.

___ 6. The occurrence of a loss contingency is probable, but the amount cannot be reasonably estimated. The loss contingency should be:
   a. recorded.
   b. disclosed in notes to the financial statements.
   c. ignored.
   d. only a and b.

___ 7. John Corporation has $1,000,000 of notes payable due on April 1, 20x5. On January 2, 20x5, John signed an agreement to borrow up to $800,000 to refinance the notes payable on a long-term basis. On the December 31, 20x4, balance sheet, John should classify:
   a. $200,000 of notes payable as short-term and $800,000 as long-term obligations.
   b. $200,000 of notes payable as long-term and $800,000 as short-term obligations.
   c. $1,000,000 as short-term obligations.
   d. $1,000,000 as long-term obligations.

___ 8. During 20x4, Bowyer Company introduced a new product carrying a two-year warranty against defects. The estimated warranty costs related to dollar sales are 2% within 12 months following the sale and 4% in the second 12 months following the sale. Sales and actual warranty expenditures for the years ended 31 December 20x4 and 20x5, are as follows:

	Sales	Actual Warranty Expenditures
20x4	$300,000	$ 4,500
20x5	500,000	15,000
	$800,000	$19,500

At 31 December 20x5, Bowyer would report an estimated warranty liability of:
a. $28,500
b. $22,500
c. $8,500
d. $5,000

____ 9. Based on the same data as in question 8, what amount should Bowyer report as estimated warranty expense at December 31, 20x5?
a. $18,000
b. $30,000
c. $4,500
d. $48,000

____10. Daga Corporation, a manufacturer of household appliances, is preparing annual financial statements at December 31, 20x4. Because of a recently proven safety hazard in one of its toasters, the government has clearly indicated its intention of having Daga recall all toasters of this model sold in the last six months. The management of Daga estimates that this recall will cost $550,000. What accounting recognition, if any, should be accorded this situation?
a. No recognition.
b. Note disclosure only.
c. Operating expense of $550,000 and liability of $550,000.
d. Appropriation of retained earnings of $550,000.

____11. When bonds are issued between interest dates:
a. accrued interest since the last interest date is deducted from the market price and the bond issue.
b. the initial journal entry at issuance is unaffected by the time of sale.
c. the determination of the price of the bonds is simplified.
d. the entry to record the issuance of the bonds will include a credit to interest expense.

____12. A gain or loss from the early extinguishment of debt is based on the assumption that any gain or loss on the transaction reflects a(n):
a. adjustment to the cost basis of the asset obtained by the debt issue.
b. amount that should be considered a cash adjustment to the cost of any other debt issued over the remaining life of the old debt instrument.
c. amount received or paid to obtain new debt instrument and, as such, should amortized over the life of the new debt.
d. difference between the reacquisition price and the net carrying amount of the debt that should be recognized in the period of extinguishment.

___ 13. XBRL Inc. has debt denominated in a foreign currency. At the balance sheet date debt is reported at the spot rate for that date and assuming the rate has changed
a. the gain or loss is recorded in income.
b. the gain or loss is recorded in other comprehensive income.
c. the gain or loss is deferred and amortized over the period of the debt.
d. there is no gain or loss to report.

___ 14. The December 31, 20x3, balance sheet of Copper Corporation includes the following items:

8% bonds payable due December 31, 2x12	$500,000
Unamortized premium on bonds payable	9,000

The bonds were issued on December 31, 20x2, at 102, with interest payable on July 1 and December 31 of each year. Copper uses straight-line amortization.

On March 1, 20x4, Copper retired $100,000 of these bonds at 98 plus accrued interest. What should Copper record as a gain on retirement of these bonds? Ignore taxes.
a. $3,800
b. $3,767
c. $5,100
d. $2,433

___ 15. Jordan Company requires advance payments with special orders from customers for machinery constructed to their specifications. Information for 20x5 is as follows:

Customer advances — balance 31 December 20x4	$295,000
Advances received with orders in 20x5	460,000
Advances applied to orders shipped in 20x5	410,000
Advances applicable to orders cancelled in 20x5	125,000

At 31 December 20x5, what amount should Jordan report as a current liability for customer deposits?
a. $0
b. $220,000
c. $345,000
d. $370,000

SOLUTIONS TO TRUE–FALSE QUESTIONS

1. T

2. T

3. F These cost are debt issue costs are not included in the initial recording of the debt.

4. F A warranty is an estimated liability where the liability exists but the amount is not known with certainty.

5. F Dividends are not legal claims. They are only received if and when the dividends are declared. Dividends in arrears are disclosed in the notes.

6. T

7. T

8. F The stated rate is used to calculate the cash interest payment on bonds.

9. T

10. F Premium on bonds payable is classified as a contra account under bonds payable. This is to show the net carrying value of the bonds at the date of the balance sheet.

11. T

12. F The opposite happens: as the premium is amortized, the carrying value of the bonds decreases; therefore, the interest expense, which is based on the carrying value, decreases.

SOLUTIONS TO MULTIPLE CHOICE QUESTIONS

1. c The three conditions are met: entails future sacrifice of assets, constitutes a present obligation, and results from past transaction.

2. b This is a contingency that is not recorded but is reported in the notes to the financial statements.

3. c Assuming a bond is sold at a discount and the effective interest method is used as maturity approaches the unamortized amount increases and the annual interest increases.

4. b The lawsuit is likely and the amount can be estimated.

5. d The outcome is likely to happen (noncancelable), and the amount is determinable (market price less the contract price.)

6. b One of the conditions is met; therefore; we must disclose in the notes.

7. a New agreement signed to refinance the notes payable on a long-term basis. Only $200,000 of the loan will be classified as current; $800,000 will be classified as long-term.

8. a The amount of the estimated warranty liability at December 31, 20x5 is $28,500. It is calculated as 20x4 warranty expense ($300,000 x 6% = $18,000) plus 20x5 warranty expense ($500,000 x 6% = $30,000) less actual warranty expenditures $19,500.

9. b The amount of warranty expense in 20x5 is $30,000 as calculated in 8.

10. c The contingency will happen (management has clearly indicated its intention), and the amount is measurable. It will be recorded as a liability and an operating expense and disclosed in the notes to the financial statements.

11. d The amount of the accrued interest must added to the market price of the bond and credited to interest expense or interest payable.

12. d This is the only choice that describes what a gain or loss is: the difference between the reacquisition price and the net carrying amount of the debt.

13. a A gain or loss will result assuming the rate changes and it is reported in income.

14. b The company paid $98,000 plus $1,333 accrued interest ($100,000 × 8% × 2/12). The carrying amount of the bonds was as follows: bonds payable = $100,000, unamortized premium = $1,767 [($9,000 × 1/5) – ($1,000 × 1/5 × 2/12)]. Total carrying amount of the bonds is $101,767 plus accrued interest of $1,333. The gain is calculated by taking the price paid plus accrued interest ($99,333), and subtracting the carrying amount plus accrued interest ($103,100), equals $3,767.

15. b The amount of the 31 December 20x5 balance of the liability for customer advances is $220,000. It is calculated as the beginning balance $295,000 plus 20x5 advances received $460,000 less advances for orders shipped $410,000 less advances for orders cancelled $125,000.

PROBLEMS

Problem 1

PURPOSE: To illustrate accounting for warranty and guarantee costs.

Fellows Limited offers a 2-year warranty on its product. In year 20x4, Simon's sales were $1,000,000. It is estimated that approximately 1/2 of 1% of sales will result in warranty cost. The actual warranty costs in 20x4 were $2,000.

Sales in year 20x5 were $1,200,000. It is estimated that the percentage of warranty cost is unchanged at 1/2 of 1% of sales. Actual warranty costs, 20x5, were $7,000.

Required
Prepare the journal entries for the 20x4 and 20x5 transactions. Show the balance on the estimated warranty liability account for the end of 20x5.

Problem 2

PURPOSE: To illustrate accounting for bonds issued at premium.

Thorne Limited (CL) issued redeemable, secured bonds with a face value of $3,000,000 on January 1, 20x4. The bonds are interest bearing at 8% interest and pay interest on June 30 and December 31 annually. The bonds mature on December 31, 20x8. Assume that the market interest rate at the time of issue is 6% and that issue costs are $300,000.

Required
    a. Calculate the price the market would pay for these bonds today, given that the market interest rates are lower that the stated rate on the bond.
    b. Prepare the journal entries to record the bond issue and the entries for accounting for the bond for the year ended December 31, 20x4. Assume that Thorne uses the effective interest method of amortization.

Problem 3

PURPOSE: To demonstrate accounting for early debt retirement.

CL sold some investments and generated sufficient cash to repay $2,000,000 of the bond issue from question 2. Since the bonds are redeemable, CL paid the bondholders out on March 31, 20x5. The bonds were retired at 101 plus accrued interest.

Required
Prepare the journal entry(ies) to record the retirement.

Problem 4
PURPOSE: To demonstrate the accounting treatment if the bonds in problem 2 were replaced by new debt instead of retired.

Assume the same information as in problem 2. In 20x5, interest rates dipped sharply and analysts were predicting that they would stay low for the short- to mid-term. Since CL's bonds were at 8%, management at CL felt that they would be paying too much for the financing over the next few years. Management decided to redeem the bonds and to issue new ones at a lower interest rate. On March 31, 2000, the bonds were retired at 110 plus accrued interest.

Required
Prepare journal entries to record the retirement of the old bonds.

Problem 5
PURPOSE: To demonstrate accounting for bonds when the issuance date is between interest dates.

Daglish Corporation issued bonds, face amount $100,000, three-year, 8% (payable semi-annually on 30 June and 31 December). The bonds were dated 1 January 20x5, and were sold on 1 November 20x5, for $100,739 (including interest of $2,667 and a bond price of $98,072) at an effective interest rate of 9%. The bonds mature on 31 December 20x7. Use the straight-line method of amortization.

Required
- a) Give the entry made by Daglish Corporation at 1 November 20x5.
- b) Give the entry for Daglish at the interest date, 31 December 20x5.
- c) Assume the accounting period ends on 28 February. Give the adjusting entry for Daglish on 28 February 20x6.
- d) On 1 March 20x6, $75,000 face value of the bond was retired for 105. Give the entry for retirement.

SOLUTIONS TO PROBLEMS

Problem 1 A warranty expense must be recorded in the year of the sale since it is a cost of sales and, therefore, must be matched with revenues. The problem is that there is uncertainty with respect to the measurement of the amount.

The journal entries for the year 20x4 are as follows:

1. Cash/accounts receivable $1,000,000
      Sales $1,000,000

2. Warranty expense   5,000
      Warranty liability (current)   5,000
      $1,000,000 x ½ % = $5,000

3. Warranty liability (current)   2,000
      Cash/A.P.   2,000

The journal entries for the year 20x5 are as follows:

1. Cash/accounts receivable   1,200,000
      Sales   1,200,000

2. Warranty expense   5,100
      Warranty liability (current)   5,100
      $1,200,000 x ½ % = $5,100

3. Warranty liability   7,000
      Cash/A.P.   7,000

The balance in estimated warranty liability at the end of 20x5 is:
$$= \$1,100 \ (\$5,000 - \$2,000 + \$5,100 - \$7,000)$$

Because it is a 2 year warranty in theory the liability should be split between current and long term.

Problem 2

Requirement a

Since the market rate is lower than the stated interest rate on the bonds, prospec-tive buyers of the bonds will find them more desirable. They cannot get a better rate on their investment by investing in another type. Prospective investors will invest to achieve an overall yield of 6%. They will likely pay more up front for the bonds.

To determine how much should be paid up front to yield 6%, we will discount the stream of payments under the bonds at 6% as follows:

   Present value $3,000,000, 10 periods (5 years
     semiannually) @ 3% = $3,000,000 × .74409   = $ 2,232,270
   + Present value annuity $3,000,000 × 4%
     10 periods @ 3% = $120,000 × 8.53020   =   <u>1,023,624</u>
                                      <u>$ 3,255,894</u>

The premium is $3,000,000 – 3,255,894 = 255,894 and will be amortized over the 5-year life of the bond (10 periods), using the effective interest method.

To prove that this will give an annual yield of 6%, the book value of the bond will now be $3,255,894 for the investor, and in Year 1 the return will be $240,000 (2 x $120,000) or 8% of $3,000,000 minus the amortization of the premium or $45,316. Therefore, $194,684/ 3,255,894 = 6%

There are other factors besides these that affect the price of bonds, but the rela-tionship between the stated interest rate and the market interest rate is the key.

Requirement b

January 1, 20x4: To record bond issue at premium

Cash	2,955,894	
Deferred bond issue costs	300,000	
Bonds payable		3,000,000
Premium on bonds		255,894

We use a partial amortization table to calculate the amortization of the premium and the amount of interest expense.

Partial amortization table for bonds issued at premium

Date	Interest payment	Interest expense	Premium amortization	Unamortized premium	Net bond liability
Jan. 1/20x4				$255,894	$3,255,894
June 30/20x4	$120,000	$97,677	$22,323	$233,571	$3,233,571
Dec. 31/20x4	120,000	97,007	22,993	210,578	3,210,578

June 30, 20x4: To record payment of interest

Interest expense	96,677	
Premium on bonds	22,323	
Cash		120,000

December 31, 20x4: To record payment of interest

Interest expense	97,007	
Premium on bonds	22,993	
Cash		120,000

December 31, 20x4: To amortize bond issue costs

Bond issue costs expense	60,000	
Unamortized bond issue costs		60,000
($300,000 / 5 years)		

The bond issue costs have been amortized using the straight-line method. This is a matter of judgment. This method is used for its simplicity.

Problem 3

March 31, 20x5: To record the interest payable as at March 31, 20x5

Interest expense	32,106	(see 1)	
Premium on bonds	7,894	(see 3)	
Interest payable			40,000 (see 4)

March 31, 20x5: To record the retirement of $2,000,000 bonds

Bonds payable	2,000,000		
Interest payable	40,000	(see 4)	
Bond issue cost expense	10,000	(see 2)	
Premium on bonds	132,49	(see 3)	
Loss on disposition	37,509	(see 5)	
Cash			2,060,000 (see 4)
Unamortized bond issue costs			160,000 (see 2)

(1) Interest expense: $3,210,578 \times 3\% \times 3/6 \times 2,000,000/ 3,000,000 = \$32,106$

(2) Unamortized bond issue costs:

$300,000/ 5$ years $\times 3/12 \times 2/3 = \$10,000$;

$300,000 - 60,000 = \$240,000 \times 2,000,000/3,000,000 = \$160,000$

    Balance at March 31, 20x5: $160,000 - \$10,000 = \$150,000$

(3)

Date	Payment 4%	Interest 3%	Book value change	Book value
12/31/20x4	120,000	97,007	22,993	3,210,578
06/30/20x5	120,000	96,317	23,683	3,186,895

Amortization of premium to March 31, 20x5: $23,683 \times 2/3 \times 3/6 = \$7,894$

Unamortized premium as at December 31, 20x4:

        $210,578 \times 2,000,000/3,000,000$

        $= 140,385$

Unamortized premium as at March 31, 20x5, for $2,000,000 bonds:

        $140,385 - 7,894 = \$132,491$

(4) Interest payment: $120,000 \times 2,000,000/3,000,000 \times 3/6 = \$40,000$.

(5) The loss is calculated as follows:

Bonds were redeemed at 101 cash		
$= \$2,020,000 + \$40,000$ interest =		$2,060,000
Less carrying value of bonds:		
Bonds payable	2,000,000	
Unamortized premium	132,491	
Unamortized issue costs	(150,000)	
Interest payable	40,000	2,022,491
Loss on redemption of $2,000,000 bonds		$ 37,509

Problem 4

The journal entries are similar as in problem 3 except that CL redeemed the entire bond issue of $3,000,000 and at a different rate.

March 31, 20x5—To record the interest payable as at March 31, 20x5

Interest expense	48,159	(see 1)
Premium on bonds	11,841	(see 2)
Cash		60,000 (see 4)

March 31, 20x5—To record the retirement of the bonds.

Bonds payable (old)	3,000,000	
Bond issue cost expense	15,000	(see 3)
Premium on bonds (old)	198,737	(see 2)
Loss on disposition	326,263	(see 5)
Bonds payable		3,000,000
Unamortized bond issue costs		240,000 (see 3)
Premium on bonds (new)		300,000 (see 6)

(1) Interest expense: $3,210,578 \times 3\% \times 3/6 = \$48,159$

(2)

Date	Payment 4%	Interest 3%	Book value change	Book value
12/31/20x4	$120,000	97,007	22,993	$3,210,578
06/30/20x5	120,000	96,317	23,683	3,186,895

Amortization of premium to March 31, 20x5: $23,683 \times 3/6 = \$11,841$

Unamortized premium as at March 31, 20x5: $210,578 - \$11,841 = \$198,737$

(3) Unamortized bond issue costs:

$300,000/5 years × 3/12 = $15,000

$300,000 − $60,000 = $240,000 − $15,000 = $ 225,000

(4) Interest payment: $120,000 × 3/6 = $60,000

(5) The loss on disposition is calculated as follows:

Bonds were redeemed and refunded by a new issue at 110:		
Bonds payable, new lower rate		$3,300,000
Less carrying value of old bonds:		
Bonds payable	$3,000,000	
Unamortized premium	198,737	
Unamortized bond issue costs	(225,000)	2,973,737
Loss on redemption of $3,000,000 bonds		$ 326,263

(6) New bond issue: Bonds payable = $3,000,000

Market value = $3,300,000 ($3,000,000 C 110)

Premium = $300,000

There are three possible accounting treatments for the $326,263 loss:

- Include the gain in income in the year the refunding occurred.
- Amortize the gain over the remaining life of the old bond issue.
- Amortize the gain over the life of the new bond issue.

Problem 5

Requirement a

1 November 20x5 (to record issuance):

Cash ($98,072 + $2,667)	100,739	
Discount on bonds payable ($100,000-$98,072)	1,928	
Bonds payable		100,000
Interest expense (or accrued interest payable)		2,667

Requirement b

Interest expense (or interest payable)	4,148	
Cash ($100,000 x .04)		4,000
Discount on bonds payable ($74 x 2)		148

Requirement c

Interest expense ($4,445 x 2/6)	1,481	
Discount on bonds payable ($445 x 2/6)		148
Interest payable ($100,000 x .08 x 2/12)		1,333

Requirement d

Bonds payable	75,000	
Loss on bond retirement	4,973	
Discount on bonds payable ($1,928 x .75 x 22/26)		1,223
Cash ($75,000 x 105%)		78,750

Interest payable	1,000	
Cash ($75,000 x .08 x 2/12)		1,000
Interest was accrued on 28 February		

CASE

In March 20x5, Armour Publications Limited completed negotiations for a 10-year $14,600,000 loan. The executive committee of the board of directors was meeting to evaluate three options:

1. A 10-year $14,600,000 long-term loan from the Canadian bank. The loan has the following terms:
   a. The interest rate is 8.2%, compounded annually. The interest rate is fixed for the life of the loan and is paid at the end of each year.
   b. Principal is to be repaid in one lump sum at the end of 10 years.
   c. The bank will charge a $19,000 up-front administrative fee.
   d. Armour will be required to move all banking activities of the company to the Canadian bank (from the Ottawa bank, its current financial institution). This will cost Armour $5,500 in fees, either at the Canadian or the Ottawa bank.
   e. Armour will agree to a maximum debt-to-equity ratio of 2 to 1, and pay no dividends in excess of 30% of reported net income during the life of the loan. Ratios are based on audited financial statements.
   f. Loan security is a second mortgage on Armour's printing facilities and personal guarantees from Armour's principal shareholders.

2. A 10-year $14,600,000 long-term loan from the Ottawa bank. The loan has the following terms:
   a. The interest rate is 6.5%, compounded annually, for the first five years of the loan. The interest rate for the second five-year term is based on prime interest rates at that time. Interest is due at the end of each year.
   b. The bank will charge a $110,000 up-front administrative fee.
   c. Armour will agree not to issue new long-term debt over the life of the loan, without the express permission of Ottawa, and maintain dividend declarations to common shareholders at no more than current levels (approximately 10-15% of net income).
   d. The loan will be secured by a second mortgage on Armour's printing facilities and a floating charge on all corporate assets.
   e. Principal is due at the end of the loan term.

3. A 10-year $14,600,000 long-term loan from a pension fund. The bond has the following terms:
   a. The interest rate is fixed at 8%, compounded semi-annually over the life of the bond. Interest is due every six months.
   b. The bond is secured by the general credit rating of Armour.
   c. Armour will agree to the following conditions:
      i.   The current ratio will go no lower than 3 to 1.
      ii. The debt-to-equity ratio will not exceed 2.5 to 1.
      iii. No dividends will be paid to common shareholders unless the current ratio is 3.5 to 1 after declaration (all ratios are based on audited financial statements).
      iv. No common shares will be issued or repurchased without the written permission of the lender.

v. No changes to management will take place without informing the lender.

vi. The lender will be given a seat on Armour's board of directors for the life of the bond.

vii. The bond will involve $227,500 in legal and other costs at inception, to be paid by Armour.

Armour Publications operates in a highly competitive printing business, known for its high rate of business failures. While Armour has had some years that have been rough financially, they now own state-of-the-art printing facilities, which were financed through government-guaranteed debt, has stabilized their position.

Armour is controlled by Jack Armour and his two sons, but there are several other shareholders, brought into the company when additional share capital was necessary for survival.

Required:
Prepare a preliminary evaluation of the financing decisions for the board.

KEY POINTS IN THE CASE

The response should be written as a report to the Board of Directors

Objectives of financial reporting
Armour operates in a highly risky business, known for business failures. While Armour itself is relatively stable, they have had loss years and have new facilities and new debt (government-guaranteed) in addition to that described. Reporting healthy, stable annual reports must be a concern in this environment, as is complying with any covenants, some of which are based on the financial statements. Lenders, would in all likelihood, require GAAP financial statements since covenants are based on audited financial statements. Lenders would also be interested in future cash flows and the ability of Armour to make interest and principal payments.

Loan Alternatives
Alternative A — Canadian Bank
    a. The effective interest rate is 8.225% (solved by spreadsheet)* over the ten-year life of the loan, after factoring in the $19,000 up-front fee, and the $5,500 transaction fees. The interest rate is fixed over the ten-year life.
    b. Principal need not be repaid until the end of the loan, allowing Armour flexibility in arranging either operating cash flow to finance the repayment or refinancing through another borrowing arrangement.
    c. Armour would have to switch current banking business to Canadian away from their current bank, which may not be attractive.
    d. The loan requires corporate guarantees but also personal guarantees from Armour's shareholders, which may be particularly unwelcome in this risky business.
    e. Debt-to-equity ratios must be kept at 2:1, but dividends can be up to 30% of net income (current levels are only 10-15% of net income). The debt-to-equity

covenant may be viewed as reasonably restrictive. The dividends covenant is more restrictive.

*x = -$14,600,000 + $19,000 + $5,500 + ($14,600,000 x .082) (P/A x%,10)

  x = 8.22526306

Alternative B

  a. The interest rate for the first five years (6.5%) is lower than the interest rate for alternative A. If the up-front fee is factored in (over 10 years), the loan would have to bear an interest rate of 10.5%* over the second five years in order to have an overall cost equivalent to alternative A. Will the interest rate in the second five-year period be below 10.5% or above 10.5%? The problem is that interest rates are unpredictable.

  b. The up-front fee is considerably larger, which is less attractive to Armour.

  c. The debt covenants are more restrictive for Armour, requiring that no new long-term debt be issued and that dividends not exceed current percentages of income.

  d. Corporate security is quite similar to alternative A, but also requires a floating charge on all corporate assets. Significantly, no personal guarantee is required, which may be a major factor for Armour.

  e. Principal payment is not required until the end of the term.

* Equivalent 8.225% return = -$14,600,000 + $110,000 + ($14,600,000 * .065) (P/A, 8.225%, 5) + ($14,600,000 x .10505) (P/A, 8.225%, 5) (P/F, 8.225%, 5) solved by spreadsheet.

Alternative C

  a. The effective interest rate on the loan is 8.4%*, considering both the fact that the interest is compounded semi-annually and there are $227,500 in legal fees, etc., paid up front. The loan cost is fixed over the life of the loan.

  b. The security is the least onerous of the alternatives only requiring a general credit rating.

  c. The covenants are severe compared to the other alternatives, e.g., no dividends unless current ratio is 3.5 or above after declaration, no changes in management.

  d. Armour would have to agree to put a representative of the lender on their Board which is potentially undesirable.

  e. Up-front fees are high, which is less attractive to Armour.

*x% = -$14,600,000 + $227,500 + ($14,600,000 x .04) (P/A x%, 20)

  x% = .041158 (solved by spreadsheet)

Annual = 8.4%

SELECTED SOLUTIONS FROM THE TEXTBOOK

Assignment 12-20

Requirement 1
1 January 20x4

Cash..	107,985	
Bonds payable...		100,000
Premium on bond payable.................................		7,985

$107,985 = \$100,000 \times (P/F, 8\%, 5) + (\$100,000 \times 10\%) \times (P/A, 8\%, 5)$

Bond issue costs..	2,000	
Cash...		2,000

Requirement 2

	Effective Interest Method		Straight-line Method	
31 December 20x4				
Interest expense..........................	8,639*		8,403	
Premium on bonds payable......	1,361		1,597***	
Cash..................................		10,000		10,000
Interest (etc.) expense...............	400**		400	
Bond issue costs		400		400

* ($107,985 × 8%)
** ($2,000 ÷ 5)
*** ($7,985 ÷ 5)

Requirement 3

	Effective Interest Method		Straight-line Method	
1 March 20x5				
Interest expense..........................	142		140	
Premium on bond payable	25		27	
Interest payable		167		167

$142 = 8\% \times (\$107,985 - \$1,361) \times 1/10 \times 2/12$
$167 = \$10,000 \times 10\% \times 2/12$
$27 = \$7,985 \times 1/5 \times 2/12 \times 1/10$

Interest (etc.) expense...............	7		7	
Bond issue costs		7		7

$7 = \$2,000 \times 1/5 \times 2/12 \times 1/10$

Interest payable..........................	167		167	

Bonds payable	10,000	10,000	
Premium on bond payable	637	612	
Loss	516	541	
Cash.....................................		11,167	11,167
Bond issue costs.................		153	153

$637 = [(\$7,985 - \$1,361) \times 1/10] - \$25$

$153 = [(\$2,000 - \$400) \times 1/10] - \$7$

$612 = [(\$7,985 - \$1,597) \times 1/10] - \$27$

$11,167 = (\$10,000 \times 1.10) + \$167$

Assignment 12-21

Case A

Requirement 1

1 January 20x5 - Issuance of the bonds at 105:

Cash ($200,000 × 1.05)...	210,000	
Bonds payable, 12%...		200,000
Premium on bonds payable		10,000

Requirement 2

31 December 20x16 - Retirement of the debt:

Bonds payable, 12%...	200,000	
Premium on bonds payable ($10,000 × 8/20).................................	4,000	
Loss, retirement of debt	2,000	
Cash ($200,000 × 1.03)...		206,000

Case B

Requirement 1

1 January 20x2

Cash ($200,000 × .98)..	196,000	
Discount on bonds payable.....................................	4,000	
Bonds payable, 10%, 10-year..............................		200,000

Requirement 2

31 December 20x2

Interest expense	20,400	
Discount on bonds payable ($4,000 × 1/10)		400
Cash ($200,000 × 10%)...		20,000

Requirement 3

1 July 20x7
    To update interest expense and discount amortization for 20x7:

Interest expense	10,200	
Discount on bonds payable ($4,000 × 1/10 × 6/12).................		200
Interest payable ($200,000 × 10% × 6/12)		10,000

To record the retirement:

Bonds payable...	200,000	
Interest payable..	10,000	
Loss, retirement of debt...	3,800	
Discount on bonds payable*		1,800
Cash ($202,000 + $10,000)..		212,000

    *Unamortized balance:
    ($4,000 / 10 years) × 4.5 years = $1,800

Requirement 4

If the bonds had been refunded, the loss could be recognized in the period of the retirement, amortized over the life of the old bond issue, or amortized over the life of the new bond issue. The alternative chosen will be dependent on the circumstances and on corporate reporting objectives.

Assignment 12-23

Requirement 1 (debtor's entries)

1 July 20x2 - Issuance of bonds:

Cash [($600,000 × .97) – $2,000]	580,000	
Discount on bonds payable ($600,000 × .03).........................	18,000	
Bond issue costs..	2,000	
Bonds payable, 5%..		600,000

Requirement 2

1 July 20x5 - Purchased $200,000 bonds at effective rate of 8%:

Bonds payable, 5%..	200,000	
Gain, retirement of debt		27,021
Discount on bonds payable..		4,200 [a]
Bond issue costs..		467 [b]
Cash		168,312 [c]

Computations:
a $18,000 × 14/20 × 2/6 = $4,200 (7 years to maturity)
b $2,000 × 14/20 × 2/6 = $467
c Purchase price:

$200,000 × (P/F, 4%, 14) = $200,000 × (.57748)		$115,496
($200,000 × 2.5%) × (P/A, 4%, 14) = $5,000 × (10.56312)......	52,816	
Purchase price (PV)..		$168,312

The gain is reported as an unusual item on the income statement. If the transaction is a refunding, the gain may be reported on the income statement in the current period, or amortized over the life of the old or new bond issue. Choice of policy depends on the circumstances and the company's reporting objectives.

Requirement 3
Economic Analysis (present value basis):

PV of old bonds (above)..	$168,312
PV of purchase price..	168,312
Economic gain (loss) on retirement (pretax)	$ 0

Neither the issuer nor investor had an economic gain or loss because the cash paid was equal to the present value of the 5% bonds. The change in market value, which caused a gain for the issuer and a loss for the investor, occurred when interest rates changed.

Assignment 12-30

Requirement 1
The exchange rate exposure to the U.S. dollar liability can be hedged by creating an offsetting U.S. dollar asset in the same amount and with the same maturity. This can happen naturally or operationally, such as by sales in U.S. dollars that create offsetting accounts receivable. To apply *hedge accounting,* however, the hedging item and the hedged item both must be formally designated by management. A formal designated hedge can be created by entering into a forward contract to receive $8 million U.S. dollars in three years. The interest obligation can also be hedged by means of a forward contract.

If the loan is hedged operationally through offsetting financial assets in U.S. dollars, the exchange gains and losses on both the financial assets and the financial liability are permitted to flow through into net income when they occur. This is a valid hedge, but it is not an a hedge to which we can apply *hedge accounting* – the deferral of gains/losses.

If the loan is formally hedged, the exchange gains and losses on the hedged item are recognized in other comprehensive income, to be recognized in income on settlement date, along with the offsetting gain or loss on the hedging item (i.e., the forward contract).

Requirement 2

Loan Balance			(Gain)/Loss
1 May 20x2	@ $1.29	$10,320,000	
31 December 20x2	@ $1.32	10,560,000	$240,000
31 December 20x3	@ $1.30	10,400,000	(160,000)

Income Statement, year ended 31 Dec. 20x2
    Exchange loss
        re: principal..   240,000

31 December 20x 2 balance sheet
    Loan payable... $10,560,000

31 December 20x3 balance sheet
    Loan payable...   10,400,000

Income statement, year ended 31 December 20x3
    Exchange (gain)
        re: principal..   (160,000)

Requirement 3

Interest Expense		
20x2	$8,000,000 × .0725 × 8/12 × $1.31	$506,533
20x3	$8,000,000 × .0725 × $1.29	$748,200

Exchange G/L (Interest)
20x2

Interest payable at 31 December 20x2 ($8,000,000 × .0725 × 8/12 × $1.32)	$510,400
Interest expense (above)	506,533
Exchange loss	$ 3,867

There is an exchange gain or loss on interest expense because it is accrued at the average rate and paid at a specific date when the exchange rate is different than the average.

SOLUTIONS TO CONCEPT REVIEW QUESTIONS

Page 740

1. The three essential characteristics of a liability are as follows: (1) It embodies a duty or responsibility to others that entails settlement by future transfer or use of assets, provision of services, or other yielding of economic benefits, at a specified or determinable date, on occurrence of a specified event, or on demand. (2) The duty or responsibility obligates the entity, leaving it little or no discretion to avoid it. (3) The transaction or event obligating the entity has already occurred.

2. A **financial liability** (payables) are debt instruments that require some form of cash payment. They give rise to a corresponding financial asset for another individual or company.

3. Contractual obligations are not recorded as liabilities because the other party has not yet performed the services required.

4. A contingent liability is recorded on the balance sheet when it is likely that a liability will be created and the amount can be estimated.

Page 745

1. A *blended payment* is a payment on a loan whereby the interest rate is fixed at the beginning of the loan term and regular, equal annuity payments are made in satisfaction of the loan. These annuity payments are a "blend" and include both principal and interest components.

2. A *debt covenant is* a restriction placed on a corporation's activities as a condition of maintaining the loan. Covenants are designed to protect the lenders' interests by limiting high-risk activities or preventing the borrower from falling into a high-risk position. Covenants may restrict dividend payments, excessive leveraging, or transfers of control of the company.

3. The sinking fund can be offset against the liability only if the company is relieved of the risk of investment losses in the sinking fund once it has made the required payments into the fund.

Page 758

1. A *premium on a bond payable* arises when the stated (nominal) rate of interest on a bond exceeds the prevailing market rate of interest. The present value of the bond will exceed the face value, and investors will be willing to pay more than the face value (a premium) to acquire the bond. A bond may offer an interest rate different from the market rate, as the bond terms are set in advance of the actual issue date.

2. For a bond the sell at par the effective rate and the nominal rate must be the same.

3. The two methods of amortizing a premium or discount are the straight line and effective interest methods. The effective interest method is recommended by the CICA. The straight line method can only be used when it is not materially different from the effective interest method.

4. Unamortized debt issue costs are normally shown as a long term deferred charge. Alternatively it may be deducted from the debt but in this case it must be disclosed in the notes.

Page 764

1. Gains and losses on debt retirement, while rare, may not be classified as extraordinary, as they are the result of normal business operations and are a management decision.

2. A *retractable bond* is one that requires repayment at the holder's (investor's) discretion.

3. *Defeasance* is the situation whereby a bond-issuing company transfers cash into an irrevocable trusted fund. The trustee invests the money in low-risk securities that will match the term and interest flow of the bonds. Such proceeds are used to retire the corporate bonds.

Page 767

1. The purpose of *hedging* is to manage risk (interest rate risk, foreign exchange risk, etc.) by arranging equal and offsetting cash flows for existing transactions. For example, a company must extinguish a note payable in U.S. dollars in three months. It may enter into a contract now to receive (buy) U.S. funds in the same amount in three months.

2. Foreign exchange gains or losses on unhedged short-term debt should be taken into income in the current period.

3. The amount of long-term debt at the time the debt is issued is $1,450,000 ($1,000,000 x $1.45). At the year-end there has been an exchange gain of $30,000 [$1,000,000 x ($1.45-$1.42)]. This would reduce the long-term debt balance to $1,420,000.

CHAPTER 13

SHAREHOLDERS' EQUITY

Shareholders' equity can be defined as "the net contributions to the firm by the owners, plus the firm's cumulative earnings retained in the business, less any adjustments, payments, or requisition of the company's own shares."

Shareholders' equity is the second part of the balance sheet equation:
Assets - Liabilities = Shareholders' equity.

Section 1000 of the *CICA Handbook* defines owners' or shareholders' equity as the difference between the assets and the liabilities of an entity.

Alternative terms for shareholders' equity include "residual interest," "net worth," and "net assets."

This chapter deals with various aspects of shareholders' equity; focusing on the accounting implications of share capital, issuance, and retirement, and the accounting for and disclosure of retained earnings and dividends. It also discusses other components of shareholders' equity with emphasis on Other Comprehensive Income (OCI).

1. THE CORPORATE FORM OF ORGANIZATION

Shareholders' equity applies only to corporations. Partnerships and proprietorships have ownership interests but not share capital.

Private versus Public Corporations
Private corporations have a limited number of shareholders and the shares cannot be publicly traded. Private companies may adopt differential disclosure with unanimous shareholder consent. They can raise share capital through private placements. *Public corporations* have debt or equity trading on the stock exchanges.

Share Capital
Share certificates represent ownership in a corporation. Shares can be bought, sold, or transferred by shareholders without the consent of the corporation.

A corporation has at least one class of shares: **common shares.** Common share normally carry the following rights:
1. The right to vote for directors.
2. The right to share profits.
3. The right to share in the distribution of assets in the event the company is liquidated or dissolved.

Preferred shares. This class has priority claim on dividends at a specified dollar amount or rate, as well as priority claim on assets upon liquidation. Dividends may be cumulative or participating. The shares may be convertible to other securities. They usually doesn't have voting rights.

WATCH! Common shares are often called **residual ownership shares,** since they get whatever is left after the creditors and the other investors have had their share in earnings and net assets.

WATCH! Common shareholders have the *risk* of ownership. They are at risk with respect to their original investment and return on that investment. They also have the *rewards* of ownership since they get the residue of earnings and have control over the company through their voting shares.

Terms and conditions

Shares are sometimes issued with special terms and conditions. Preferred shares are sometimes structured to look a lot like debt – this is discussed in chapter 14.

Par Value Shares versus No-par Value Shares

Par value shares have a designated dollar amount per share, as stated in the articles of incorporation and as printed on the face of the share certificates.

No-par value shares do not carry a designated or assigned value per share.

WATCH! If a corporation is incorporated under the CBCA (Canadian Business Corporations Act), it is prohibited from using par value shares. No-par value shares are common in the United States.

2. FUNDAMENTAL SHARE EQUITY CONCEPTS AND DISTINCTIONS

The fundamental concepts that underlie accounting and reporting of shareholders' equity are:

- *Separate legal entity.*
- *Sources of shareholders' equity.* Includes contributed capital from shareholders, retained earnings and other comprehensive income.
- *Cost-based accounting.*
- *No impact on income.*

WATCH! Equity may be **contributed** or **earned.**

Important terms relating to share capital are:
- *Authorized share capital.* If a corporation chooses to place a limit on authorized shares, this should be stated in the articles of incorporation.
- *Issued share capital.* The number of shares issued and outstanding.
- *Unissued share capital.* Difference between authorized and issued shares.
- *Outstanding share capital.* The number of shares issued and owned.
- *Treasury shares.* Issued but not outstanding.
- *Subscribed shares.* Unissued shares set aside to meet a subscription contract.

3. ACCOUNTING FOR SHARE CAPITAL AT ISSUANCE

Accounting for shareholders' equity emphasizes source. If a corporation has more than one share class, separate accounts should be maintained for each.

Authorization. When the articles of incorporation authorize an unlimited or limited number of shares, this will be recorded as a memo entry.

No-par value shares issued for cash. A share certificate, specifying the number of shares represented, is prepared. The amount is recorded in the share capital account.

Shares sold on a subscription basis. Prospective shareholders sign a contract to purchase a specified number of shares at a specified price to be paid in installments. Then:

> *On date of subscription*—The stock subscriptions receivable account is debited and share capital subscribed is credited.
>
> *On date of collection*—Cash is debited and stock subscriptions receivable is credited.
>
> *On date of issuance of shares*—Share capital subscribed is debited and common shares is credited.

Share capital subscribed is classified in the shareholders' equity section. The stock subscriptions receivable can be classified in two acceptable ways. The *first* alternative is to treat it as an asset: receivable; the *second* is to classify the account as shareholders' equity since it is related to capital share transactions. The preferred approach is to classify it as an equity account.

Default of Subscriptions

If the subscriber defaults after a partial fulfillment of the subscription, the corporation may decide to:

> (a) return all payments received to the subscriber,
> (b) issue shares equivalent to the number paid in full, rather than the total number subscribed,
> (c) keep the money received.

Non-cash Sale of Share Capital

The transaction must be recorded at the most reliable fair value:

- Fair value of the asset received.
- Fair value of the shares issued.

The general rule is that the cost of the assets is the value of the consideration given up – the shares in this case. In order to apply this the shares must have a determinable market value. It may be easier to determine the market value of the asset. The lower-of-cost-ore market must always be applied. The final authority rests with the company's board of directors. Watered stock occurs when the asset is overvalued and secret reserves are created by undervaluing.

Private companies have a limited number of shareholders and the shares cannot be publicly traded. Market values for shares of private companies are essentially nonexistent or not reliable. Public companies are those whose securities are traded on stock exchanges. Market values for shares of public companies are usually more reliable if the shares are frequently traded.

Basket Sale of Share Capital (lump sum)

When selling two or more classes for one lump sum amount, we must use either the **proportional method** or the **incremental method** to allocate the proceeds.

The *proportional method* is preferred. It be used when we have a fair value for all the classes of shares involved in the transaction. We use the *incremental method* when we know the fair value of all but one class involved in the transaction.

If no market values are known, the board of directors may arbitrarily split the proceeds between the securities.

If the basket sale involves only equity the allocation is not really important. However when the basket includes debt and equity the allocation is more significant as it changes the liabilities on the balance sheet. The market value of debt can generally be determined using the market value of the company's other debt with similar risk.

Share Issue Costs

Share issue costs include the following: registration fee, underwriter commissions, legal and accounting fees, printing costs, clerical costs, and promotional costs.

There are two methods of accounting, both of which are used in practice,:
- Offset method—reduce the amount received for the sale.
- Retained earnings method.

4. RETIREMENT OF SHARES

Retractable shares. At the option of the shareholder, at a contractually arranged price, a company is required to buy back its shares.

Callable or Redeemable shares. These involve specific buy-back provisions at the option of the company.

Reasons for share redemption include:
- Increase EPS.
- Provide cash flow to shareholders in lieu of dividends.
- Acquire shares when they appear to be undervalued.
- Buy out one or mort particular shareholders or thwart a takeover bid.
- Reduce future dividend payments.

Retirement accounting rules

When shares are **purchased and immediately retired**, all capital items relating to the specific shares are removed from the accounts.

The CICA Handbook, paragraphs 3240.75 and 3240.17, requires:
  1. *When the reacquisition cost is higher than the average price per share issued to date, the cost should be charged in this sequence:*
     a. *first, to share capital, at the average price per issued share*
     b. *second, to any **contributed surplus** that was created by earlier share transactions in the same class of shares, and then,*
     c. *if any remaining amount, to retained earnings.*

  2. *When the reacquisition cost is lower than the average price per share issued to date, the cost should lie charged in this sequence:*
     a. *first, to share capital, at the average price per issued share*
     b. *any remaining amount, to contributed surplus.*

   The important point to notes is that a corporation does not report any gain or loss on buying back its own shares.

Conversion of shares are accounted for at book value, with an equal decrease to one share class and an increase to another. No gain or loss is reported.

5. TREASURY STOCK

Treasury stock arises when a company buys its own shares and holds them for resale. Treasury shares do not have voting rights and are not entitled to dividends.

The CBCA provides that if a company reacquires its own shares, it must retire those shares immediately.

When a company buys treasury shares, the cost of shares acquired is debited to treasury stock. This account is classified at the end of the shareholders' equity section, after retained earnings. When shares are resold, treasury stock is credited for the cost and the gain or loss impacts on contributed surplus or retained earnings. There is no impact on the income statement.

One of the fundamental principles in accounting for shareholders' equity is that it does not have an impact on net income.

6. RETAINED EARNINGS

Retained earnings represents a corporation's accumulated net income, net loss, error corrections, and retroactive changes in accounting policy, less dividends and amounts transferred to the contributed capital accounts, as illustrated in the table be below.

RETAINED EARNINGS	
Decreased by (*debits*)	**Increased by (*credits*)**
Net loss (including extraordinary items and/or discontinued operations).	Net income (including extraordinary items and/or discontinued operations).
	Removal of deficit in a financial reorganization.
	Unrealized appreciation of investments valued at market.
Error correction.	Error correction.
Effect of an accounting policy change applied retroactively.	Effects an accounting policy change applied retroactively.
Cash or other dividends. Stock dividends.	
Share retirement and treasury stock transactions.	
Share issue costs.	

Appropriations and Restrictions of Retained Earnings

WATCH! An **appropriation of retained earnings** is a result of a discretionary management action. A **restriction of retained earnings** is a result of a legal contract or corporate law.

An appropriation or restriction of retained earnings reduces the amount of retained earnings that financial statement readers might consider available for dividend distribution.

Appropriations and restrictions are made (a) to fulfil a contractual agreement, (b) to comply with corporate legislation, or (c) to indicate a specific purpose for a specified portion of retained earnings.

WATCH! Appropriations and restrictions do not involve any segregation of assets—only allocation of retained earnings.

7. DIVIDENDS

A **dividend** is a distribution of earnings, in the form of assets or shares, to shareholders. It typically results in a *credit* to the account that represents the item distributed and a *debit* to retained earnings.

Corporations are *not* required to pay dividends.

Relevant Dividend Dates

There are 4 relevant dividend dates, as follows:

1. *Declaration Date.* The board of directors formally announces the dividend distribution. A cash or property dividend declared is recorded on this date. A journal entry is required. In the case of a stock dividend, there is no liability and an entry is not required on the declaration date. However, accountants sometimes prefer to make an entry on the declaration date to recognize the intention to issue additional shares.

2. *Record Date.* On a specified date selected by the board of directors, a list of shareholders of record is prepared. No entry is made on the date of record.

3. *Ex-dividend date:* To provide time to transfer the shares, stock exchanges advance the effective ex-dividend date by three or four days beyond the date of record. Thus, those who hold the shares on the day prior to the stipulated ex-dividend date receive the dividend.

4. *Payment Date:* This date, which is determined by the board of directors, is stated in the declaration. A journal entry is required to record the payment and remove the liability.

Legality of Dividends

There must be retained earnings or contributed capital before dividends can be declared.

   a. Dividends may not be paid from legal capital without permission from the creditors.

   b. Retained earnings are available for dividends unless there is a contractual or statutory restriction.

A liquidity test must be met: Dividends may not be declared or paid if (1) the result would be that the corporation became unable to meet its liabilities as they came due, (2) if there is a deficit, or (3) if it would result in the company going bankrupt.

WATCH!

Forms (types) of Dividends

1. *Cash dividends*

Cash dividends are the usual form of distributions to shareholders.

Cash dividends are usually reported on the balance sheet as a current liability. Preferred shared have first preference on amounts declared as dividends. To record cash dividends:

a. On date of declaration:

Retained earnings	xxxx	
Cash dividends payable, preferred		xxxx
Cash dividends payable, common		xxxx

b. On date of payment:

Cash dividends payable, preferred	xxxx	
Cash dividends payable, common	xxxx	
Cash		xxxx

WATCH! It is important to distinguish the portion of the dividend payable to the *preferred* shares versus the *common*. When the cash dividends are recorded separately, it is clear that the preferred shareholders have been given first preference on amounts declared as dividends.

Cumulative Dividends on Preferred Shares

Any dividends not declared in a given year, accumulate at the specified rate of such shares. The accumulated amount must be paid in full *if and when* dividends are declared in a later year before any dividends can be paid on the common shares.

WATCH! Dividends in arrears are *not* liabilities but must be disclosed in the notes to the financial statements.

Participating Dividends on Preferred Shares

Participating preferred shares provide that the preferred shareholders participate above the stated preferential rate on a pro rata basis in dividend declarations with the common shareholders, as follows:

1. *First,* the preferred shareholders receive their preference rate.
2. *Second,* common shareholders receive a specified matching dividend.
3. *If the total is larger than the two amounts,* the excess is divided on a pro rata basis between the two share classes.

Participation terms must be specified in the articles of incorporation. The shares may be fully participating or partially participating.

ILLUSTRATION

Common and Preferred Dividends

The balance sheet of Sun Corporation included the data shown below for the year 20x4. No dividends were declared in 20x4. During 20x5, Sun declared cash dividends of $320,000. Share capital is as follows:

Preferred shares, no-par value, dividend entitlement,
$3 per share, 12,000 shares outstanding $240,000
Common shares, no-par value, 36,000 shares outstanding 720,000

Allocate and declare dividends in each of the following cases:

Case 1 The preferred shares are noncumulative and nonparticipating.

	Preferred	Common	allocated
Dividends declared			$320,000
Preferred, current	$36,000		(36,000)
			$284,000
Common, remainder	–0–	$284,000	(284,000)
	$36,000	$284,000	–0–

Case 2 The preferred shares are cumulative and nonparticipating.

	Preferred	Common	allocated
Dividends declared			$320,000
Preferred, in arrears	$36,000		(36,000)
			$284,000
Preferred, current	36,000		(36,000)
			248,000
Common, remainder		$248,000	(248,000)
	$72,000	$248,000	–0–

Case 3 The preferred shares are noncumulative and fully participating. The matching dividend is $3 per share.

	Preferred	Common	allocated
Dividends declared			$320,000
Preferred, current	$36,000		(36,000)
			$284,000
Common, matching[a]		$108,000	(108,000)
			176,000
Preferred, participating[b]	44,000		(44,000)
(25% × 176,000)			132,000
Common, participating[b]		132,000	(132,000)
(75% × 176,000)			
	$80,000	$240,000	–0–

[a] Common, matching dividend
   Preferred dividend
      12,000 shares × $3 = $36,000
      36,000 common shares × $3 = $108,000
[b] Participating-pro rata ratio

	Dividend	Ratio
Preferred shares	$ 36,000	25%
Common shares	108,000	75%
	$144,000	100%

Case 4 The preferred shares are cumulative and fully participating.

	Preferred	Common	To be allocated
Dividends declared			$320,000
Preferred, in arrears	$36,000		(36,000)
			$284,000
Preferred, current	36,000		(36,000)
			248,000
Common, matching		$108,000	(108,000)
			140,000
Preferred, participating (25% × $140,000)	35,000		(35,000)
			105,000
Common, participating (75% × $140,000)		105,000	(105,000)
	$107,000	$213,000	–0–

Case 5 The preferred shares are cumulative and partially participating, with maximum participation rate of $2 above the stated rate of $3.

	Preferred	Common	To be allocated
Dividends declared			$320,000
Preferred, in arrears	$36,000		(36,000)
			$284,000
Preferred, current	36,000		(36,000)
			248,000
Common, matching		$108,000	(108,000)
			140,000
Preferred, participating[a] ($2 ceiling)	24,000		(24,000)
			116,000
Common, remainder		116,000	(116,000)
	$96,000	$224,000	–0–

[a] Participation–pro rata ratio–ceiling $2
Preferred maximum participation:
Lesser of participation or maximum:
1) 12,000 shares x $2 = $24,000, $24,000/$240,000 = 10%
   or
2) Preferred 25% of $140,000 = $35,000
Limit = $24,000

Property Dividends and Spin-offs

When a corporation pays dividends with non-cash assets, the dividends are called *property dividends*. Property dividends are recorded at the current market value of the assets transferred. Corporations recognize a gain or a loss on disposal of the assets as of the declaration date.

On the date of declaration:
    a. To record revaluation of the property:

Investment in equity securities	xxxx	
Gain on disposal of security investment		xxxx

b. To record the dividend:

Retained earnings	xxxx	
Property dividend payable		xxxx

At the distribution date:

Property dividend payable	xxxx	
Investment in equity security		xxxx

A *spin-off* is where the shares of a subsidiary are distributed to the parent company's shareholders. This is in effect a capital transaction which means that a gain or loss cannot be recognized.

Liquidating Dividends
Liquidating dividends occur when the dividend is paid out of equity other than retained earnings. Shareholders must be informed of the portion of any dividend that represents a return of capital.

Script Dividends
These arise when a corporation declares dividends and issues promissory notes (scripts) to the shareholders.

Stock Dividends
These entail a proportional distribution to shareholders of additional common or preferred shares of the corporation. They increase the number of shares outstanding but have no effect on total shareholders' equity. Your text explains some for the reasons for issuing stock dividends.

Accounting Issues Relating to Stock Dividends
There are two issues with respect to accounting for stock dividends – value and timing.

There are three alternatives for recording a stock dividend.
1. Market value method.
2. Stated value method.
3. Memo entry.

The AcSB has made no recommendation on the matter; however, the *Canada Business Corporations Act* requires shares to be issued at fair market value.

Recognition of the dividend could be at declaration or at issue date. The difference is trivial. Disclosure would accompany both alternatives.

The stock dividend distributable account is not a liability but an account in the equity section. The declaration of a stock dividend can be revoked prior to the issuance date.

WATCH!

ILLUSTRATION

Beta Ltd. has 100,000 common shares outstanding, and declares a 10% common stock dividend. The board of directors directed that the dividend be recorded at market value. The market value after issuance was $8 per share.

Entry at declaration date:

Retained earnings	80,000	
Stock dividend distributable[a]		80,000

[a] Reported as a credit in shareholders' equity.

Entry at issuance date:

Stock dividend distributable	80,000	
Common shares		80,000

Fractional Share Rights

When a small stock dividend is issued, not all shareholders will own exactly the number of shares needed to receive whole shares. Fractional shares may be issued of a cash distribution can be made.

ILLUSTRATION

Instead of issuing 10,000 shares, the corporation issued 8,000 shares and enough fractional share rights for the remaining 2,000 shares. That is, 2,000 shares x 10 rights each = 20,000 rights.

If the market value of one share is $8, then the market value of 10 rights must be $8. Therefore, $8/10 rights = $.80 is the value of one right.

To record the issuance of 8,000 shares and 20,000 share rights:

Retained earnings (10,000 shares × $8)	80,000	
Common shares (8,000 shares × $8)		64,000
Common shares fractional		
share rights (20,000 × $.80)		16,000

To record 10% stock dividend for 10,000 shares—
8,000 shares issued plus 20,000 share rights
for the remaining 2,000 shares.

To record redemption of 15,000 share rights:

Common share fractional share rights		
(15,000 × $.80)	12,000	
Common shares (15,000/10		
= 1,500 shares)		12,000

To record redemption of 15,000 rights for 1,500 shares.

To record lapse of the remaining rights:

Common share fractional share rights		
(20,000 − 15,000 = 5,000, × $.80)	4,000	
Contributed capital, lapse of		
share rights		4,000

To record the lapse of the remaining 5,000 share rights.

An alternative to issuing fractional share rights requires the corporation to pay the cash equivalent for the 20,000 share rights (2,000 × $.80 = $16,000). To obtain the cash, the corporation sells the equivalent number of shares: (20,000/10 = 2,000 shares). The entry is then:

Cash	16,000	
Common shares (200 shares × $8)		16,000
Retained earnings (10,000 shares × $.80)	80,000	
Common shares (8,000 shares × $.80)		64,000
Cash		16,000

8. STOCK SPLITS

A stock split is a change in the number of shares outstanding with no change in the recorded capital accounts. No capitalization of retained earnings is involved. The main purpose of a stock split is to increase the number of shares, reduce the market price per share, and improve the marketability of the stock.

A stock *split* is similar to a stock *dividend* in that additional shares of stock are distributed. No accounting entry is needed, only a memo.   WATCH!

9. ADDITIONAL CONTRIBUTED CAPITAL

CONTRIBUTED CAPITAL	
Decreased by (debits):	Increased by the following (credits):
	Receipt of a donation of assets (donated capital).
Retirement of shares at a price greater than average issue price to date, when previous contributed capital has been recorded.	Retirement of shares at a price less than average issue price to date.
	Issue of par value shares at a price or assigned value higher than par.
Treasury stock transactions, shares issued below cost, when previous contributed capital has been recorded.	Treasury stock transactions, shares reissued above cost.
A financial restructuring.	

10. OTHER COMPONENTS OF SHAREHOLDERS' EQUITY

Accumulated Other Comprehensive Income (OCI)
The only items that can be recorded in OCI are the items that GAAP requires to be included. They are:

1. Gains and losses on available-for-sale financial instruments (Chapter 7).
2. Gains and losses on certain hedging instruments (Chapters 12 and 14).
3. Translations gains and losses on self-sustaining foreign operations (Chapter 11).

Revaluation Adjustment

One more source of amounts reported in shareholders' equity is a **comprehensive revaluation of assets and liabilities from cost to market value.** This type of revaluation is permitted *only* when there is (a) a change in control or (b) a financial reorganization (see also discussion in chapter 10).

11. SHAREHOLDERS' EQUITY DISCLOSURE

Corporations must disclose the items and conditions of all share classes. They must also disclose the changes in their equity accounts.

TRUE–FALSE QUESTIONS

T F **1.** Owners of common shares are more likely to possess voting rights than owners of preferred shares.

T F **2.** The dividend preference of preferred shares generally is a fixed percentage of its market price.

T F **2.** In the event of liquidation, preferred shareholders always have a right over common shareholders to the assets of the corporation.

T F **4.** If preferred shares are retractable, the corporation has an option to acquire a specified number of common shares within a specified time period at a specified price.

T F **5.** At the time a common shares subscription contract is signed, the common shares account is credited for the issue price of the shares.

T F **6.** The existence of a credit balance in the unappropriated retained earnings indicates that a corporation has cash available for paying dividends.

T F **7.** The declaration of a cash dividend creates a legal obligation to pay the dividend that did not exist prior to the declaration.

T F **8.** A stock dividend does not affect assets, liabilities, or total shareholders' equity.

T F **9.** A stock split is a change in the number of shares outstanding, with a corresponding change in the recorded capital accounts.

T F **10.** Other comprehensive income (OCI) is a component of retained earnings.

MULTIPLE CHOICE QUESTIONS

_____ **1.** Shareholders' equity is generally classified into two major categories:
   a. Contributed capital and donated capital.
   b. Appropriated capital and restricted retained earnings.
   c. Retained earnings and unrestricted capital.
   d. Contributed capital and earned capital.

___ 2. When a corporation is incorporated under the CBCA and that company purchases its own shares on the market:
   a. they are recorded as treasury shares.
   b. the excess of purchase price over cost is a loss.
   c. they must be cancelled.
   d. the gain or loss is recorded on the income statement.

___ 3. Various features and restrictions are often attached to preferred shares. Which of the following combinations of features are most typical of preferred shares with primarily debt characteristics rather than equity characteristics?
   a. Noncumulative, participating, nonredeemable, voting.
   b. Cumulative, participating, redeemable, voting.
   c. Noncumulative, nonparticipating, nonredeemable, nonvoting.
   d. Cumulative, nonparticipating, redeemable, non-voting.

___ 4. Bartlett Co. is authorized to issue 100,000 no-par common shares. Subscribers have contracted to purchase the shares at $50 per share with a 30% down payment. Assume that Eric Bone subscribed to 2,000 shares but defaults after paying his 30% down payment. The terms of the agreement afford the subscriber shares on a pro rata basis. The journal entry for disposition of the balances in the accounts related to Bone includes a:
   a. credit to common shares for $30,000.
   b. credit to subscriptions receivable for $100,000.
   c. debit to common shares for $30,000.
   d. debit to common shares subscribed for $30,000.

___ 5. Using the same data as in question 4, assume that Tina Duncan subscribed to 1,000 shares but defaults after paying her 30% down payment. The 1,000 shares will be sold and Tina's down payment will be returned. The journal entry to record Tina's default on 1,000 shares includes a:
   a. debit to common shares subscribed for $15,000.
   b. debit to common shares subscribed for $50,000.
   c. credit to due to defaulting subscriber for $35,000.
   d. credit to subscriptions receivable for $50,000.

___ 6. The basic rights of common share ownership generally do *not* include:
   a. the right to vote for directors.
   b. the right over preferred shares to receive a specified rate or amount of dividends.
   c. the right to share in the distribution of assets in the event of liquidation.
   d. the right to the residual amount of dividends as declared by the board of directors.

_____ 7. If the fair value of a donated operational asset is known, it should be recorded as a debit to operational assets and a credit to:
a. other contributed capital.
b. retained earnings.
c. a deferred charge.
d. other revenue.

_____ 8. When all the preferred shares are purchased and formally retired by the issuing corporation for less than the original issue price, accounting for the retirement increases:
a. retained earnings.
b. contributed capital unrealized.
c. net income for the period.
d. contributed capital from share retirement.

_____ 9. Dividends in arrears:
a. are reported in a note to the financial statements.
b. are reported in contributed capital.
c. are reported as a current liability.
d. are reported as a long-term liability.

_____ 10. The City of Manford donated land to XYZ Corporation. Manford's book value of the land was $400,000 at the time of the transfer. The land was appraised for property tax purposes at $500,000. A similar parcel of land recently sold for $600,000. XYZ will likely show the donated land on its books at:
a. $400,000
b. $600,000
c. $500,000
d. $0

_____ 11. Megan Ltd. has 10,000 cumulative and fully participating $7 preferred shares issued and outstanding (issue price $100 each). It also has 50,000 common shares issued and outstanding (issue price $20 each). The December 31, 20x1, preferred dividends are in arrears. The common matching dividend is $1.40. What total dividend must Megan declare on December 31, 20x2, to ensure that the common shareholders receive a dividend of $2 per share?
a. $100,000
b. $170,000
c. $200,000
d. $270,000

_____ 12. Combine Ltd. had a lump sum (basket) sale of two of its securities, common and preferred shares. The market value of the common shares sold was $20,000, and the market value of the preferred shares sold was $25,000. The total proceeds were $40,500. Combine should record the issue of these shares at:

	Common shares	Preferred shares
a.	$15,500	$25,000
b.	18,000	22,500
c.	20,000	20,500
d.	20,000	25,000

_____ 13. Storm Corporation reported shareholders' equity on its balance sheet at December 31, 20x4, as follows:

Common shares, 20,000 shares outstanding	200,000
Contributed capital in excess of cost over price	100,000
Retained earnings	200,000
Total contributed capital	$500,000

In 20x5, Storm earned income of $25,000, declared cash dividends of $15,000, and retired 2,000 shares of its outstanding stock for $20 per share. At the end of 20x5, Storm's contributed capital in excess of cost over price and retained earnings should have the following balances:

	Contributed capital	Retained earnings
a.	$ 90,000	$ 200,000
b.	100,000	110,000
c.	80,000	210,000
d.	–0–	210,000

_____ 14. Assume the same data as in question 13, except that Storm intended to reissue those reacquired shares, and that the single transaction method is used to account for treasury stock transactions. Storm's contributed capital and retained earnings at the end of 20x2 should have the following balances:

	Contributed capital	Retained earnings
a.	$ 90,000	$ 200,000
b.	100,000	110,000
c.	80,000	210,000
d.	100,000	210,000

15. Assume the same data as in question 13. What is the total amount of shareholders' equity at the end of 20x5?
- a. $470,000
- b. $500,000
- c. $510,000
- d. $525,000

SOLUTIONS TO TRUE–FALSE QUESTIONS

1. T

2. F The dividend preference of preferred shares is usually at a stated rate, based not on the market price but on the carrying value or an amount per share.

3. T

4. F Retractable preferred shares have specific buy-back provisions, at the option of the shareholder.

5. F The common shares account is not credited until the shares are issued. The shares are issued when paid in full.

6. F The balance in retained earnings does not give any information related to cash availability.

7. T

8. T

9. F A stock split is a change in the number of shares outstanding with no change in the recorded capital accounts.

10. F Other comprehensive income (OCI) is a component of shareholders' equity but not part of retained earnings.

SOLUTIONS TO MULTIPLE CHOICE QUESTIONS

1. d

2. c

3. d These characteristics are closer to a debt characteristics.

4. a The original payment made by Bone was = 2,000 x $50 x 30% = $30,000. The terms of the agreement afford the subscriber shares on a pro rata basis. The number of shares issued will be 600 shares @ $50 = $30,000. The journal entry will be as follows: debit to common shares subscribed, $100,000, credit to common shares, $30,000, and credit to subscriptions receivable, $70,000.

5. b The original payment made by Tina Duncan was 1,000 shares x $50 x 30% = $15,000.The shares will be sold on the market, and Tina will get the money when this happens. The journal entry will be as follows: debit to common shares subscribed, $50,000, credit to due to defaulting subscriber, $15,000, and credit to subscriptions receivable, $35,000.

6. b Preferred shareholders are the first to receive dividends if declared.

7. a

8. d According to the *CICA Handbook,* paragraph 3240.15.

9. a The dividends in arrears are not liabilities until declared.

10. b The recorded amount should be the value that is the most reliable value. The recent sale of a similar parcel of land is the most reliable fair market value. The book value is totally irrelevant.

11. d First the preferred dividends in arrears must be paid: 10,000 shares $7 = $70,000, plus current preferred dividends = $70,000, then matching common dividends = 50,000 shares @ $1.40 = $70,000. Participating pro rata ratio = Preferred shares = $1,000,000 (50%), common shares = $1,000,000 (50%). Total dividend to be received by common shareholders = $2.00, less matching dividend of $1.40 = $0.60 x 50,000 = $30,000. The preferred shares are fully participating and represent 50% of total contributed capital ($1,000,000/$2,000,000), so the preferred shareholders will receive the same additional dividend as the common shareholders = $30,000. Total dividend payment: Preferred shares = $70,000 + S70,000 + $30,000 = $170,000; Common shares = $70,000 + $30,000 = $100,000 ($100,000/50,000 shares = $2.00). Total dividend Megan must declare is $270,000.

12. b Market value of the lump sum sale = $20,000 + $25,000 = $45,000. The value assigned to the common shares = $40,500 x 20,000/$45,000 = $18,000, and the value assigned to preferred shares = $40,500 x $25,000/$45,000 = $22,500.

13. c To record the purchase of its own shares: debit to common shares 2,000 shares x ($200,000/20,000 = $10) = $20,000; debit to contributed capital in excess of cost over price 2,000 shares x ($20 – $10 = $10) = $20,000, and credit to cash = $40,000. The balance in the contributed capital in excess of cost over price = $100,000 – $20,000 = $80,000. Retained earnings balance is $200,000 + 25,000 – $15,000 = $210,000.

14. d To record the acquisition of 2,000 shares of common treasury shares at $20 per share: debit to treasury stock $40,000, and credit to cash $40,000. The balance in retained earnings will be $200,000 + $25,000 – $15,000 = $210,000. The balance in the contributed capital in excess of cost over price is not affected by the original transaction.

15. a Common shares = $200,000 – $20,000 = $180,000; contributed capital in excess of cost over price = $80,000; retained earnings = $210,000. So, $180,000 + $80,000 + $210,000 = $470,000.

PROBLEMS

Problem 1

PURPOSE: To illustrate accounting for share issuance: cash and subscriptions.

Barrows Corporation was authorized to issue unlimited preferred shares, 80 cents, no-par value, and unlimited common shares, no-par. During the first year, the following transactions occurred:

    (1) 50,000 common shares were sold for cash at $15 per share.
    (2) 5,000 preferred shares were sold for cash at $30 per share.

(3) Subscriptions were received for 5,000 common shares at $16 per share; 50% was received as a down payment, and the balance was payable in two months. The shares will be issued upon collection in full. As part of the agreement, if the second payment is not made, the first will be forfeited to the company.

(4) 5,000 common shares, 500 preferred shares, and $80,000 cash were given as payment for some land the company needed. This land originally cost $75,000 and had a net book value in the selling company's books of $50,000.

(5) The second payment on subscriptions was received with one exception: a subscriber for 100 shares defaulted on her payment.

Required

a. Prepare the journal entries to record the above transactions.

b. Prepare the shareholders' equity section of the balance sheet at year end. Retained earnings at the end of the year amounted to $160,000.

Problem 2

PURPOSE: To demonstrate accounting for share reacquisition.

McNally Corporation had the following account balances on January 1, 20x5:

Common shares, no-par, 40,000 shares outstanding	$200,000
Preferred shares, no-par, 9%, cumulative and nonparticipating, 5,000 shares outstanding	100,000
Contributed surplus on retirement of common shares	5,000
Contributed surplus—donated assets	40,000
Retained earnings	210,000

During the year, the following transactions took place, in chronological order.

(1) Acquired and retired 1,000 preferred shares at $15.

(2) Acquired and retired 5,000 common shares at $10.

(3) Acquired and retired 2,000 preferred shares at $22.

(4) Acquired and retired 1,000 common shares at $6.

Required

a. Prepare journal entries to record the above transactions.

b. Give the resulting balance in each shareholders' equity account.

Problem 3

PURPOSE: To illustrate the accounting for appropriations and restrictions of retained earnings.

Miller Corporation carries separate accounts for appropriations and restrictions of retained earnings. One such account is the reserve for profits invested in property, plant and equipment—$840,000. Share capital outstanding, 20,000 shares of no-par value common, amounted to $800,000.

The company had bonds payable outstanding of $400,000. The following accounts were also carried: bond sinking fund, $200,000; and bond sinking fund reserve, $200,000.

Required

Prepare the journal entries for the following, using preferable titles:

      a. To establish the reserve related to operational assets.

      b. To establish the bond sinking fund.

      c. To establish the reserve for the bond sinking fund.

      d. To record payment of the bonds, assuming the bond sinking fund and the reserve each have a $360,000 balance at retirement date.

SOLUTIONS TO PROBLEMS

Problem 1

Requirement a

Memo: Common shares, no-par, unlimited shares authorized.

Memo: Preferred shares, no-par, $0.80, unlimited shares authorized.

(1)	Cash	750,000	
	Common shares (50,000 × $15)		750,000
(2)	Cash (5,000 shares × $30)	150,000	
	Preferred shares (5,000)		150,000
(3)	Cash (5,000 × 16 × 50%)	40,000	
	Subscriptions receivable, common	40,000	
	Common shares subscribed (5,000)		80,000
(4)	Land[a]	175,000	
	Common shares (5,000 × $16)		80,000
	Preferred shares (500 × $30)		15,000
	Cash		80,000

[a] Assumes the current market value of the share capital was realistic to value the land: (5,000 × $16) + (500 x $30) + $80,000 = $175,000.

(5)	Cash: $40,000 − (100 × $16 × 50%)	39,200	
	Common shares subscribed (5,000)	80,000	
	Subscriptions receivable, common		40,000
	Common shares (5,000 − 100) × $16		78,400
	Contributed surplus (100 × $16 × 50%)		800

The amount initially contributed by the subscriber of 100 shares who defaulted has been forfeited under the agreement. And since it is nonrefundable and did not result in any shares being issued, it has been booked as contributed capital.

Requirement b

BARROWS CORPORATION
Shareholders' Equity

Contributed capital:
  Share capital
    Preferred shares, no-par, $0.80, unlimited shares
      authorized, 5,500 shares issued and outstanding $ 165,000
    Common shares, no-par, unlimited shares authorized,
      59,900 shares issued and outstanding   908,400
                                                                                               1,073,400
  Contributed capital on defaulted subscription   800
    Total contributed surplus   1,873,400
    Retained earnings   160,000
      Total shareholders' equity $2,033,400

Problem 2

Requirement a

(1) Preferred shares (1,000 × $20)   20,000

       Cash (1,000 × $15)   15,000
       Contributed surplus on retirement
         of preferred shares   5,000

(2) Common shares (5,000 × $5)   25,000

       Contributed surplus on retirement
         common shares (balance)   5,000
       Retained earnings ($50,000 – $25,000
         – $10,000)   20,000
           Cash   50,000

(3) Preferred shares (2,000 × $20)   40,000

       Contributed surplus on retirement
         of preferred shares   4,000
           Cash (2,000 × $22)   44,000

(4) Common shares (1,000 × $5)   5,000

       Retained earnings ($6,000 – $5,000)   1,000
           Cash (1,000 × $6)   6,000

Requirement b

Common shares ($200,000 – $25,000 – $5,000) $170,000
Preferred shares ($100,000 – $20,000 – $40,000)   40,000
Contributed surplus on retirement of shares
  Common ($5,000 – $5,000)   –0–
  Preferred ($5,000 – $4,000)   1,000
Retained earnings ($210,000 – 20,000 – $1,000)   189,000

Problem 3

Requirement a

To establish the appropriation of retained earnings related to property, plant and equipment—

Retained earnings   840,000
    Appropriated retained earnings invested
      in property, plant and equipment   840,000

Requirement b
To establish the bond sinking fund—

Bond sinking fund	200,000	
Cash		200,000

Requirement c
To establish the appropriation for bond sinking fund—

Retained earnings	200,000	
Appropriated retained earnings, bond sinking fund		200,000

Requirement d
To record payment of bonds—

Bonds payable	400,000	
Bond sinking fund		360,000
Cash		40,000

To return the appropriation for bond sinking fund to the unappropriated retained earnings account—

Appropriated retained earnings, bond sinking fund	360,000	
Retained earnings		360,000

CASE

Edward Banfield, an engineer, developed a special safety device to be installed in backyard swimming pools that, when turned on, would set off an alarm should anything (e.g., a child) fall into the water. Over a two-year period, Banfield's spare time was spent developing and testing the device. After receiving a patent, three of Banfield's friends, including a lawyer, considered plans to produce and market the device. Accordingly, a company was formed that was authorized to issue an unlimited number of no-par value common shares. Each of the four organizers contributed $20,000, and each received in return 2,000 shares. They also agreed that, for other consideration, each would receive 5,000 additional shares. Each organizer made a proposal as to how the additional 5,000 shares would be paid for. These individual proposals were made independently, then the group considered them as a package. The four proposals were as follows:

Banfield. The patent would be turned over to the corporation as payment for the 5,000 shares. An independent appraisal of the patent could not be obtained.

Bill Lui. Mr. Lui, a lawyer, has suggested that 1,000 shares would be received for legal services already rendered during organization, 1,000 shares would be received as advance payment for legal retainer fees for the next three years, and the balance would be paid for in cash at $10 per share.

Frank Spalding. A small building, suitable for operations, would be given to the corporation for the 5,000 shares. It is estimated that $20,000 would be needed for renovations prior to use. Spalding estimates that the market value of the building is $750,000. There is a $580,000 mortgage on it to be assumed by the corporation.

Jennifer Franconi. Ms. Franconi has suggested that she pay $10,000 cash for the shares and provide a non-interest bearing note for $40,000, to be paid out of dividends on her common shares over the next five years.

Mr. Banfield has come to you, an independent accountant, for advice on two issues:

1. How would the above proposals be recorded in the accounts? Assess the valuation basis for each, including alternatives.
2. Do you think that the proposals made are equitable? Explain the basis for your reasoning.

Required: Respond to Mr. Banfield.

KEY POINTS IN THE CASE

The case should be written as a report to Mr. Banfield.

Overview

This is a company in a startup where there are four initial investments to value and record. Fairness and equity must be considered when evaluating the relative contributions to each party. The accountant has an ethical responsibility to ensure, to the extent possible, that all shareholders are treated fairly.

Analysis

Recording the initial share acquisitions requires only a straightforward journal entry.

To record the cash sale of shares to organizers (four separate transactions)
Cash..	80,000	
Common shares (8,000 shares).................		80,000

This initial recording of the transactions can be used to value the remaining shares. Support for using this basis is the transaction occurred recently and each contributor paid cash for these shares. However, the $10 per share value is questionable because the 8,000 shares may not have been issued at fair market value. This is not an arm's-length transaction. Each of the journal entries below assumes that the $10 per share is a valid value to use. The numbers and amounts would differ if one of the four proposals was seen as a more valid starting point. It is also key to realize that all the 5,000 shares for each of the investors must have the same value.

Banfield Proposal

Patent	50,000	
Common shares (5,000 shares).....................		50,000

Under the cost principle $10 per share is the best estimation of market value since so few capital transactions have occurred and there is no appraisal available.

Appraisals would provide support for this entry. Two appraisals would be preferable. This proposal is equitable if the patent is worth something in the range of $50,000. Ethically the concern is that Banfield could be shortchanged if the product is very successful and the valuation is too low. Alternatively, the other shareholders may be shortchanged if the product is not a success.

Lui Proposal

Organization costs (1,000 shares x $10)..............	10,000	
Prepaid legal fees (1,000 shares x $10)................	10,000	
Cash..	30,000	
Common shares (5,000 shares)......................		50,000

This entry is also based on the $10 per share market value. It may not be appropriate to issue shares for service not yet performed since consideration is not yet received. This would mean the consideration by the lawyer is only $40,000.

The appropriateness of this proposal is difficult to assess. It must be considered if the past legal fees were worth $10,000. Independent evidence of this value needs to be obtained. Records of hours spent times Lui's usual billing rate may give an approximation of the value. A problem arises if no legal services are required over the next few years. It may be preferable for Lui to pay an extra $10,000 in cash, and then be formally hired as the lawyer for any additional work.

Spalding Proposal

Building ($50,000 + $580,000)	630,000	
Common shares (5,000 shares)......................		50,000
Mortgage payable, 12% (assumed by co.) ...		580,000

This entry presumes that the building is valued on the basis of $10 per share plus the PV of the mortgage. The $750,000 estimate provided by Spalding is questionable because there is no evidence that an independent appraisal was completed. The cost principle has been observed by recognizing the cost as the sum of the market value of the shares plus the debt. The required renovations could also be seen as a reason to reduce the value of the building.

To ensure this proposal is fair, there should be two independent appraisals obtained for the building. If the appraisals are lower than $630,000, they should require cash, or a reduction of the loan assumed for the difference. If the appraisals are higher than $630,000, Spalding may require additional compensation.

Fraconi Proposal

Cash..	10,000	
Subscription (note) receivable	40,000	
Common shares subscribed		50,000

Shares cannot be issued since proceeds have not been received. This transaction would be seen as being shares in installments or as subscription shares. Also note that discounting techniques are usually not applied to equity transactions. Therefore, this shareholder is paying less than $50,000 in real terms for her shares.

The proposal that the note be "paid out of dividends" is a problem since nothing is stipulated about what if dividends are not declared. Also, no dividends would be paid on the subscribed (unissued) shares. Franconi would have to use dividends from the original, paid shares only.

Assignment 13-5

Case A:

Machinery	50,000	
Common shares (600 shares × $70)..............................		42,000
Preferred shares (100 shares × $80)..............................		8,000

The recent share prices are assumed to reliably measure market value of the shares issued as well as the cost of the machinery.

The value placed on the machinery is assumed to not be higher than the fair market value of the machinery.

Case B:

Machinery	45,000	
Common shares (600 shares × $70)..............................		42,000
Preferred shares (residual)..............................		3,000

The machine should be recorded at market value. Common shares are recorded at market value, using the incremental method for the preferred shares.

Case C:

Machinery	44,000	
Common shares (600 shares)		24,000
Preferred shares (100 shares)		20,000

The appraised value is accepted as market value of the asset acquired because no reasonable value is available on the shares. Consider adjusting the entry if the market values of the shares are determinable in the near future.

Computation of relative values:

Common:	600 × $10 =	$ 6,000	54.5% × $44,000 =	$24,000
Preferred:	100 × $50 =	5,000	45.4% × $44,000 =	20,000
		$11,000		$44,000

Assignment 13-17

Requirement 1

a) Number of Ace Corporation shares required for the dividends in arrears:

$10,000 \times \$1.20 \times 2$ years $= \$24,000$
$\$24,000 \div \$60$ per share $= \underline{400}$ shares of Ace Corporation required for the property dividend to preferred shareholders (in arrears).

b) Cash dividends for the current year:

Preferred:	$10,000 \times \$1.20 =$	$12,000
Common:	50,000 shares $\times \$1.00 =$	50,000
	Total cash required	$62,000

Requirement 2
15 January 20x5 - declaration date:

Investment, Ace Corporation [400 shares $\times$ ($60 – $20)]	16,000	
Retained earnings (or dividends) ($24,000 + $62,000)	86,000	
Gain on disposal of shares of Ace Corporation		16,000
Cash dividends payable...		62,000
Property dividends payable (Ace Corporation shares)............		24,000

Note: the Ace Corporation shares should be revalued to fair value at the *declaration date* and the gain recognized at that time.

1 March 20x5, payment date:		
Property dividends payable	24,000	
Cash dividends payable..	62,000	
Investment, Ace Corporation (400 shares $\times$ $60)......................		24,000
Cash		62,000

Requirement 3
The investment in Ace shares would be recorded at book value in a spin-off; there would be no gain on disposal.

Assignment 13-25
Requirement 1

HAWKEN SUPPLY CORPORATION
Income Statement
for the year ended

	20x5	20x4
Revenues:		
Sales revenue...	$260,000	$240,000
Expenses:		
Cost of goods sold	143,000	134,000
Expenses	77,000	71,000
Total expenses	220,000	205,000
Income from operations, pretax....................................	40,000	35,000
Income tax expense (45%)	18,000	15,750
Income before extraordinary items	22,000	19,250
Extraordinary items:		
Loss (net of tax of ($2,000 × .45) $900)	(1,100)	
Loss (net of tax of ($7,000 × .45) $3,150)		(3,850)
Net income...	$ 20,900	$ 15,400
Earnings per share (10,000 common shares outstanding)		
Income before extraordinary items..............................	$2.20	$1.93
Extraordinary losses...	(.11)	(.39)
Net income	$2.09	$1.54

Requirement 2

HAWKEN SUPPLY CORPORATION
Retained Earnings Statement
for the year ended

	20x5	20x4
Retained earnings balance 1 January	$287,100	$ 295,000
Adjustments applicable to prior years:		
Deduct: Error correction [net of tax of ($6,000 × 45%) $2,700].....		(3,300)
Corrected balance..	287,100	291,700
Net income for year	20,900	15,400
Total...	308,000	307,100
Deductions:		
Cash dividend..	--	(20,000)
Stock dividend	(30,000)	--
Retained earnings, 31 December (Note A)..	$278,000	$287,100

Note A - Appropriations	and restrictions: Bond Fund Restriction	Expansion Appropriation	Unappropriated	Total
Balance 1 Jan. 20x4	$70,000	$65,000	$160,000	$295,000
Additions during 20x4	10,000	0	(17,900)	(7,900)
Balance 31 Dec. 20x4	80,000	65,000	142,100	287,100
Additions during 20x5	10,000	0	(19,100)	(9,100)
Balance 31 Dec. 20x5	$90,000	$65,000	$123,000	$278,000

**Additions to unappropriated:x4 $15,400 – $3,300 – $20,000 – $10,000 = ($17,900)
x5 $20,900 – $30,000 – $10,000 = ($19,100)

SOLUTIONS TO CONCEPT REVIEW QUESTIONS

Page 801

1. The essential difference between a *public corporation* and a *private corporation* is that the shares of the latter cannot be publicly traded.

2. Private corporations can obtain equity from external investors without having to register with provincial securities commissions through private placements with institutional investors. Another alternative may be to ensure that each individual investor invests capital of at least a certain amount ($97,000 in Alberta and British Columbia, $150,000 in Ontario and Quebec). Such investors are presumed to be sophisticated and do not require the protection offered by provincial regulators.

3. *Restricted shares* are a type (or class) of common share with no voting rights or limited voting rights.

4. *Treasury shares* are outstanding shares that are reacquired by corporation, and held pending resale.

Page 809

1. In general, when shares are issued for non-cash assets the transaction should be recognized at the fair value of the consideration given (i.e., the value of the shares issued). When the value of the shares cannot be determined, the value of the assets received may be used.

2. A *basket sale* of share capital is the sale and issue of two or more classes of shares for one lump-sum amount.

3. When shares are redeemed or retired, the cost of the redemption should be charged to the shareholder equity accounts as follows: *first,* to share capital at the average price per issued share; *second,* to contributed capital, if any has been created by previous treasury stock transactions in the same class of shares; and *finally,* any remaining amount to retained earnings.

1. The dates that require entries are the declaration date and the payment date. The entries are:

On date of declaration:

Retained earnings	xxxx	
Cash dividends payable		xxxx

On date of payment:

Cash dividends payable	xxxx	
Cash		xxxx

2. In paying a cash dividend, retained earnings are reduced by the amount of the dividend paid, as is the cash account. A stock dividend will also reduce retained earnings but will not affect assets, liabilities, or the total shareholders' equity of the issuing corporation. A stock dividend is a proportional distribution to shareholders of additional common or preferred shares of the corporation. Retained earnings are reduced by the amount of the stock dividend; the common or preferred stock accounts are increased by the same amount.

3. A *participating preferred dividend* allows the holder to participate in dividends above the stated preferential rate on a pro rata basis in dividend declarations with common shareholders. First, the preferred shareholders receive their preference rate. Second, the common shareholders receive a specified matching dividend. Then, if the total dividend declaration is larger than the aggregate of these two amounts, the excess is divided pro rata between the two share classes.

1. A *stock split* is change in the number of shares outstanding with no change in the recorded capital. A stock dividend is the capitalization of retained earnings to share capital. The former does not affect shareholders' equity accounts. A stock dividend will affect shareholders' equity accounts by reducing retained earnings by the amount of the dividend declared, and increasing share capital by the same amount.

2. Transactions that may result in additions to contributed capital include the following: receipt of donated assets, retirement of shares at a price more than average issue price, the issue of par value shares at a price or assigned value higher than par, and treasury transactions with shares reissued above cost.

3. The following items are included in accumulated other comprehensive income:

- Gains and losses on available-for-sale financial instruments.
- Gains and losses on certain hedging instruments.
- Translations gains and losses on self-sustaining foreign operations .

CHAPTER 14

COMPLEX DEBT AND EQUITY INSTRUMENTS

When preparing financial statements, a major task is to classify and organize the financial statement accounts into categories. Unfortunately, some things are hard to classify.

Many modern financing instruments have characteristics of both debt and equity. This chapter examines instruments used in raising capital that do not fit neatly into the debt and share equity categories.

The Appendix looks at accounting for financial restructuring, in which debt instruments may be converted involuntarily to share equity.

1. THE DEBT-TO-EQUITY CONTINUUM

Accountants traditionally relied on the legal description of capital instruments for classification. This method works as long as debt and equity conform to expectations:

- Debt carried a firm commitment to interest payments and repayments of capital at maturity.
- Equity was a residual interest in net assets, with rights only to dividends as declared and no guaranteed return of capital.

Some types of financing don't fit neatly into these categories. For example:

Income bonds are bonds that pay interest, but only when the corporation has earned sufficient income in a year to enable payment of interest. While the principal amount of income bonds must be paid at maturity, the interest is contingent upon earnings.

Convertible debt is a debt intended by the issuing corporation to be exchanged for shares by the investors at some time prior to maturity. The option rests with the holder, but sometimes a corporation will issue convertible debt in which it is the issuer who decides whether the debt will be satisfied through the issuance of shares rather than cash payment.

Derivative instruments are contracts that specify an exchange of financial instruments at a specified price. They can be used to hedge interest rate risk and exchange risk. They derive their value from the underlying security that can be acquired by exercising the rights, futures contracts for commodities, and forward contracts for foreign currency. The may or may not result in the physical transfer of the underlying instrument either at inception of the contract or on settlement.

Hybrid securities are securities that have characteristics of both debt and equity. Examples are shares issued with many of the characteristics of debt and debt instruments that function like equity.

The balance sheet does draw a definite line between debt and equity and the accounting profession is in the process of developing a set of comprehensive standards to deal with the reporting problems of hybrid securities.

2. FINANCIAL INSTRUMENTS—GENERAL PRINCIPLES

There are been recent developments and new standards in this area. Section 3860 of the CICA handbook Financial Instruments – Disclosure and Presentation came into effect on 1996. This section deals only with *presentation and disclosure* issues and not with *measurement and recognition* issues. Section 3855 Financial Instruments – Recognition of Measurement becomes effective in 2007. This section will require fair value measurement for most assets and financial liabilities held for trading. It will require all derivatives instruments to be measured at fair value.

A **hybrid** instrument has a liability and an equity component. Hybrid financial instrument must be classified as debt or equity in accordance with their substance. This holds true for the balance sheet presentation and the income statement presentation relating to payments on the instruments. If an instrument contains components of debt and equity it must be split. Note the accounting treatment does not impact the tax treatment.

3. DEBT VERSUS EQUITY—THE GENERAL PROBLEM

The impact of the difference in classifying a financial instrument as debt or equity is presented in a table on page 860 of your text. Classification impacts the balance sheet and the income statement.

To determine whether a hybrid security is debt or equity in substance, it is necessary to answer the following questions:

1. Is the periodic return on capital obligatory?
2. Is the debtor legally obligated to repay the principal, either at a fixed, pre-determined date or at the option of the creditor?

- If the answer to both is "yes", then it is a liability.
- If the answer to both is "no", then it is an equity.
- If you get one "yes" and one "no", you have a hybrid security that must be split between debt and equity.

WATCH! Accountants cannot rely on the apparent *form* of any contract between a corporation and its suppliers of capital. Instead a security should be reported in accordance with the *substance of* its contractual provisions.

4. SPECIFIC EXAMPLES OF HYBRID SECURITY CLASSIFICATION

Retractable Preferred Shares

Retractable shares can be redeemed at the option of the holder. If they must be redeemed on or before a certain date they are term-preferred shares.

Preferred shares are likely to be classified as debt if:
- (a) redemption is contractually required, *or*
- (b) redemption can be forced by the investor, *or*
- (c) terms of the shares are such that redemption is essentially forced, even if the entity is financially sound.

If the shares are classified as debt the payments on them are classified as interest rather than dividends. If the shares are redeemed at a premium, the premium should be accrued over the life of the debt.

Private companies electing to use differential reporting can classify these shares as equity.

TCH! Preferred shares that are redeemable at the company's option are NOT a liability.

Perpetual Debt

Perpetual debt is a loan that never has to be repaid or is highly unlikely ever to be repaid. There is a stated interest rate for the perpetual debt, and the corporation is obligated to pay the interest regularly, as required by the agreements with the lender.

The *CICA Handbook,* para. 3860.A19, states that perpetual debt should be classified as a liability at the present value of the stream of future interest payments.

Present value of future interest payments should be equal to the face value of the debt.

Convertible Debt

Bonds with a provision that they may be converted into shares at a specified price and ratio of exchange are an example of a convertible debt. A key element of convertible bonds is that management fully expects that investors will convert. Therefore, the company will never repay the principal.

Convertible Debt, at the Investor's Option

Convertible debt that is convertible at the option of the investor is: (1) a promise to pay interest and principal and (2) an option that gives the investor the right to use the principal to buy a certain number of common shares.

Proceeds from issuance of convertible bonds must be divided between the **liability** and the **option,** and the two must recorded **separately.**

Conversion

When convertible bonds are submitted for conversion:

1. Update any accounts relating to the bond premium or discount, accrued interest, and foreign exchange gains or losses on foreign currency denominated debt.
2. Transfer, to the share account, the balance of the liability account that pertains to the converted bonds .
3. Transfer, to the share account, the proportionate balance of the stock option account.

There are two alternative methods in recording the conversion: book value method and market value method.

To demonstrate the **book value** method, let's assume that $100,000 of bonds payable are outstanding that can be converted into 1,000 common shares. The following entry will be made when the bonds are first issued:

Cash	106,000	
Discount on bonds payable	9,200	
Bonds payable		100,000
Common stock conversion rights		15,200

Later the bonds are converted. Let's assume that the conversion occurs at interest date. On conversion date, the stock price is $105 per share and $6,000 of discount remains unamortized after updating the discount account. The entry to record the conversion is:

Bonds payable	100,000	
Common stock conversion rights	15,200	
Discount on bonds payable		6,000
Common shares		109,200

The difference between the original proceeds of the bond issue ($106,000) and the capitalized value for the shares into which it has been converted ($109,200) is the $3,200 of amortized discount.

If we used the **market value** method:

Bonds payable	100,000	
Common stock conversion rights	15,200	
Loss on conversion of bonds[a]	11,000	
Discount on bonds payable		6,000
Common shares		120,200

[a] Market value of shares issued (1,000 shares × $105 = $105,000) less book value of bonds ($94,000) equals loss of $11,000.

The common share value is arrived at by taking the book value of the bonds ($109,200) plus the loss on conversion of bonds ($11,000) equals $120,200.

Measurement

The *CICA Handbook* [CICA 3860.29) suggests two methods may be used to measure the two components:

> - *the incremental method in which the stock option is valued at the difference between the total proceeds of the bond issue and the market value of an equivalent "ordinary" bond issue; or*
> - *the proportional method, in which the proceeds of the bond issue are allocated on the basis of the relative market values of the ordinary bond and the imbedded stock option.*

CICA

Demonstration of the *incremental* method

Assume a convertible 5-year bond with face value $100, issue price $106, stated interest 7%, interest payable annually, and market interest 9%. The value of the bond is calculated as follows:

Present value $100, 5 years, 9%	=	$65.00	(100 × .64993)
+ Present value annuity, $7, 5 years, 9%	=	27.22	(7 × 3.88965)
		$92.22	
Conversion privilege: $106 – $92.22	=	$13.78	

The issuance will be recorded as follows:

Cash	106.00	
Discount on bonds payable[a]	7.78	
Bonds payable		100.00
Common stock conversion rights		13.78

[a] 100 – 92.22 = 7.78

The account *common stock conversion rights,* is an equity account that will be reported as contributed capital on the balance sheet. In later years the amount in that account will be transferred to share equity if and when the conversion rights are exercised, and transferred to other contributed capital if the conversion rights lapse.

Demonstration of the *proportional* method

Assume, using the above example, that the option pricing model produced a market value of $15.78 for the conversion feature. Allocation of the $106 proceeds is as follows:

	Market value	Proportion	Allocation
Liability component	$92.22	85.4%	$90.52
Stock option component	15.78	14.6%	15.48
	$108.00	100.0%	$106.00

Using the allocation approach, the bond issuance will be recorded as follows:

Cash	106.00	
Discount on convertible bonds	9.48	
Convertible bonds payable		100.00
Common stock conversion rights		15.48

Convertible Debt, at the Issuer's Option

When debt is convertible at the issuer's option there are three possible classifications, summarized in the following table:

	Return of principal	Periodic return on capital
1. Debt	Paid in cash or # of shares dependent on their market value at time of conversion	Paid in cash
2. Equity	Fixed conversion price	Fixed conversion price
3. Part debt and part equity	One component fixed in dollars , the other in shares	

If the company's option to repay the debentures through the issuance of common shares, the principal component of these bonds clearly is equity. The obligation to pay interest is a liability and should be measured at the present value of the interest stream.

Interest will be accounted for by the effective interest method, *calculated only on the outstanding balance of the interest liability.* The carrying value of the interest liability and the share equity portion will be increased each year. At maturity there will be a debit to share equity account and a credit to common shares or cash.

When a company can pay the interest as well as the principal in shares, the entire proceeds of the "debt" issue are classified as equity.

Exhibit 14-4 in the textbook summarizes the various types of convertible debt and the accounting for each.

5. STOCK OPTIONS

Stock options give the holder the right to buy shares at a fixed price. They are the most common form of derivative instruments.

Stock Rights and Warrants

Stock rights provide the holder with an option to acquire a specified number of shares in a corporation under prescribed conditions and within a stated time period.

Stock warrants are issued as an attachment to other securities.

Stock rights and warrants may be:
- (a) exercised, *or*
- (b) sold at the market value of the rights, *or*
- (c) allowed to lapse on expiration date.

Accounting for Stock Rights

The issuance of stock rights raises accounting issues for both the recipient and the issuing corporation.

The *investor* records the acquisition as an asset.

In accounting for the rights, the *issuing corporation* has a choice between two basic patterns. One involves **recognition;** the other involves **memorandum entries** regarding the rights.

Recognition

Assume that a corporation issues 20,000 rights allowing the holder(s) to acquire common shares in five years' time at an acquisition price of $40 per share, which is the current market price of the common shares. It takes one right to acquire a share, so 20,000 shares could be issued when the rights become exercisable. The corporation receives $10,000 for the rights.

Relevant dates:

1. Announcement date: only a memorandum entry.

2. Issuance date or grant date:

Cash	10,000	
Stock rights outstanding		10,000

3. If exercised: Assuming that the current market price of the common shares was $58 and that all rights are exercised:

Cash (20,000 × $40)	800,000	
Stock rights outstanding	10,000	
Common shares		810,000

4. At expiration: Assuming that the current market price of the common shares was $38 and all rights expired:

Stock rights outstanding	10,000	
Contributed capital, lapse		
of stock rights		10,000

Options are valued using the **fair value based method.** The options are valued at fair value of consideration received or the fair value of the option issued, whichever is more reliably determinable.

Memorandum Entries

This pattern is followed if the rights or warrants are issued for no consideration or no measurable consideration.

At the date of announcement and the date of issuance, only memorandum entries are used.

If the rights are exercised and cash is received, the journal entry will be as follows:

Cash	800,000	
Common shares		800,000

If rights expire, there will be a further memorandum entry to record the lapse of the rights.

Exhibit 14–5 summarizes accounting for stock options.

6. EXAMPLES OF STOCK OPTION REPORTING

The textbook provides the accounting for the following seven cases:

Memorandum Entries
1. *Issuance of stock rights to existing shareholders*—preemptive rights which are issued in advance of a planned sale of common shares or financial reorganization to allow shareholders to maintain their relative voting position in company.
2. *Rights issued as a "poison pill"*—rights issued to existing shareholders for no consideration to try and prevent hostile takeover bid.
3. *Stock rights issued with a stock dividend*
4. *Non-compensatory stock rights issued to employees*

Recognition Required
5. *Stock rights issued with other financial instruments*—debt is issued with detachable stock warrants that can be exercised without having to trade in or redeem the debt. General practice is to value the separate components of the basket based on their relative market values. The proportional and the incremental method can be used for this allocation.
6. *Compensation to outside parties*—to conserve cash during start-up a company may issue shares or stock rights as payment for professional services.
7. *Compensatory stock rights issued to employees*—two alternatives for recognition are the intrinsic value method and the fair value based method. U.S. companies are allowed to choose between these two methods. In Canada, AcSB concluded that the fair value based method is preferable but allows companies a choice.

7. DISCLOSURE OF STOCK OPTIONS

The *CICA Handbook*, paragraph 3240.04, states that options are a financial instrument—an equity instrument—and that details of terms and conditions must be disclosed. For stock-based compensation the *CICA Handbook* requires disclosure of:
- The accounting policy for option plans (intrinsic value or fair value).
- A description of the plan(s), including the terms and prices of the options.
- Specific information about the options outstanding.
- The amount of compensation expense recognized.

8. OTHER DERIVATIVES

A **derivative** is a secondary financial instrument whose value is linked to a primary financial instrument or commodity. They are either *options* (right to buy or sell something in future) or *forward contracts* (obligation to buy or sell something in the future). The basic principles underlying the recognition and measurement of derivative financial liabilities are the same as for primary financial liabilities. The initial recognition is generally zero, as there is normally no cost. The value of the derivative changes as the intrinsic value changes and this change is recognized in income. Section 3860 lists extensive disclosure that focuses on terms and conditions, interest rate risk, credit risk and fair value.

US and International Developments

FASB has issued extensive standards on reporting for derivative instruments and hedging activities, which require recognition of all derivatives measured at fair value. Canadian standards are the same as international standards.

9. CASH FLOW STATEMENT

The cash flows relating to complex financial instruments must be reported in the cash flow statement in a manner that is consistent with their substance.

Net proceeds from the issuance of any financial instruments must be reported as a financing activity. Conversions do not represent cash flow and therefore do not appear on the cash flow statement.

TRUE–FALSE QUESTIONS

T F 1. Retractable shares include an option to redeem them that can be exercised at the option of the investor.

T F 2. Perpetual debt is classified as a liability because it will never have to be repaid.

T F 3. Convertible securities offer holders greater choice and therefore are generally more valuable.

T F 4. The term "financial instruments" is excluded from the liabilities classification and should be classified as equity.

T F 5. The *recognition and measurement* for financial instruments are discussed in the *CICA Handbook,* paragraph 3860.

T F 6. There are no differences between a convertible bond and a bond with detachable warrants.

T F 7. The general characteristic of convertible bonds is that management issues them fully intending that the conversion privilege will eventually be attractive to the investors.

T F 8. Common stock conversion rights is an equity account that will be reported as contributed capital on the balance sheet.

T F 9. Recognition is required for all stock options issued to employees.

T F 10. Most preferred shares have a call provision whereby the corporation can call in the shares and redeem them at a given price.

MULTIPLE CHOICE QUESTIONS

___ 1. Retractable preferred shares are likely to be reported as debt if
a. Redemption is contractually required.
b. Redemption can be forced by the investor.

c. Terms of the shares are such that redemption is essentially forced by the terms of the shares, even if the entity is financial sound.

d. Either of the above conditions are met.

_____ 2. Options are valued using the
  a. Incremental method.
  b. Proportional method.
  c. Fair value-based method.
  d. Intrinsic value method.

_____ 3. Which of the following is a financial liability?
  a. Warranty liabilities.
  b. Accounts payable.
  c. Unearned revenue.
  d. Obligation to deliver product.

_____ 4. Which of the following stock options require memorandum entries?
  a. Rights issued as a poison pill.
  b. Stock rights issued with other financial instruments.
  c. Rights issued as compensation to outside parties.
  d. Compensatory stock rights issued to employees.

_____ 5. Toller Company issues $1,000,000 of $1,000 bonds dated January 1, 20x3, due December 31, 20x5, at par. Interest at 6% is payable annually, and each bond is convertible at any time up to maturity into 250 common shares. When the bonds are issued, the prevailing interest rate for similar debt without conversion options is 8%. The fair market value of the conversion feature is not known. The issuance of the convertible bonds will be recorded as follows:

a.
Cash	1,000,000	
Discount on convertible bonds	51,544	
Convertible bonds payable		1,000,000
Common stock conversion rights		51,544

b.
Cash	948,456	
Discount on convertible bonds	51,544	
Bonds payable		1,000,000

c.
Cash	1,000,000	
Bonds payable		1,000,000

d.
Cash	930,057	
Discount on convertible bonds	75,943	
Convertible bonds payable		1,000,000
Common stock conversion rights		6,000

_____ 6. Assume Bobo Company issued 100,000 rights allowing the holder(s) to acquire common shares at an acquisition price of $20 per share, which is the current market price of the common shares. It takes two rights to acquire a share. The company received $10,000 for the rights. At the issuance date the following will be recorded:

a. Only a memorandum entry.

b. Cash, debit, $10,000, and stock rights outstanding, credit, $10,000.

c. Cash, credit, $10,000, and common shares, debit, $10,000.

d. Cash, debit, $10,000, and common shares, credit, $10,000.

___ 7. Use the same data from question 6, and assume that the current market price of the common shares is $22 and that all the rights are exercised. The following will be recorded:

a. Debit cash $1,000,000, credit common shares $1,000,000.

b. Debit cash $1,000,000, debit stock rights outstanding $10,000, debit loss on sale of shares $90,000, credit common shares $1,100,000.

c. Debit cash $1,000,000, debit stock rights outstanding $10,000, credit common shares $990,000.

d. Debit cash $2,000,000, credit common shares $2,000,000.

___ 8. Use the same data from question 6, and assume that the current market price of the common shares is only $16 and that all rights have expired. The following will be recorded:

a. Debit stock rights outstanding $10,000, credit common shares $10,000.

b. Debit cash $800,000, credit common shares $800,000.

c. Debit stock rights outstanding $10,000, credit cash $10,000.

d. Debit stock rights outstanding $10,000, credit contributed capital, lapse of stock rights, $10,000.

___ 9. A lender is owed $1,400,000 and agrees, as part of a restructuring plan, to accept capital assets with a market value of $1,200,000 and a book value of $950,000. How is this transaction recorded in the books?

a. Debit debt $1,400,000, credit capital assets $1,200,000, credit gain on debt restructure $200,000.

b. Debit debt $1,400,000, credit capital assets $950,000, credit gain on asset disposal $250,000, credit gain on debt restructure $200,000.

c. Debit capital assets 250,000, credit gain on asset disposal.

d. Debit debt $1,400,000, credit capital assets $950,000, credit gain on restructuring $450,000.

10. The value of a derivative changes as the underlying value changes. These changes are recognized

a. in net income.

b. in other comprehensive income.

c. in contributed capital.

d. as a deferred credit.

SOLUTIONS TO TRUE–FALSE QUESTIONS

1. T

2. F The interest payments on perpetual debt do represent a liability and the debt should be classified as a liability – the present value of the interest payments should be equal to the face value of the debt.

3. T

4. F The *CICA Handbook,* Section 3860, defines a **financial instrument** as any contract that gives rise to both a **financial asset** of one party and a **financial liability** or **equity instrument** of another party.

5. F The *CICA Handbook,* Section 3860, deals only with **presentation and disclosure** issues and not with **measurement and recognition** issues.

6. F The difference between convertible bonds and bonds with warrants are: Warrants usually are detachable, and warrants can be exercised without having to trade or redeem the bonds.

7. T

8. T

9. F Recognition is required only when stock options are issued to employees as compensation for current performance or as an incentive for future performance (i.e. compensatory stock rights).

10. T

SOLUTIONS TO MULTIPLE CHOICE QUESTIONS

1. d If either of the conditions in a, b or c are met the shares are likely classified as debt.

2. c Options are valued using the fair value-based method.

3. b The only liability that will result in a future payment of cash.

4. a Rights issued as a poison pill required memorandum entries. The other rights listed require recognition entries..

5. a The market value of the bonds is calculated by taking the present value of $1,000,000 discounted at 8% for a period of 3. ($1,000,000 × .79383) = $793,830 plus the present value of the interest payments, discounted at 8% for 3 periods. ($60,000 × 2.57710) = 154,626 for a total of $948,456. The discount is calculated by subtracting $948,456 from $1,000,000 = $51,544. Because the bonds were issued at par, the common stock conversion rights = $51,544.

6. b Cash received must be recorded, and stock rights outstanding is an equity account.

7. c Cash = $20 × 50,000 shares (100,000 rights/2) = $1,000,000. Close the stock rights outstanding account by crediting it $10,000. The difference is then credited to common shares = $990,000.

8. d When stock rights lapse, the account is closed to a contributed capital account.

9. b The debt and the assets will be removed from the books. A $250,000 gain on asset disposal and a $200,000 gain on debt restructure will be recognized to balance the entry.

10. a The changes in value of derivatives are recognized in net income.

PROBLEMS

Problem 1
PURPOSE: To illustrate accounting for convertible bonds issued at premium.

Astrowall Corporation issued $50,000 of 5%, 10-year convertible bonds. Each $1,000 bond was convertible to 10 shares of no-par value common stock of Astrowall at any interest date after 3 years from issuance. The market value of the bonds without the conversion feature was 94. The bonds were sold at 105 to Jason Corporation, which intends to hold the bonds as a long-term investment.

Required
- a. Give the entry for the issuer at the date of issuance.
- b. Give entries for the issuer, assuming that the conversion privilege is subsequently exercised by Jason Corporation immediately after the end of the third year. Assume that 30% of any premium has been amortized and that, at date of conversion, the common stock was selling for $125 per share. Show entries for both the book value method and market value method.

Problem 2
PURPOSE: To illustrate sale of shares, stock rights issued, and some lapses.

Showdon Corporation has outstanding 200,000 common shares, no-par value. On January 31, 20x3, the company announced it was selling a further 50,000 unissued common shares at $25 per share and to give the current shareholders first chance to buy shares proportionally equivalent to the number now held. To this end, on February 15, 20x3, each shareholder was issued one right for each common share currently held. Four rights must be submitted to acquire one additional share for $25. Rights not exercised lapse on July 15, 20x3.

Required
- a. Give any entry or memorandum that should be made in the accounts of Showdon Corporation on each of the following dates:
  - (1) January 15, 20x3, the date of the announcement.
  - (2) February 15, 20x3, issuance of all the rights. At this date, the shares of Showdon Corporation were quoted on the stock market at $26 per share.
  - (3) July 6, 20x3, exercise by current shareholders of 98% of the rights issued.
  - (4) July 15, 20x3, the remaining rights outstanding lapsed.
- b. Repeat requirement 1, assuming that the rights were sold by the company for $82,000 to outside investors on February 15, 20x3.

Problem 3

PURPOSE: To discuss accounting for convertible bond.

Colombos Company

Columbos Company's 10-year convertible bonds, issued and dated October 20x5, are convertible into 20 shares of Columbos' no-par value common stock, at the holder's option. The bonds were issued at a premium when the common stock traded at $45 per share. After payment of interest on October 1, 200x6, 30% of the bonds were tendered for conversion when the common stock was trading a $57 per share. Columbos uses the book value method to account for the conversion.

Required

1. How would the issue price of Columbos's convertible bonds be determined?
2. How should Columbos account for the issuance of the convertible bonds? Give the rationale for this accounting practice.
3. How should Columbos account for the conversion of the bonds into common stock?

Problem 4 (material covered in appendix)

PURPOSE: To illustrate a restructuring by modification of terms.

On January 1, 20x5, Overdue Corporation issued to Liquid Corporation a $100,000, 8% (payable annually on December 31), 10-year note to yield 10% interest. After paying interest for 20x5 and 20x6, Overdue Corporation encountered severe financial difficulties, which made it apparent that Liquid Corporation would have to make concessions as to the debt terms. Therefore, a debt restructuring was agreed to on January 1, 20x7, that provided (a) the remaining term to maturity would be 20 years from January 1, 20x7, and (b) interest would be reduced so that the same total dollar amount of interest would be paid over the new term to maturity (20 years) as would have been paid over the remaining portion of the old term (8 years).

Required

a. Give the entry by each party to record issuance of the note on January 1, 20x5. Show computation of the original note issuance price. Overdue received cash from Liquid in exchange for the note. Use the net method.
b. Compute the carrying amount of the note for the debtor and the creditor on January 1, 20x7.
c. Compute the new effective rate of interest for Overdue. Use straight-line interpolation to compute the approximate interest rate to two decimal places.
d. Give any required entries for the debtor and for the creditor on the date of the restructuring, January 1, 20x7.
e. Give all entries for both the debtor and the creditor on the two interest dates, December 31, 20x7, and December 31, 20x8. Liquid records the change in present value over time as interest revenue.

SOLUTIONS TO PROBLEMS

Problem 1

Requirement a

Cash[a]	52,500	
Discount on bonds payable [b]	3,000	
Bonds payable		50,000
Common stock conversion rights[c]		5,500

[a] $50,000 \times 1.05 = \$52,500$
[b] $\$50,000 - \$47,000 \ (\$50,000 \times .94) = \$3,000$
[c] $\$52,500 - \$47,000 = \$5,500$

Requirement b
Book value method

Bonds payable	50,000	
Common stock conversion rights	5,500	
Discounted bonds payable[a]		2,100
Common shares		53,400

[a] $\$3,000 \times (1 - .30) = \$2,100$

Market value method

Bonds payable	50,000	
Common stock conversion rights	5,500	
Loss on conversion of bonds payable[a]	14,600	
Discounted bonds payable		2,100
Common shares		68,000

[a] $\$50,000/\$1,000 \times 10 = 500$ shares @ $\$125 = \$62,500$
Bonds payable carrying value = $\$50,000 - \$2,100 = \$47,900$
Loss on conversion of bonds payable = $\$62,500 - \$47,900 = \$14,600$

Problem 2

Requirement a

January 15, 20x3—Date of announcement; no entry in the accounts is required at this date. (A memorandum entry may be made.)

February 15, 20x3—Date of issuance of the stock rights; memorandum entry:
    Issued 200,000 common share rights for 50,000 common shares. Each common share requires 4 rights plus $25. After July 15, 20x3, all rights not exercised will lapse.

July 6, 20x3—Exercise of 98 percent of the outstanding rights:

Cash ([200,000 × 98%/4] × $25)	1,225,000	
Common shares (no-par, 49,000 shares)		1,225,000

July 15, 20x3—Expiration of rights not exercised by July 15, 20x3; memorandum only:
    Lapse of 4,000 common stock rights for 1,000 common shares due to nonexercise deadline date, July 15, 20x3.

Requirement b

January 15, 20x3—as above.

February 15, 20x3:

Cash	82,000	
Stock rights outstanding		82,000

July 6, 20x3:

Cash	1,225,000	
Stock rights outstanding		
($82,000 × 98%)	80,360	
Common shares, no-par		1,305,360

July 15, 20x3:

Stock rights outstanding		
($82,000 × 2%)	1,640	
Contributed capital, lapse of		
stock rights		1,640

Problem 3

Requirement 1

The bond issue price is the present value of expected future cash flows of principal and interest, discounted at the market rate of interest on date of issuance. The price will be influenced by the conversion feature and will be higher than the market value of the bond without the conversion feature.

Requirement 2

Columbos should account for the issuance of the convertible bonds by increasing cash for the issue price, increasing bonds payable by the face amount, increasing premium or discount on bonds payable, and increasing common stock conversion rights for the balance. A convertible debt must be accounted for as debt and equity. The market value of the bonds without the conversion feature is recorded as debt. The conversion option is recorded in the account "Common stock conversion rights," as an equity account that will be reported as contributed capital on the balance sheet.

Requirement 3

Columbos should account for the conversion of the bonds into common stock by decreasing bonds payable, unamortized bond premium or discount, and common stock conversion rights by 30%, and by increasing common stock.

Problem 4

Requirement a

January 1, 20x5—Issuance of note
(a) Overdue Corporation (debtor)

Cash	87,711	
Notes payable, 7%		87,711

(b) Liquid Corporation (creditor)

Note receivable	87,711	
Cash		87,711

Computation of proceeds on note:
PV of principal:	
$100,000 × (PV1, 10%, 10)(.38544)	$38,554
PV of interest:	
($100,000 × 8% = $8,000) ×	
(PVA, 10%, 10)(6.14457)	49,157
Bond issue price	$87,711

Requirement b

Debtor's liability and the creditor's receivable:
= $100,000 (PV1, 10°/a, 8) + $8,000 (PVA, 10%, 8)
= $100,000 × .46651 + $8,000 × 5.33493
= $46,651 + $42,679 = **$89,330**

Requirement c

Inspection of the several values given below suggests that the new effective interest rate is relatively low. Therefore, we will try 2%, 3%, and 4% as follows:

Present Value at

	2%	3%	4%
PV of principal: $100,000 × PV1, n = 20			
2% = .67297	$67,297		
3% = .55368		$ 55,368	
4% = .45639			$45,639
PV of interest: $8,000 × 8 years			
= $64,000 ($64,000/20 years			
= $3,200 × PVA, n = 20 years)			
2% = 16.35143	$53,325		
3% = 14.87747		47,608	
4% = 13.59033			$43,489
Total present value	$119,622	$102,976	$89,128

The effective rate of interest (rounded to the nearest percent) interpolated, is:

$$3\% + \frac{\$102,976 - \$89,330}{\$102,976 - \$89,128} (4\% - 3\%) = 3.98\%$$

Requirement d

January 1, 20x7, date of restructure of the debt:

New loan carrying amount
= $100,000(PV1, 10%, 20) + $3,200 (PVA, 10%, 20)
= $100,000 × .14684 + $3,200 × 8.51356
= $14,684 + $27,243
= $41,927

Overdue Corporation:
January 1, 20x7
Notes payable ($89,330 − $41,927)   47,403
    Gain on debt restructuring   47,403

Liquid Corporation:

January 1, 20x7
Bad debt expense   47,403
    Allowance for decline in note value   47,403

Requirement e

Overdue Corporation (debtor)			**Liquid Corporation (creditor)**		
December 31, 20x7—Interest date:					
Interest expense	4,740		Cash	3,200	
Cash		3,200	Allowance for		
Notes payable		1,540	decline in note		
			value	1,540	
			Interest revenue		4,740

Computations:

($100,000 × 8% × 8 years/20 years = $3,200
$47,403 × 10% = $4,740
$4,740 − $3,200 = $1,540

December 31, 20x8

Interest expense	4,894		Cash	3,200	
Cash		3,200	Allowance for		
Notes payable		1,694	decline in note		
			value	1,694	
			Interest revenue		4,894

Computations:
($47,403 + $1,540) × 10% = $4,894 (rounded)

CASE

Trouble Inc. (TI) is a private company, incorporated 20 years ago. They have experienced financial difficulties over the past year and needed to obtain additional financing. They anticipate a loss in 20x5 for the first time in 20 years. Due to the uncertainties of their financial position, creditors have required covenants for their debt-to-equity ratio and a minimum current ratio of 2:1. Dividends are not allowed to be paid out to shareholders until the loan has been repaid. Management has a bonus based on net income before extraordinary and discontinued items.

Once their financial position has improved Trouble Inc. would like to have a public share offering.

It is now November 20x5. TI's fiscal year-end is December 31, 20x5. The Vice-President of TI has provided you (CA) with the following accounting issues facing the company for 20x5. He would like you to prepare a report outlining the alternative accounting policies and your recommendations. Your discussion should identify measurement and disclosure issues.

1. TI does not accrue for warranty costs for their products.

2. TI issued preferred shares to investors, who also owned common shares, during 20x5. The preferred shares must be redeemed, or bought back, at their $100 stated value per share, in 20x6. The dividends are cumulative. If there are any dividends in arrears they must be paid before the redemption date.

3. To conserve cash, an arrangement was made to exchange 4,000 common shares in TI for equipment from their supplier. The book value of the equipment was $200,000 and the listed selling price was $350,000. Common shares were last issued at $150 per share.

4. TI uses the taxes payable method of accounting for income taxes, not the liability method.

5. Again, to conserve cash, TI has reduced salaries to top management staff and issued stock options as compensation. TI provides note disclosure of their stock options. At the end of the year TI bought back some of their own shares at a profit. These shares are expected to be reissued when employee stock option plans are exercised. The gain from the sale has been included in other income.

Required: Prepare the requested report.

KEY POINTS IN THE CASE

The solution should be written as a report to the Vice-President of Trouble Inc.

Overview

There is no GAAP constraint now since private but GAAP needed for IPO. Since TI is a private company they may follow the differential reporting guidelines. Management will want financial statements to look good for going public. It may not be feasible for TI to go public at this time since they are encountering financial difficulties. In addition, due to the bank covenants they are not allowed to issue dividends. These covenants also indicate that their banker views their business as high risk. Creditors and management will want to ensure the covenants have been complied with for debt-to-equity and the current ratio. A past objective may have been tax minimization. This will not be a factor this year since they expect a loss in 20x5. Management will want to maximize net income for bonus in the future. Since there is a loss expected this year there will not be a bonus. Therefore, they want to get as many expenses through the income statement in 20x5 to make the future bonus payments higher. A conclusion needs to be made on which user and objective is most important with support. Special reports could be used to satisfy some users, e.g., bank.

Issues

Going Concern

The following are indications that TI may have a going concern issue:
- significant loss expected in 20x5
- difficulties with financing
- barter transaction completed with supplier to conserve cash
- stock options issued and salaries reduced to management

The following are indications that TI does not have a going concern issue:
- first loss in 20 years
- expect public share offering
- were able to issue preferred shares

Conclusion supported by analysis on going concern issue. Provide a conclusion supported by the analysis on the going concern issue and discuss accounting implications, e.g., note in financial statements, liquidation values.

Warranty Costs

GAAP requires an estimate for warranties. This provides matching of revenues and expenses. If the amount was immaterial no accrual would be appropriate. The company has been in business for 20 years, therefore, there is past history for an estimate. An accrual would have a negative impact on debt-to-equity ratio and current ratio. After an analysis of the facts a recommendation should be made tied back to the most important user and objective.

Preferred Shares

The legal form is equity but it is important to look at substance over form. In deciding how to classify the preferred shares we should ask the following two questions:
1) Is the periodic return on capital (interest) obligatory?
   Yes—In 20x6 any dividends in arrears must be paid before the redemption date.
2) Is the debtor legally obligated to repay the principal?
   Yes—the preferred shares must be redeemed or bought back in 20x6.

Since the answer is yes to both questions, these shares should be classified as debt. The only exception will be if TI is using differential reporting. In that situation these shares could be classified as equity. If classified as debt this would have a negative impact on the debt-to-equity ratio. After an analysis of the facts a recommendation should be made tied back to the most important user and objective.

Barter Transaction

The exchange of equipment for common shares would be a non-monetary transaction. Since the assets are dissimilar there would be culmination of the earnings process and the equipment would be valued at its fair value or the fair value of the shares given up. Since TI is a private company a value based on their shares may not be reliable. We do not know when the shares were last traded. A fair value for the shares of $600,000 is probably high due to recent financial difficulties. The listing price of the equipment for

$350,000 could be used for fair value. There is no impact on the current ratio since equipment would be classified as a long-term asset. After an analysis of the facts a recommendation should be made tied back to the most important user and objective.

Income Taxes

The taxes payable method of accounting for income taxes is allowed under differential reporting. If the company is not using differential reporting they will need to change to the liability method. This may result in future income tax liabilities which would have a negative impact on the debt-to-equity ratio.

Stock Option

Note disclosure of the stock options is GAAP. Currently, TI is not required to measure and record the liability. The shares which are bought back are called treasury shares. The gain cannot go through the income statement. The gain must be shown as contributed surplus in equity section.

SELECTED SOLUTIONS FROM THE TEXTBOOK

Assignment 14- 8

Requirement 1

Cash...	5,325,000	
Discount on bonds payable (2)..	760,000	
Bonds payable		5,000,000
Contributed capital: common stock		
conversion rights (1)..		1,085,000

(1) $5,325,000 – $4,240,000
(2) $5,000,000 – $4,240,000

The conversion rights are valued at the difference between the actual proceeds and the amount that would have been received had the bond not been convertible.

Requirement 2

Cash...	5,325,000	
Discount on bonds payable ($5,000 – $4,100)....................	900,000	
Bonds payable		5,000,000
Contributed capital: common stock		
conversion rights..		1,225,000

Relative value:

Bond	$4,240	77%	×	$5,325	$4,100
Option	1,250	23%	×	5,325	1,225
	$5,490				$5,325

Requirement 3
Present value:

Principal	$5,000	(P/F,10%,15 yrs,) (.23939)	$1,197
Interest	400	(P/A,10%,15 yrs) (7.60608)	3,042
Price			$4,239 (rounded to $4,240)

An option pricing model (such as the Black-Scholes model) would have been used to value the conversion option.

Requirement 4
Interest expense, based on requirement 1

Cash cost ($5,000,000 × .08)	$400,000
Discount amortization ($760,000/15)	50,667
Total expense...	$450,667

Interest expense, based on issuance price

Cash cost	$400,000
Premium amortization ($325,000/15)...	(21,667)
Total expense...	$378,333

Assignment 14-9

Requirement 1
Convertible bonds are hybrid instruments in that they have some characteristics of debt (guaranteed interest payments, minimum cash payout at maturity) and some characteristics of equity (ability to participate in residual interest in net assets).

Requirement 2
The conversion option can be valued using an option pricing model (Black-Scholes is often cited). The bond is valued (PV) based on interest rates on similar issues, and the two relative values are used to allocate the actual proceeds to the two component parts. More commonly, only the bond is valued and the residual proceeds allocated to the option: $400,000 ($4,300,000 – $3,900,000) in this case.

Requirement 3

Cash...	4,300,000	
Discount on bonds payable	100,000	
Bonds payable...		4,000,000
Contributed capital: common stock conversion rights		400,000

Requirement 4

Bonds payable	4,000,000	
Contributed capital: common stock conversion rights.............	400,000	
Contributed capital: lapse of rights......................................		200,000
Common stock ($2,000,000 + $200,000)		2,200,000
Cash..		2,000,000

Requirement 5
A split is unusual because it is usually either a better deal to take the stock, in which case all convert, or the money, in which case all cash out.

Assignment 14-14

Requirement 1

Cash...	11,450,000	
Discount on bonds payable (1)...	278,004	
Bonds payable		10,000,000
Contributed capital: common stock conversion		
rights (2)		1,728,004

PV of the bond at market rates:

Principal $10,000,000 (P/F, 4%,15) .55526..............................	$5,552,600	
Interest $375,000 (P/A, 4%,15) 11.11839	<u>4,169,396</u>	
........<u>$9,721,996</u>		

(1) $10,000,000 – $9,721,996
(2) $11,450,000 – $9,721,996

Requirement 2
Revised share entitlement:
25 shares × 3/2 = 37.5 shares

Requirement 3

Bonds payable	3,000,000	
Contributed capital: common stock conversion rights (1)	518,401	
Discount on bonds payable (2)		33,360
Common shares (112,500 shares); ($3,000,000/$1,000 × 37.5)		3,485,041

(1) $1,728,004 × 3/10
(2) $278,004 × 3/10 × 6/15 (interest periods remaining)

Requirement 4
Liabilities

Bonds payable	$7,000,000	
Discount on bonds payable (1)	<u>(77,841)</u>	
....		$6,922,159

Equity

Common shares (2)..		38,485,041
Contributed capital: common stock conversion		
rights (3)		1,209,603

(1) $278,004 × 7/10 × 6/15
(2) $35,000,000 + $3,485,041
(3) $1,728,004 × 7/10

Assignment 14-27

Requirement 1

1 February 20x4—Date of issuance of the stock rights; memorandum entry:

Issued 100,000 common share rights for 50,000 common shares. Each common share requires 2 rights plus $15. After 30 June 20x4, all rights not exercised will lapse.

27 June 20x4—Exercise of 98 percent of the outstanding rights:

Cash [(100,000 × 98%) ÷ 2] × $15	735,000	
Common shares, no-par (49,000 shares)		735,000
(Remaining rights outstanding, 2,000 for 1,000 shares)		

30 June 20x4—Expiration of rights not exercised by 30 June 20x4; memorandum only: Lapse of 2,000 common stock rights for 1,000 common shares due to nonexercise by deadline date, 30 June 20x4.

Requirement 2

1 February 20x4

Cash...	62,000	
Contributed capital: stock rights outstanding		62,000

27 June 20x4

Cash...	735,000	
Contributed capital: stock rights outstanding ($62,000 × .98)...	60,760	
Common shares, no-par..		795,760

30 June 20x4

Contributed capital: stock rights outstanding ($62,000 × .02)...	1,240	
Contributed capital: lapse of stock rights.............................		1,240

Assignment 14-36

Requirement 1

a) To increase allowance for doubtful accounts:

Retained earnings	2,000	
Allowance for doubtful accounts.....................................		2,000

b) To write down inventory:

Retained earnings	50,000	
Inventory ($150,000 – $100,000).......................................		50,000

c) To write down operational assets:
Retained earnings ($500,000 – $400,000)............................. 100,000
    Accumulated depreciation... 100,000

d) To reduce liabilities:
Current liabilities ($150,000 × 5%)........................... 7,500
Long-term liabilities ($240,000 × 5%)................................ 12,000
    Retained earnings... 19,500

e) To transfer $70,000 from the preferred share account to retained earnings:
Preferred shares 70,000
    Retained earnings... 70,000

f) To transfer from common share account to retained earnings:
Common shares 282,500*
    Retained earnings... 282,500

*Computation:
Debits in retained earnings	$372,000
Credits in retained earnings	(89,500)
Credit required to reduce to zero balance	$282,500

g) Long-term debt.. 200,000
    Common shares 200,000

Requirement 2

Norwood Corporation
Balance Sheet
Immediately after Reorganization

Assets

Cash..	$ 20,000
Accounts receivable...	94,000
Allowance for doubtful accounts.......................................	(6,000)
Inventory...	100,000
Operational assets...	800,000
Accumulated depreciation...	(400,000)
Land...	40,000
Total assets...	$648,000

Liabilities and Shareholders' Equity

Current liabilities	$142,500
Long-term liabilities..	28,000
Preferred shares, no-par (1,000 shares)............................	60,000

Common shares, no-par (70,000 shares) 417,500
Retained earnings (Note A) .... _____0_
    Total liabilities and shareholders' equity .... $<u>648,000</u>

Note A:

On (date) the corporation completed a reorganization to eliminate the deficit in retained earnings and to achieve a more realistic accounting basis for assets, liabilities, and shareholders' equity. Thus, the balance in retained earnings is the balance beginning with the date given above and accordingly does not reflect the entire earnings and loss history of the company.

SOLUTIONS TO CONCEPT REVIEW QUESTIONS

Page 859

1. Some types of financial instruments are known as hybrid securities because they are primary securities (i.e., not derivatives) that have characteristics of both debt and equity.

2. Financial liabilities are initially measure at fair value.

3. The exceptions to this rule are financial liabilities that are held for trading and derivatives that are liabilities. These items should be measured at fair value.

Page 874

1. Retractable preferred shares may be reported as debt rather than equity, as cash repayment may be forced at the option of the investor. When repayment is required or is at the option of the investor (i.e., retractable), the potential (unavoidable) cash pay out effectively qualifies the preferred shares as a liability.

2. $5,000/$20 per share = 250 shares.

3. Under the *incremental* method, the value attributed to the conversion privilege is the difference between the total proceeds of the bond issue and the market value of an equivalent "straight" bond issue (i.e., a bond issue without the conversion privilege).

4. The principal portion of a convertible bond may be reported as shareholders' equity when the conversion of the bond is at the issuer's option—that is, the corporation may avoid repayment by issuing common shares. The interest associated with the convertible bond, however, is a liability that must be paid by the corporation.

Page 883

1. If the option price equals, or exceeds, the market price of the shares at the date of issue, no accounting entry is required. Only a memo entry is made to record the issue of the options. If the option price at the time of issue is less than the market price, the stock option issue is considered compensatory. The difference between the option price and the market price is recorded as a compensation expense incurred by the company.

2. The issue of rights may act as a poison pill and lower the likelihood of a hostile takeover by increasing the shares outstanding and severely diluting the value of the shares held by a hostile acquiror, which is not entitled to exercise rights. The rights are issued to existing ("friendly") shareholders, allowing them to acquire additional shares at a discount. The hostile acquiror is thus forced to acquire more shares in its attempt to acquire a controlling percentage of outstanding shares. The poison pill rights are intended to make the unwanted acquisition prohibitively expensive.

3. The value of the warrants will be the difference between the exercise and the current market price and is initially charged to the "stock warrant account," a liability account. If the exercise price of the warrants is less than the market price of the common shares, it is highly likely that the warrants will be exercised and their value charged to share capital. However, this entry to should not be made until the warrants are exercised. Therefore, at the time of issue of the warrants no amount should be charged to shareholders' equity. If the warrants are not exercised, the value of the warrants will be charged to contributed surplus, also a shareholders' equity account.

Page 888

1. A derivative financial instrument is one whose value is tied to a primary financial instrument or a commodity.

2. A derivative financial liability should be recorded at fair value on the balance sheet.

3. Gains and losses from derivative instruments are recognized in income in the period in which they arise.

CHAPTER 15

ACCOUNTING FOR CORPORATE INCOME TAX

This area is complicated by the fact that the income tax payable by a corporation is determined as a single amount, but the revenues, expenses, gains and losses that give rise to taxable income are reported in different sections of the income statement (intraperiod income tax allocation). A second complication arises when the income tax expense differs from the income tax payable which results in future income tax liability or asset (interperiod income tax allocation). A third complication arises when a corporation has an operating loss for tax purposes.

This chapter deals with intraperiod and interperiod tax allocation. Tax benefits of accounting losses will be covered in Chapter 16.

1. INTRAPERIOD TAX ALLOCATION

Interperiod tax allocation deals with allocating taxes between different lines on the income statement. Financial statements are reported in accordance with the nature of the revenues, expenses, gains, and losses that gave rise to the tax.

Total income tax expense must be allocated to the following:

INCOME STATEMENT	STATEMENT OF CHANGES IN RETAINED EARNINGS
• continuing operations	• capital transactions
• discontinued operations (net of tax)	• restatements of prior periods
• extraordinary gains and losses (net of tax)	

2. INTERPERIOD TAX ALLOCATION—INTRODUCTION

Interperiod tax allocation deals with allocating taxes between different reporting periods, such as this year and future years.

One objective of financial statement users and preparers is to measure net income. The objective of the Income Tax Act and Regulations is to generate revenue for the government. Both accounting net income and taxable income are the net result of matching the revenues and expenses of a period. Most items of revenue and expense are recognized in the same period for both accounting and tax purposes. But there are some differences, which can be categorized as follows:

- Permanent differences.
- Temporary differences.

Permanent differences enter in the computation of either taxable income or pretax accounting income, but *never* both.

A **temporary difference** arises when the tax basis of an asset or liability differs from its accounting carrying value.

The *CICA Handbook,* Section 3465.09, defines temporary differences as follows:

CICA

Differences between the tax basis of an asset or liability and its carrying amount in the balance sheet that will result in taxable or deductible amounts in determining taxable income of future periods when the carrying amount of the asset or liability is recovered or settled.

A temporary difference *originates* in the period in which it first enters the computation of either taxable income or accounting income. It *reverses* in the subsequent period when it enters into the computation of the other measure.

Examples of temporary differences include: revenue on long term contracts, deferred development costs and, accounting amortization and CCA. Exhibit 15-1 in the textbook provides common examples of permanent and temporary differences.

International Perspective
Canada has changed the terminology and definition of the differences that affect both accounting and taxable income. We now use the term temporary differences instead of timing differences. This reflect the change in emphasis from an income statement approach to a balance sheet approach.

3. CONCEPTUAL ISSUES IN INTERPERIOD TAX ALLOCATION
There are three basic underlying issues:
1. The extent of allocation.
2. The measurement method.
3. Discounting.

The Extent of Allocation
Extent of allocation refers to the range of temporary differences to which interperiod tax allocation is applied. There are three basic options:
1. *Taxes payable method.* The amount of taxes assessed each year are recognized as income tax expense for that year.
2. *Comprehensive method.* The tax effects of all temporary differences are allocated, regardless of the timing or likelihood of their reversal.
3. *Partial allocation.* This method takes the middle ground. Material non-recurring temporary differences that are likely to reverse in the near future are accorded tax allocation.

The *CICA Handbook* requires the comprehensive method, except for qualifying corporations that elect to use the taxes payable method under differential reporting.

International Perspective
Most countries use comprehensive allocation. The UK is a notable exception. It uses partial allocation, although a proposed change in is process.

Your text provides an example that illustrates the impact of the taxes payable method and comprehensive tax allocation.

WATCH! Temporary differences *reverse*. Future income tax liability/asset that relate to the temporary differences is *drawn down,*

Measurement Method
What should the tax rate be?
- The rate in effect at the time that the temporary difference first arises (deferral method), *or*
- The rate that is expected to be in effect when the temporary difference reverses (liability method).

The **deferral method** uses the rate in effect when the difference originates. The **liability** or **accrual method** uses the tax rate that will be in effect in the year of reversal. The emphasis is on the balance sheet. Under the liability method when the tax rate changes the liability must be adjusted. The offset to the adjustment goes to income tax expense in the year of adjustment.

The liability and deferral methods are illustrated in the text.

The *CICA Handbook,* Section 3465.56, states:

CICA *Future income tax liabilities and income tax assets should be measured using the income tax rates and income tax laws that, at the balance sheet date, are expected to apply when the liability is settled or the asset is realized, which would normally be those enacted at the balance sheet date.*

Discounting
In general, GAAP requires that future monetary assets and liabilities be shown at their discounted present value. With future tax liabilities it is difficult to determine which interest rate to use and the time period for discounting.
The *CICA Handbook,* paragraph 3465.57, states that:

CICA *Future income tax liabilities and future income tax assets should not be discounted.*

4. APPROACH TO INCOME TAX QUESTIONS
Using the liability method there are three basic steps:
1. Calculate taxable income and taxes payable
   - Start with accounting income and adjust for permanent differences to get accounting income subject to tax.
   - Then adjust for temporary differences to arrive at taxable income.
   - Multiply taxable income by the tax rate to get taxes payable
2. Determine the change in future taxes
   - Identify the tax carrying value and accounting carrying value for assets and liabilities with differences and calculate the difference.

- Calculate the future tax liability as the difference in values calculated above times the tax rate. The tax rate used is the enacted tax rate expected in the year of reversal.
- Calculate the difference between the future tax liability calculated above and the opening balance. This is the adjustment required.

3. Combine income taxes payable with the change in future income tax to determine the expense for the year.

- Credit taxes payable (from step 1).
- Debit/credit future taxes (from step 2).
- Debit income tax expense to balance.

Your text provides an example of the application of these steps.

Step 2 Determining the change in future income tax involves determining the accounting basis and the tax basis for assts and liabilities. Determining the accounting basis should be relatively straight forward. The handbook provides guidance in determining the tax basis. The chart following summarizes this information.

	MONETARY	NON-MONETARY
ASSETS	Accounting carrying value less any amount that will enter tax in the future	Tax deductible amount less all amounts already deducted in determining taxable income in current and prior periods
LIABILITIES	Accounting carrying value less any amount that will be deductible for income tax in the future.	Carrying amount less any amounts that will not be taxable in future periods

For permanent differences the tax basis is equal to the accounting basis.

EXAMPLE #1

Assume the following for Company ABC:

Company ABC
Balance Sheet
December 31, 20x5

	20x5	20x4
Cash	$150	$120
Inventory	50	40
Capital assets	100	110
	$300	$270
Liabilities	$120	$130
Shareholders' equity	180	140
	$300	$270

COMPANY ABC
Income Statement
for the Year Ended December 31, 20x5

Revenue	$90
Cost of Sales	(30)
Amortization	(10)
Net income	50

Other information: CCA = $15. Tax rate = 40%.

NOTE: CCA refers to **capital cost allowance**, which is amortization for tax purposes.

Capital assets were purchased in Year 20x4 for $120. Amortization for 20x4 was $10 and CCA was also $10. Therefore, the carrying value for 20x4 was $110 and the tax basis for 20x4 was $110. The future tax asset (liability) at the end of Year 20x4 was zero.

Step 1: Calculate taxable income and income tax payable:
Begin with net income before taxes (accounting income) per the financial statements and add/ deduct permanent and temporary differences.

Taxable income is calculated as follows:

Net income	$50
Add back amortization	10
Deduct CCA	(15)
Taxable income	$45

The tax rate to use is the current tax rate. This amount is the current amount of taxes that the company must pay the government according to its tax return.

$$\text{Taxable income} \times \text{Tax rate} = \text{Taxes payable}$$
$$\$45 \times 40\% = \$18$$

Step 2: Prepare a tax balance sheet and compare it to the financial statement balance sheet. Calculate future tax assets or future tax liabilities.

	Tax basis	Carrying values	Temporary differences deductible (taxable)
Cash	$150	$150	–0–
Inventory	50	50	–0–
Capital assets	95	100	(5)
Liabilities	120	120	–0–

WATCH! You only look at assets and liabilities, since shareholders' equity is a balancing figure.

The tax basis amounts are the opening balances adjusted for items from the tax return or reconciling items from Step 1 above. Therefore tax capital assets equal $110 – CCA

($15) = $95. Note that inventory is the same for the carrying value and tax, since there were no reconciling items in Step 1 relating to those items.

The temporary difference relating to capital assets is a temporary *taxable* difference, since we have already had the benefit of accelerated tax deduction in the current year. This means the company will have to pay more taxes in future years—that is, it faces a **future income tax liability**.

We are assuming that no future tax rates have been enacted. That being so, we multiply the temporary taxable difference by the current tax rate, since the current rate is the best estimate of the future rate.

$$\$5 \times 40\% = \$2 \text{ FTL}$$

Step 3
The resulting journal entry is as follows:

```
dr. Income tax expense (I/S)            20
    cr. Income tax payable (B/S)              18
    cr. Future income tax liability (B/S)      2
```

EXAMPLE #2
Use the same data for Company ABC in the "simple example" above. Assume also that in the Year 20x6, everything is the same as in Year 20x5 except that the expected future tax rate decreases to 30% and amortization = CCA at $10.

Assume that net income is $50 (also the same as in 20x5) and that there are no additional temporary differences.

Step 1
```
Net income              $50
Add back amortization    10
Deduct CCA              (10)
Taxable income          $50
```

Income tax payable = $50 × 30% = $15

Step 2
Note that the balance sheet keeps track of cumulative temporary differences and then re-estimates the tax impact using the new tax rate.

	Tax basis dr.(cr.)	Carrying values dr.(cr.)	TD D(T)	Tax rate	Future tax assets (liability)	Less beg. balance	Adj. for year
20x4							
Capital assets	$110	$110	–0–	40%	–0–	–0–	–0–
20x5							
Capital assets	95	100	($5)	40%	($2.00)	–0–	(2)
20x6							

| Capital assets | 85 | 90 | ($5) | 30% | ($1.5) | (2) | (0.5) |

At this point we will take the new balance in future income tax liability of $1.5, deduct the amount already booked = $2, and enter the adjustment, which is dr. $0.5.

Step 3

The journal entry is as follows for year 2003:

dr. Income tax expense   14.5

dr. Future income tax liability   .5

       cr. Income tax payable   15

Note that the income tax expense is a residual (i.e., a *plug* to balance the entry).

WATCH! Under the liability method, a change in tax rate flows through to the effective tax rate in the year that the rate changes.

EXAMPLE #3

This example will demonstrate accounting for income taxes under the liability method of comprehensive allocation when there are both permanent and temporary differences and when tax rates change. A 3-year period will be used.

The following facts pertain to accounting and taxable income for Nigel Ltd. in the year 20x4, Nigel's first year of operations:

- Net income before taxes is $750,000; there are no extraordinary items or discontinued operations,
- Net income includes dividends of $50,000 received from a taxable Canadian corporation.
- In determining pretax accounting income, Nigel deducts the following expenses:
  - —golf club membership dues of $35,000
  - —accrued estimated warranty expense of $95,000
  - —amortization of $150,000
- For tax purposes, Nigel deducts the following expenses:
  - —actual warranty costs incurred of $75,000
  - —CCA of $250,000
- The tax rate is 40%.
- Nigel acquired capital assets costing $1,500,000.
  - —The assets will be amortized on a straight-line basis over 10 years, assuming zero residual value, with a full year's amortization in the year of acquisition ($150,000 per year).
  - —For income tax purposes, Nigel deducted CCA of $250,000 in 20x4.

The intercorporate dividend is a permanent difference, because it is not taxable.

The golf club membership expense is also a permanent difference because this expense is never deductible for tax purposes.

Step 1A: Remove the permanent differences from the accounting income to obtain the *accounting income subject to tax:*

Pretax accounting income	$750,000
Permanent differences:	
Intercorporate dividends	−50,000
Golf club dues	+35,000
Accounting income subject to tax	$735,000

Step 1B: Calculate the taxable income:

Accounting income subject to tax		$735,000
Temporary differences:		
Warranty expense, accrued, not deductible	+ 95,000	
Warranty cost incurred, deductible	−75,000	+20,000
Amortization expense, not deductible	+150,000	
CCA, deductible	−250,000	−100,000
Taxable income		$655,000

Step 1C: Calculate Income tax payable:

Taxable income × Tax rate = Income tax payable
$655,000 × 40% = $262,000

Step 2: Prepare a tax balance sheet and compare it to the financial statement balance sheet. Calculate future income tax assets and liabilities:

	Tax basis	Carrying value	Temporary difference deductible (taxable)	Future tax asset (liability) yr.-end	Less beginning balance dr. (cr.)	Adjustment for current year dr. (cr.)
20x4						
Capital assets	$1,250,000	$1,350,000	$(100,000)	$(40,000)	–0–	$(40,000)
Accrued warranty liability	–0–	(20,000)	20,000	8,000	–0–	8,000

Step 3:

The summary income tax journal entry, 20x4:

dr. Income tax expense	294,000	
dr. Future income tax asset (current)	8,000	
cr. Future income tax liability (long-term)		40,000
cr. Income tax payable		262,000

In 20x5:
- The tax rate increases to 45%.
- Nigel claims CCA of $230,000.
- The actual warranty costs were $80,000.
- Amortization expense was $150,000.
- Accrued warranty expense was $105,000.
- Net income before tax was $800,000.
- Net income included dividends of $75,000 received from a taxable Canadian corporation.

Step 1A: Calculate Accounting income subject to tax:

Net income before tax	$800,000
Permanent differences	
Intercorporate dividends	−75,000
Accounting income subject to tax	$725,000

Step 1B: Calculate taxable income:

Accounting income subject to tax		$725,000
Temporary differences:		
Warranty expense, accrued, not deductible	+105,000	
Warranty cost, incurred, deductible	− 80,000	+25,000
Amortization expense, not deductible	+150,000	
CCA, deductible	−230,000	− 80,000
Taxable income		$670,000

Step 1C: Calculate Income Tax Payable:

Taxable income × Tax rate = Income tax payable
$670,000 × 45% = $301,500

Step 2: Prepare a tax balance sheet:

20x5	Tax basic	Carrying value	Temporary difference deductible (taxable)	Future tax asset (liability) yr.-end	Less beginning balance dr. (cr.)	Adjustment for current year dr. (cr.)
Capital assets	$1,020,000	$1,200,000	$(180,000)	$(81,000)	$(40,000)	$(41,000)
Warranty liability	−0−	45,000	45,000	20,250	8,000	12,250

Step 3:

The summary income tax journal entry, 20x5:

dr. Income tax expense	330,250	
dr. Future income tax asset (current)	12,250	
Future income tax liability (long-term)		1,000
cr. Income tax payable		301,500

In 20x6:

Exactly the same procedure is used. In that year, there are reversals.
- Net income before tax is $650,000.
- Net income includes dividends of $100,000 received from a taxable Canadian corporation.
- Accrued warranty expense is $90,000.
- Amortization expense is $150,000.
- Actual warranty costs are $120,000.
- Nigel claims CCA of $130,000.
- The tax rate increases to 46%.

Step 1A: Calculate accounting income subject to tax:

Net income before tax	$650,000
Permanent difference:	
Intercorporate dividends	−100,000
Accounting income subject to tax	$550,000

Step 1B: Calculate taxable income:

Accounting income subject to tax		$550,000
Temporary differences:		
Warranty expense, accrued, not deductible	+ 90,000	
Warranty cost incurred, deductible	−120,000	−30,000
Amortization expense, not deductible	+150,000	
CCA, deductible	−130,000	+.20,000
Taxable income		$540,000

Step 1C: Calculate income tax payable:

Taxable income × Tax rate = Income tax payable

$540,000 × 46% = $248,400

Step 2: Prepare a tax balance sheet:

	Tax basis	Carrying value	Temporary difference deductible (taxable)	Future tax asset (liability) yr.-end	Less beginning balance dr.(cr.)	Adjustment for current year dr.(cr.)
20x6						
Capital assets	$890,000	$1,050,000	$(160,000)	$(73,600)	$(81,000)	$7,400
Warranty liability	–0–	15,000	15,000	6,900	20,250	(13,350)

Step 3:

The summary income tax journal entry, 20x6:

dr. Income tax expense	254,350	
dr. Future income tax asset (current)	7,400	
cr. Future income tax liability (long-term)		13,350
cr. Income tax payable		248,400

5. BALANCE SHEET ELEMENTS

FUTURE INCOME TAX ASSET (DEBIT BALANCE)	FUTURE INCOME TAX LIABILITY (CREDIT BALANCE)
Tax paid is more that accrual based accounting expense	Tax paid is less than accrual based accounting expense
Revenue is recognized for accounting purposes after it is taxable	Revenue is recognized for accounting purposes before it is taxable
Expenses are deducted for tax after it is deducted for accounting purposes	Expenses are deducted for tax before it is deducted for accounting purposes
Limited to the amount that is more likely than not to be realized.	

Rule of Thumb Future income tax often appears on the balance sheet on the opposite side from the balance sheet account to which it relates.

When future income tax assets or liabilities are reported on a balance sheet in which the current and long-term assets and liabilities are segregated, they must be classified as either current or long-term. The classification of future income tax balances as current or long-term does not depend on the period of reversal. The key to classifying future income tax balances is based on the classification of its related asset or liability. The future taxes related to all current assets and liabilities are netted and shown as one figure. Likewise the future taxes related to long term items are netted. Current and long term future taxes are not netted.

6. DISCLOSURE

The amount of income tax expense or benefit that is included in net income before discontinued operations and extraordinary items should be reported separately in the income statement. Income tax expense should not be combined with other items of expense.

The amount of income tax expense that is attributable to future income taxes should be disclosed, either on the face of the statements or in the notes.

The amount of income tax expense that relates to each of discontinued operations, extraordinary items, and capital transactions should be disclosed.

Public companies must disclose the nature of temporary differences. They must also reconcile the statutory tax rate and the effective tax rate.

7. SHORTCUT APPROACH

This approach is best suited to situations where the income tax rate has not changed. The steps are as follows:

1. Calculate taxable income and tax payable.
2. Determine the change in future income tax through a direct calculation.
3. Combine income tax payable with the change in future income tax to determine the tax expense for the year.

Your text provides an example of this approach.

8. DIFFERENTIAL REPORTING

Differential reporting may be used by a corporation that is not publicly accountable. Qualifying companies may elect to use the taxes payable method instead of comprehensive allocation where income tax paid is the income tax expense. This is an option not a requirement. Differential reporting for income taxes is an all-or-nothing affair. A company should disclose it is using differential reporting in its accounting policy note, along with the specific accounting policies being used. The company should also reconcile its income tax expense to the average statutory income tax rate.

9. CASH FLOW STATEMENT

All tax allocation amounts must be reversed out of transactions reported in the cash flow statement. The cash flow statement must include only the actual taxes paid.

APPENDIX: THE INVESTMENT TAX CREDIT

The Income Tax Act provides for **investment tax credits (ITCs)** for specified types of expenditures relating to capital investments and to qualifying R&D expenditures. The expenditures that qualify vary on three dimensions:
1. Type of expenditure.
2. Type of corporation.
3. Geographic region.

A **tax credit** is directly offset against income taxes payable.

There are two possible approaches to accounting for ITCs:
1. The *flow-through approach,* whereby the ITC for which the corporation qualifies is reported as a direct reduction in the income tax expense for the year.
2. The *cost-reduction approach,* whereby the ITC is deducted from the expenditures that gave rise to the ITC. The benefit of the ITC is thus allocated to the years in which the expenditures are recognized as expenses.

The *CICA Handbook,* Section 3805.12 recommends the cost reduction approach.

ITCs on expenditures that are reported as current expenses are usually deducted from income tax expense rather than from the functional expense itself.

When qualifying expenditures are made in order to acquire an asset, the ITC can either be (1) deducted from the asset's carrying value, with depreciation based on the net amount, or (2) deferred separately and amortized on the same basis as the asset itself.

TRUE–FALSE QUESTIONS

T F 1. Future income tax liabilities result when revenue is recognized on the books before it is taxable.

T F 2. Interperiod tax allocation is mandatory for both permanent and temporary differences using the liability method.

T F 3. The *CICA Handbook* requires the use of comprehensive allocation for public companies.

T F 4. Interperiod income tax allocation involves deciding how the total income tax amount should be reported in the current financial statements.

T F 5. A temporary difference, once originated, will result in either taxable or deductible amounts in future years when the difference reverses.

T F 6. In the absence of temporary differences, there should be no difference between income tax expense and income tax payable.

T F 7. *Intraperiod* tax allocation refers to determining the appropriate income tax expense for each reporting period; whereas *interperiod* tax allocation refers to allocating a given year's tax expense among the financial statement items giving rise to the expense.

T F 8. Private companies may elect to use the taxes payable method.

MULTIPLE CHOICE QUESTIONS

_____ 1. At the most recent year-end, Johnston Limited's income tax liability relating to a non-current asset exceeded its future income tax asset relating to a current asset. Which of the following is reported in Johnston's balance sheet?
   a. The future tax asset is a current asset.
   b. The excess of the future tax liability over the future tax asset is a long-term liability.
   c. The future tax liability is excluded from liabilities and is shown after long-term liabilities but before shareholders' equity.
   d. The excess of the future tax asset over the future tax liability is a current asset.

_____ 2. An example of an item requiring intraperiod tax allocation is:
   a. Bond discount amortization.
   b. Non-deductible golf dues included on the income statement.
   c. Loss from discontinued operations.
   d. Non-taxable dividend revenue included on the income statement.

_____ 3. At the beginning of 20x5, Rundle Ltd. reported a future tax liability of $300,000. The net book value of the capital assets was $2,600,000, while UCC was $1,600,000. In 20x5, amortization was $400,000, while CCA was $625,000. The tax rate is unchanged in 20x5. Which of the following statements is **incorrect**?
   a. The tax rate up to the beginning of 20x5 was 30%.
   b. The UCC at year-end was $975,000.
   c. The future tax liability increased by $225,000 in 20x5.
   d. The NBV at year-end was $2,200,000.

_____ 4. Return to the facts in question 3. If the tax rate was 45% in 20x5, which of the following statements is true?
   a. The future tax liability will decline in 20x5.
   b. The future tax liability has to be increased only to the effect of the change in tax rates on the opening balance.
   c. The future tax liability will increase by $251,250 in 20x5.
   d. The future tax liability will have a balance of $401,250 at 20x5.

_____ 5. Taxable income of a corporation:
   a. differs from accounting income due to differences in interperiod allocation and permanent differences between the two methods of income determination.
   b. is based on generally accepted accounting principles.
   c. is reported on the corporation's income statement.
   d. differs from accounting income due to differences in intraperiod allocation between the two methods of income determination.

___ 6. Interperiod income tax allocation causes:
   a. tax expense in the income statement to be presented with the specific revenues causing the tax.
   b. tax expense shown on the income statement to equal the amount of income taxes payable for the current year plus or minus the change in the future tax asset or liability balances for the year.
   c. tax expense shown in the income statement to bear a normal relation to the income taxes payable.
   d. income taxes payable in the income statement to be presented with the specific revenues causing the tax.

___ 7. Assume that Able Corporation has paid and expensed several speeding fines for its salespeople. Fines are never deductible for tax purposes. This will result in which of the following?
   a. Deductible temporary difference and future income tax liability.
   b. No temporary difference.
   c. Taxable temporary difference and future income tax liability.
   d. Taxable temporary difference and future income tax asset.

___ 8. Shelley Corporation's taxable income differed from its pretax financial income computed for this past year. An item that would create a perma-nent difference in pretax financial and taxable incomes for Shelley is:
   a. a balance in the accrued warranty expense account at year end.
   b. deducted golf club dues as a business expense for accounting purposes and not deducting for tax purposes.
   c. using accelerated amortization for tax purposes and straight-line amortization for accounting purposes.
   d. development cost deferred for accounting purposes and deducted for tax purposes.

___ 9. Future income tax asset or liability amounts that are related to specific assets or liabilities should be classified as current or long-term based on:
   a. their expected reversal dates.
   b. their debit or credit balances.
   c. the length of time the future income tax asset or liability amounts will generate future tax benefits.
   d. the classification of the related asset or liability.

___ 10. Palm Corporation purchased a computer on January 2, 20x4, for $300,000. The computer has an estimated 5-year life with no salvage value. The straight-line method of amortization is being used for financial statement purposes, and the following CCA amounts will be deducted for tax purposes:

20x4	$ 75,000
20x5	112,500
20x6	56,250
20x7	28,125
20x8	28,125

Assume an income tax rate of 40% for all years. The net future income tax liability that should be reflected on Palm's balance sheet at December 31, 20x5, should be:

	Future income tax liability	
	Current	Long-term
a.	$0	$27,000
b.	$21,000	$6,000
c.	$6,000	$21,000
d.	$	$6,000

SOLUTIONS TO TRUE–FALSE QUESTIONS

1. T

2. F Only temporary differences enter into the computation of taxable income, but they do so in a different period than they are recognized for financial reporting.

3. T

4. T

5. T

6. T

7. F The opposite is true. *Interperiod* tax allocation refers to allocating a given year's tax expense among the financial statement items giving rise to the expense; *interperiod* tax allocation refers to determining the appropriate income tax expense for each period.

8. T

SOLUTIONS TO MULTIPLE CHOICE QUESTIONS

1. a Current and non-current items cannot be netted.

2. c Intraperiod tax allocation deals only with the components of income.

3. c CCA versus amortization was $225,000 in the year; $225,000 x 30% does not equal $225,000.

4. c NBV versus UCC is $1,225,000 ($2,200,000–$975,000). A balance of $551,250 ($1,225,000 x .45) is needed in FIT. Existing balance of $300,000. Adjustment needed: $251,250 ($551,250–300,000) b is not correct because the FIT also has to be increased for the temporary difference.

5. a One objective of financial statement users and preparers is to measure net income according to GAAP. The objective of the Income Tax Regulations is to generate revenue for the government. There are some differences between GAAP and the Income Tax Regulations.

6. b This is how the comprehensive allocation method works. The tax effect of all temporary differences are allocated regardless of the timing or likelihood of their reversal.

7. b When an expense is not deductible for tax purposes, it is a permanent difference and therefore, there is no temporary difference at all. This amount is eliminated when calculating the accounting income subject to tax.

8. b Golf club dues are not allowed as a deduction for tax purposes. This is a permanent difference.

9. d According to the *CICA Handbook*, paragraph 3465.87, the key to classifying future income tax balances is the classification of their related assets or liabilities. The rapidity of the reversal is irrelevant.

10. a Amortization expense = $300,000/5 years = $60,000 per year. Using the balance sheet approach to calculate future income tax liability:

	Tax basis	Carrying value	Temporary difference deductible (taxable)	Future tax asset (liability) yr.-end	Less beginning balance dr. (cr.)	Adjustment for current year dr. (cr.)
20x4						
Capital asset	$225,000	$240,000	$(15,000)	$(6,000)	–0–	$(6,000)
20x5						
Capital asset	$112,500	$180,000	$(67,500)	$(27,000)	$(6,000)	$(21,000)

The net future income tax liability reflected on Palm's balance sheet at December 31, 20x5, should be a long-term liability of $27,000.

PROBLEMS
Problem 1

PURPOSE: To illustrate the steps to be taken in calculating and preparing income tax journal entries.

Sandals Corporation was formed in 20x3. Following is relevant information pertaining to 20x3, 20x4, and 20x5:

	20x3	20x4	20x5
Net income before tax	$200,000	$250,000	$225,000
Accounting income includes:			
Amortization (assets have a cost of $400,000)	40,000	40,000	40,000
Pension expense	6,000	8,000	11,000
Warranty expense	4,000	3,000	5,000
Dividend income	5,000	6,000	7,000
Taxable income includes the following:			
Capital cost allowance	45,000	60,000	35,000
Pension funding (amount paid)	5,000	6,000	10,000
Warranty costs paid	2,000	4,000	3,000
Tax rate—enacted in each year	40%	40%	45%

Required
Prepare the journal entry to record the income tax expense for each year.

Problem 2

PURPOSE: To illustrate the financial statement balance sheet presentation for future taxes.

Using the same information as in problem 1, show how the future income taxes would be classified on the balance sheet for each year.

SOLUTIONS TO PROBLEMS

Problem 1

We calculate accounting income subject to tax, taxable income, and current income taxes payable. (See table) Using the balance sheet approach, we then calculate the carrying values, tax basis, and summary income tax journal entries. (See table.).

	Tax basis	Carrying value	Temporary difference deductible (taxable)	Future tax asset (liability) yr.-end	Less beginning balance dr. (cr.)	Adjustment for current year dr. (cr.)
20x3						
Capital assets	$355,000	$360,000	$(5,000)	$(2,000)	–0–	$(2,000)
Pension liability	–0–	(1,000)	1000	400	–0–	400
Warranty liability	–0–	(2,000)	2,000	800	–0–	800
20x4						
Capital assets	$295,000	$320,000	$(25,000)	$(10,000)	$(2,000)	$(8,000)
Pension liability	–0–	(3,000)	3,000	1,200	400	800
Warranty liability	–0–	(1,000)	1,000	400	800	(400)
20x5						
Capital assets	$260,000	$280,000	$(20,000)	$(9,000)	$(10,000)	$1,000
Pension liability	–0–	4,000)	4,000	1,800	1,200	600
Warranty liability	–0–	(3,000)	3,000	1,350	400	950

Summary income tax journal entries:

20x3

Income tax expense	78,000	
Future income tax asset—pension	400	
Future income tax asset—warranty	800	
Future income tax liability—capital assets		2,000
Income taxes payable		77,200

20x4

Income tax expense	97,600	
Future income tax asset—pension	800	
Future income tax asset—warranty		400
Future income tax liability—capital assets		8,000
Income taxes payable		90,000

20x5

Income tax expense	99,150	
Future income tax asset—pension	600	
Future income tax asset—warranty	950	
Future income tax liability—capital assets	1,000	
Income taxes payable		101,700

Problem 2

	20x3	20x4	20x5
Assets			
Current:			
Future income tax assets	$ 800	$ 400	$1,350
Long-term:			
Future income tax assets	400	1,200	1,800
Liabilities			
Long term:			
Future income tax assets	$2,000	$10,000	$9,000

	20x3	20x4	20x5
Net income, before tax	$200,000	$250,000	$225,000
Permanent differences:			
Dividends	–5,000	–6,000	–7,000
Accounting income subject to tax	$195,000	$244,000	$218,000
Timing differences:			
Amortization expense	+40,000	+40,000	+40,000
CCA	–45,000	–60,000	–35,000
Pension expense	+6,000	+8,000	+11,000
Pension funding	–5,000	–6,000	–10,000
Warranty expense	+4,000	+3,000	+5,000
Warranty costs paid	–2,000	–4,000	–3,000
Taxable income	$193,000	$225,000	$226,000
Enacted tax rate	40%	$40%	45%
Current taxes payable	$77,200	$90,000	$101,700

> Classification of the future income tax assets and liabilities is a function of how **WATCH!** the underlying asset or liability is classified on the balance sheet. The pension accrual is classified as a long-term liability; therefore the related future income tax asset is also classified as a long-term asset. The warranty accrual is classified as current liability so the related future income tax asset is classified as a current asset. The net book value versus the unamortized capital cost is classified as a long-term asset, so the related future income tax liability is classified as long-term liability.

CASE: Forged Chemicals Inc.

You are the new accountant for Forged Chemicals Inc. (FCI). You have been asked to consider the tax impacts on the financial statements for the year ended December 31, 20x5. For that year, FCI had income of $2 million before the items that follow. The company's tax rate is 40%, as it has been every year since incorporation 10 years ago.

During the year, FCI sold its plant in Toronto and relocated to Barrie, Ontario. It bought the land in Toronto in 19x6 for $500,000 and built the plant for $4 million at the end of that year The plant was amortized on a 5% straight-line basis for a total of $1,800,000, including $200,000 in 20x5. The land and building were sold for a net of $8 million, the land being worth $3 million. The unamortized capital cost (UCC) of the building is $2,827,000.

Although the company has reported the gain for accounting purposes, for tax purposes it is entitled to the gain on the building and the recapture from the sale of the building, since in 20x5 it built a new plant in Barrie for $5 million on land purchased for $600,000. Its maximum CCA claim in 20x5 is $50,000. The new building was occupied at year end and is to be amortized on a 4% straight-line basis commencing in 20x6.

The taxable gain on the sale of the land is to be included in the taxable income.

FCI's product development expenses of $1 million have been deferred, to be amortized over the anticipated product life of four years starting two years from now. For tax purposes, the company has written off the development costs in 20x5 and claimed a 30% refundable investment tax credit, taxable in the next year.

Required

As the new accountant for FCI Inc., compute the income tax consequences of the above and describe how they will be reported on the company's financial statements. Note: 25% of capital gains are not taxable. The balance of capital gains is taxable at normal rates.

KEY POINTS IN THE CASE

This question requires students to identify and calculate temporary differences for income tax purposes and to determine the impact these differences will have on a company's financial statements. Included in the scenario is the sale of capital assets on which there are nontaxable permanent differences.

Sale of land and building: Computations—

Land:
Proceeds		$3,000,000
Book value		
Cost		500,000
Gain on sale		$2,500,000
Permanent difference		
1/4 of gain ($2,500,000 × 25%)		$ 625,000

Building:
Proceeds		$5,000,000
Book value		
Cost	$4,000,000	
Accumulated amortization	1,800,000	2,200,000
Gain on sale		$2,800,000
Permanent difference		
1/4 of gain (proceeds over cost)		
($5,000,000 − $4,000,000)		$ 250,000

Accounting gain included in accounting income:
$$($2,500,000 + $2,800,000) = $5,300,000$$

Taxable gain: [75% × ($2,500,000 + $1,000,000)] = $2,625,000
Breakdown of taxable gain:
       Land: 75% × $2,500,000 = $1,875,000
       Building: 75% × $1,000,000 = $750,000

Recapture on sale of building: The lesser of proceeds and cost, less UCC.

    Proceeds: $5,000,000

    Cost: $4,000,000

    UCC: $2,827,000

    Recapture: $4,000,000 – $2,827,000 = $1,173,000

Recapture is fully taxable.

COMMENTS

The income statement will record a gain on the sale of capital assets of $5,300,000. This gain should be deducted from the income. The taxable amount to be added is the taxable capital gain on the sale of the land of $1,875,000. The taxable capital gain on the sale of the building and the recapture will be deferred by deducting it from the cost of the new building. Therefore, these two amounts are not included in income for 20x5.

Accounting gain: $5,300,000

Less taxable gain: $(1,875,000)

Difference: $3,425,000

Deferred capital gain and recapture: ($750,000 + $1,173,000)		$1,923,000
Permanent differences calculated above: ($625,000 + $250,000)		$875,000
Tax basis of the capital assets (building): UCC	$2,827,000	
Carrying value of the building (NBV):	2,200,000	
Temporary difference (taxable):		$ 627,000
Reconciliation of the difference:		$3,425,000

The company is entitled to defer all taxable capital gain of $750,000 and the taxable recapture of $1,173,000 for tax purposes as a consequence of the purchase of replacement property. A note to the financial statements will be required to disclose this deferral. The tax basis for the building will be cost of $5,000,000, less $750,000 (taxable capital gain on sale of building), and less $1,173,000 (recapture), to equal $3,077,000.

SUMMARY

Next we will calculate the accounting income subject to income tax, the taxable income, and the current taxes payable.

Income for accounting purposes:

Accounting income before adjustments		$2,000,000
Accounting gain on sale of assets		5,300,000
Less: amortization		(200,000)
Accounting income before tax		$7,100,000

Permanent difference:

Nontaxable gain (1/4 of capital gain)		(875,000)
Accounting income subject to tax		$6,225,000

Temporary differences:

Amortization expense	+200,000	
CCA	− 50,000	+ 150,000
Product development-deductible		−1,000,000
Accounting gain on sale of assets		
($5,300,000 − 875,000)		−4,425,000
Taxable gain on sale of land		+1,875,000
Taxable income		$2,825,000
Tax rate		40%
Income tax payable		$ 1,130,000
Less: investment tax credit		$ (300,000)
Tax payable		$ 830,000

Product Development Expenses: Computations

Deferred development expenses	$1,000,000
Cost	300,000
Investment tax credit	$ 700,000

Deferred tax credit	
Deferred deduction/deferred for accounting	$1,000,000
Tax basis	−0−
Future income tax liability	$ 400,000

COMMENTS

The balance sheet will show deferred development expenses of $700,000. The net amount will be amortized on the basis selected for development costs. The $400,000 will be added to the long-term future income tax liabilities on the balance sheet. This temporary difference will reverse as development costs are amortized.

The amount of investment tax credits recognized in the financial statements will be disclosed in the notes thereto.

The fact that development expenses have been written off for income tax purposes will be disclosed in the notes to the financial statements.

Investment Tax Credit: Computations—

Investment tax credit taxable next year	$300,000
Tax @ 40%	$120,000

COMMENTS

As the $300,000 will be taxable next year, the balance sheet will show a current deferred income tax credit of $120,000. This amount will reverse next year when the company will have to declare the income for tax purposes and pay the tax thereon.

The amount of $120,000 will be deducted from long-term future income tax liabilities on the balance sheet.

Balance in the building account at the end of 2004:

UCC balance	$2,827,000	
Net book value	2,400,000	($2,200,000 + $200,000 amortization)
	$ 427,000	
	40%	
Future income tax asset balance:	$ 170,800	

Using the balance sheet approach, we calculate the future income tax liabilities:

	Tax basis	Carrying value	Temporary difference deductible (taxable)	Future tax asset (liability) yr.-end	Less beginning balance dr. (cr.)	Adjustment for current year dr. (cr.)
20x4						
Building	$2,827,000	$2,400,000	$427,000	$170,800	–0–	–0–
20x5						
Building	$3,027,000	$4,800,000	$(1,773,000)	$(709,200)	170,800	$(880,000)
Development expenses	–0–	$1,000,000	$(1,000,000)	$(400,000)	–0–	$(400,000)

SUMMARY INCOME TAX JOURNAL ENTRY FOR 20x5

Income tax expense	2,530,000	
Income tax payable		830,000
Future income tax liability—building		880,000
Future income tax liability—development expense		400,000
Future income tax liability—deferred income tax credit		120,000
Deferred development expense		300,000

SELECTED SOLUTIONS FROM THE TEXTBOOK

Assignment 15-7

Requirement 1

	20x4	*20x5*	*20x6*	*20x7*
Revenues	$110,000	$124,000	$144,000	$164,000
Expenses.....................................	(80,000)	(92,000)	(95,000)	(128,000)
Depreciation, straight line............	(10,000)	(10,000)	(10,000)	(10,000)
Pretax accounting income (given)	20,000	22,000	39,000	26,000
Temporary differences for depreciation:				
Add accounting depreciation expense................................	10,000	10,000	10,000	10,000
Less capital cost allowance....	(16,000)	(12,000)	(8,000)	(4,000)
Net temporary difference.............	(6,000)	(2,000)	2,000	6,000
Taxable income..............................	$ 14,000	$ 20,000	$ 41,000	$ 32,000

Computation of income tax payable:

Taxable income..............................	$ 14,000	$ 20,000	$ 41,000	$ 32,000
Income tax rate	x .40	x .40	x .40	x .40
Income tax payable	$ 5,600	$ 8,000	$ 16,400	$ 12,800

Net income, taxes payable method

	20x4	*20x5*	*20x6*	*20x7*
Income before income tax	$20,000	$22,000	$39,000	$26,000
Income tax expense........................	5,600	8,000	16,400	12,800
	$14,400	$14,000	$22,600	$13,200

Requirement 2

Future income tax, balance sheet

Net temporary differences (see req 1)	(6,000)	(2,000)	2,000	6,000
Tax rate...	.4	.4	.4	.4
Change in period..............................	(2,400)	(800)	800	2,400
Cumulative balance in FIT	(2,400) cr	(3,200) cr	(2,400) cr	0

A table can also be used for calculations:

(in 000's)	Tax Basis	Carrying Value	Temp Diff	Future Tax	Op. Bal.	Adjustment
20x4 40%						
Cap.Assets	$ 24	$ 30	$(6)	$ (2.4)	0	$ (2.4)
20x5 40%						
Cap.Assets	12	20	(8)	(3.2)	(2.4)	(.8)
20x6 40%						
Cap.Assets	4	10	(6)	(2.4)	(3.2)	.8
20x7 40%						
Cap.Assets	0	0	0	0	(2.4)	2.4

Income tax expense, liability method of tax allocation:

	20x4	20x5	20x6	20x7
Income tax expense:				
Income tax payable......................	$5,600	$8,000	$16,400	$12,800
Temporary differences.................	2,400	800	(800)	(2,400)
	$8,000	$8,800	$15,600	$10,400

Net income, liability method of tax allocation

	20x4	20x5	20x6	20x7
Pretax...	$20,000	$22,000	$39,000	$26,000
Income tax expense.......................	8,000	8,800	15,600	10,400
	$12,000	$13,200	$23,400	$15,600

Requirement 3

The taxes payable method records tax paid as the expense, reflecting cash flow. Tax allocation methods accrue tax as income is recognized for accounting purposes, regardless of when it will be paid. Matching is well served, and future taxes are reflected on the balance sheet, thus providing a more accurate portrayal of the company's financial position. Since all individual temporary differences do reverse, accrual of tax is appropriate.

Assignment 15-13

Income tax payable:

	20x4	20x5	20x6
Accounting income..	$550,000	$123,000	$310,000
Temporary difference...	(300,000)	150,000	150,000
Taxable income...	250,000	273,000	460,000
Tax rate	.30	.35	.42
Income tax payable	$75,000	$95,550	$193,200

Income tax expense:

	20x4	20x5	20x6
Income tax payable (above)...................................	$75,000	$95,550	$193,200
Change in future income tax			
See calculations, below	90,000	(37,500)	(52,500)
Income tax expense...	$165,000	$58,050	$140,700
Future income tax liability balance	$ 90,000 cr.	$52,500 cr.	None

Future income tax:

	Tax Basis	Accounting Basis	Temporary Difference	Future tax Liability	Opening Balance	Adjustment
20x4						
Accounts receivable	0	$300,000	($300,000)	($90,000)	0	($90,000)
20x5						
Accounts receivable	0	150,000	(150,000)	(52,500)	(90,000)	37,500
20x6						
Accounts receivable	0	0	0	0	(52,500)	52,500

Assignment 15-14

Requirement 1

This is a temporary difference because (a) pretax accounting income and taxable income are different for each year, and (b) the difference will reverse in subsequent years.

Requirement 2

	20x4	20x5	20x6	20x7
Accounting net book value	$90,000	$60,000	$30,000	$0
Tax basis (UCC)	72,000	36,000	12,000	0

Requirement 3

Accounting and taxable income 20x4–20x7

	20x4	20x5	20x6	20x7
Pretax income (excluding depreciation)	$60,000	$80,000	$70,000	$70,000
Depreciation	30,000	30,000	30,000	30,000
Income before tax	30,000	50,000	40,000	40,000
Add back depreciation	30,000	30,000	30,000	30,000
Deduct depreciation for tax purposes (given):				
20x4	$(48,000)			
20x5		$(36,000)		
20x6			$(24,000)	
20x7				$(12,000)
Taxable income	12,000	44,000	46,000	58,000
Tax rate	30%	30%	40%	40%
Income tax payable	$ 3,600	$13,200	$18,400	$23,200

Assignment 15-21

	20x3	20x4	20x5
Net income before tax..	$75,000	$ 90,000	$80,000
Timing differences:			
Warranty: expense	60,000		
tax deduction..............................	(15,000)	(20,000)	(25,000)
Franchise: accounting fee revenue.................	(90,000)		
fees for tax purposes....................	9,000	51,000	30,000
Taxable income...	$39,000	$121,000	$85,000
Income tax payable (.38,.40,.45)	$14,820	$48,400	$38,250
Income tax expense:			
Income tax payable..	$14,820	$48,400	$38,250
Change in future income tax (see schedule)	13,680	(11,680)	(2,000)
Income tax expense..	$28,500	$36,720	$36,250

Future income tax:

	Tax Basis	Accounting Basis	Temporary Difference	Future tax (Liab)/Asset	Opening Balance	Adjustment
20x3 (38%)						
Warranty	$0	($45,000)	$45,000	$17,100	$0	$17,100
Franchise	0	81,000	(81,000)	(30,780)	0	(30,780)
						(13,680)
20x4 (40%)						
Warranty	0	(25,000)	25,000	10,000	17,100	(7,100)
Franchise	0	30,000	(30,000)	(12,000)	(30,780)	18,780
						11,680
20x5 (45%)						
Warranty	0	0	0	0	10,000	(10,000)
Franchise	0	0	0	0	(12,000)	12,000
						2,000

Entries:

20x3	Income tax expense	28,500	
	Future income tax - warranty..................	17,100	
	Future income tax- franchise		30,780
	Income tax payable		14,820
20x4	Income tax expense	36,720	
	Future income tax- franchise...................	18,780	
	Future income tax- warranty..............		7,100
	Income tax payable		48,400
20x5	Income tax expense.................................	36,250	
	Future income tax - franchise..................	12,000	
	Future income tax- warranty.............		10,000
	Income tax payable		38,250

SOLUTIONS TO CONCEPT REVIEW QUESTIONS

Page 933

1. *Intraperiod* allocation is the allocation of the total income tax expense for the accounting period to the various income statement items giving rise to the income tax—for example, operating income, extraordinary gains/losses, discontinued operations—within an accounting period. *Interperiod* allocation accounts for the differences in the tax value versus the carrying (book) values of assets and liabilities through several accounting periods. Interperiod allocation is concerned with temporary differences in the accounting and tax treatment of transactions and recognizes the effect of those differences on a year-to-year basis.

2. A *permanent difference* is an element of the income statement—a revenue, gain, expense, or loss—that enters the computation of *either* taxable income *or* pretax accounting income, but never both. Examples of permanent differences include 50% of meals and entertainment costs, 25% of capital gains/losses not taxable, and intercorporate dividends.

3. The temporary difference originates in 20X0, the year it first affects either accounting or taxable income. It reveres in 20X1.

Page 936

1. The *flow-through method* (taxes payable method) of accounting for income tax expense recognizes the amount of taxes assessed in each year as the income tax expense for that year. Thus, income tax expense equals current income tax.

2. Comprehensive tax allocation because the income ax effect of revenue and expenses is recognized in the same period as the revenue or expense.

3. Partial tax allocation usually omits temporary differences that are unlikely to reverse in the near future. There recurring temporary differences include, for example, NBV/UCC.

Page 939

1. The essential difference between the deferral method and the liability method is that the former records the future tax impact of temporary differences by using the corporation's effective average tax rate in the year that the temporary difference first arises; whereas the latter records the future tax impact at the tax rate that will be in effect in the year of reversal of the temporary difference. The result of the liability method is that the future tax impact is re-evaluated each year and may be revised as the expected future tax rate is enacted.

2. Using the liability method the impact of the rate change is recognized in 20X2, the year the change occurred.

3. The CICA's position on the discounting of future income tax amounts is that "future income tax liabilities and future income tax expense should not be discounted."

Page 948

1. The distinction between current future income tax liabilities and long-term future income tax liabilities is as follows: to qualify as a *current* future income tax balance, the temporary differences giving rise to the future income taxes must be current assets or liabilities (e.g., accounts receivable, inventories, notes payable). *Long-term* future income tax liabilities are those not qualifying as current future income tax liabilities (or those for which the underlying items giving rise to the temporary difference are long-term in nature).

2. The future income taxes relating to all long-term assets and liabilities are grouped together and reported as a single amount. The asset and liability are not shown individually.

Page 954

1. The amount of income tax expense or benefit that is attributable to net income before discontinued operations and extraordinary items should be reported separately on the face of the income statement. The income tax expense should not be combined with other items of expense. The amount of income tax expense that is attributable to future income taxes should be disclosed, either on the face of the statements or in the notes.

2. The CICA recommends that all public companies provide a reconciliation of the effective tax rate. Stakeholders of a public company may not be able to determine the factors affecting the tax rate without such communication. Private companies are not required to provide such a reconciliation, as it is presumed that the stakeholders have the ability to influence the company to disclose such information if they require.

3. The purpose of the effective tax rate reconciliation is to provide an explanation as to why the income tax expense reported by the company on its income statements may bear little resemblance to the expected level of taxes under the prevailing statutory rate. The reconciliation explains the factors causing the variation in the tax rate such as permanent differences, special taxes, and changes in tax rates relating to temporary differences that will reverse in future periods.

4. The amounts to be reported in the operating activities section of the cash flow statement are only those amounts that are actually paid by the company. Under the direct method, the actual amount of tax paid (or received) is reported; under the indirect method, the effect of tax allocations and benefits recognized for the future benefits of tax loss carry forwards are reversed.

CHAPTER 16

ACCOUNTING FOR TAX LOSSES

The previous chapter dealt with temporary differences—the differences between carrying values and tax basis for assets and liabilities. Another issue in interperiod tax allocation arises when a corporation experiences a loss. This creates a matching issue. A loss will normally have tax benefits, but the benefits may be realized in a period other than that of the loss. This chapter discusses when and how to recognize the income tax benefits that arise from a loss.

1. TAX BENEFITS OF A LOSS

When a corporation prepares its tax return and ends up with a taxable loss instead of taxable income, the loss may be used against past and/or future taxable income, as follows:

- The loss can be *carried back* for 3 years.
- Any remaining loss can be *carried forward* for 10 years.

The taxes recovered from the loss carry-back are recognized on the income statement as a *tax recovery,* and this item is shown on the balance sheet as a current asset. Recognition occurs in the period of the loss.

If the carry-backs do not fully utilize the loss, a recognition problem arises. Income taxes can be reduced in *future* periods as a result of the tax loss carry-forward. The benefit can be measured with reasonable assurance. The issue that arise relates to likelihood of the benefit being realized. Will sufficient taxable income be earned in the carryforward period?

The general principle is that the tax benefits of tax losses should be recognized in the period of the loss, *to the extent possible.* Current Canadian practice gives precedence to matching over conservatism and the loss is recognized when it is probable (greater than 50% probability).

Tax Loss versus Tax Benefits
Separate records should be kept for the amount of the **tax loss** and the amount of the **tax benefit**. The *tax loss* is the final number of taxable income (loss) on the income tax return. The *tax benefit* is the total present and future benefit that the company will be able to realize from the tax loss through a reduction of income taxes paid to governments. It is calculated as the loss times the tax rate.

2. TAX LOSS CARRYBACKS

Loss carrybacks entitle a company to receive tax paid in the previous three years. It is normally carried back to the earliest year first and then applied to subsequent years. Tax is recovered at the rate that was in effect in the year it was paid.

3. TEMPORARY AND PERMANENT DIFFERENCES IN A LOSS YEAR

Step 1: Calculate Taxable Loss According to the Income Tax Act.

Begin with the net loss according to the financial statements and add/deduct reconciling items. *The existence of a loss has no impact on accounting for the temporary differences;* temporary differences are recorded exactly as illustrated in the previous chapter.

> **1.** Amortization will always be added back to accounting income, since it is not deductible for tax purposes. **2.** CCA is an *optional* deduction that may not be taken in a loss year. This is a key point for tax planning.

WATCH!

Step 2: Determine the change to future income tax (using a table or the shortcut method).

Step 3: Prepare the journal entries

> The *credit* to income tax expense reflects the fact that it is a recovery of taxes paid in earlier years.

WATCH!

4. TAX LOSS CARRYFORWARDS

The Basic Principle "More likely Than Not"
If after the carry-back there is still a loss left over, it may be carried forward to future tax benefits. This amount of future tax benefits "recognized should be limited to the amount that is **more likely than not** to be realized" (3465.24).

> At each balance sheet date, ... a future income tax asset should be recognized for all deductible temporary differences, unused tax losses and income tax reductions. The amount recognized should be limited to the amount that is more likely than not to be realized. [3465.24]

CICA

> An event is more likely than not when the probability that it will occur is greater than 50%.[3465.09(1)]

CICA

Tax planning strategies that could be used to realize a future income tax asset include the following:

- Reducing or eliminating CCA in the year of the loss and future years.
- Amending prior years' tax returns to reduce or eliminate CCA.
- Recognizing taxable revenues in the carry-forward period that might ordinarily be recognized in later periods.

In deciding whether recognition is more likely than not companies should evaluate all favourable and unfavourable evidence. Whether or not the over-50% criterion is met is a matter of professional judgement.

The asset, future tax benefit, must be reviewed annually. If the asset has been set up and it is judged that the 50% test is not longer met the asset is removed. Alternatively if it was not previously recorded because the 50% test was not met but this changes the asset is recorded. Examples of various recognition scenarios are presented in your text.

5. USING A VALUATION ALLOWANCE

An alternative to adjusting the future income tax benefit is to use an allowance account. This account is similar to the allowance for doubtful accounts. The amount of the future benefit is assessed in the usual manner but instead of adjusting the account directly, necessary adjustment is made to the allowance account. The allowance account is a contra account and only the net amount is reported on the balance sheet.

When a loss carryfoward expires it must be written off, along with any allowance account.

6. WHICH TAX RATE?

The CICA recommends the use of the rate expected to apply when the temporary differences reverse. This is referred to as the **substantively enacted income tax rate**. The rate must be updated as tax rates change, with the offset going to income tax expense in the period of the rate change. If the rate decreases it will result in a credit to income tax expense; if it increases tax expense will be debited.

7. BASIC ILLUSTRATION

Your text provides basic illustrations of recognition of loss carryforward benefits that have no other temporary timing differences but does include rate changes. It includes a situation where realization is likely and another where realization becomes likely.

8. EXTENDED ILLUSTRATION

Your text also provides an illustrations of recognition of loss carryforward benefits with more complications. It compares the result under the assumption that realizations is likely and not likely. Matching is better served when realization is likely. When realization is not likely but the benefit is realized in subsequent periods a swing in income results.

ILLUSTRATION

Lockheed Inc. has the following information:

- In 20x2, Lockheed begins operations and acquires equipment costing $1,200,000.
- The equipment is being amortized straight-line at 5% (i.e., $60,000 per year).
- Lockheed claims CCA of $120,000 in 20x2, $216,000 in 20x3, $172,800 in 20x4, and $138,240 in 20x5.

- The tax rate is 30% in 20x2 and 20x3. During 20x4, Parliament increases the tax rate to 35%, applicable to 20x4 and following years.
- Lockheed's income before income tax for 20x2 through 20x5 is as follows:
  - 20x2 $200,000
  - 20x3 $(700,000) [loss]
  - 20x4 $300,000
  - 20x5 $700,000

Step 1: Calculate taxable income (loss).

	20x2	20x3	20x4	20x5
Accounting income (loss) subject to tax	$200,000	$(700,000)	$300,000	$700,000
Temporary differences:				
+ amortization	60,000	60,000	60,000	60,000
– CCA	–120,000	–216,000	–172,800	–138,240
Taxable income (loss), current year	$140,000	$(856,000)	$187,200	$621,760

Step 2: Calculate the temporary difference, based on the difference between the tax basis and the carrying value of the equipment. Assume that probability of realization is equal to or less than 50%.

	20x2	20x3	20x4	20x5
Tax basis of equipment	$1,080,000	$ 864,000	$ 691,200	$ 552,960
Carrying value of equipment	1,140,000	1,080,000	1,020,000	960,000
Temporary difference—equipment	(60,000)	(216,000)	(328,800)	(407,040)
Tax rate	30%	30%	35%	35%
F.I.T. asset (liability balance for year)	$ (18,000)	$ (64,800)	$ (115,080)	$ (142,464)

In 20x2, taxable income is $140,000. At 30%, the current income tax payable is $42,000. The F.I.T. liability goes from zero to a credit of $18,000. The journal entry for 20x2 is as follows:

Income tax expense	60,000	
Income tax payable		42,000
Future income tax liability		18,000

In 20x3, Lockheed has a loss.
- Tax loss = $856,000, of which $140,000 is carried back and $716,000 is carried forward.
- Future income tax liability increases by $46,800.

	Tax basis	Carrying value dr. (cr.)	Temporary difference, asset (liability) dr. (cr.)	Future tax asset (liability)	Beginning balance	Adjustment
20x2						
Equipment	$1,080,000	$1,140,000 1	$(60,000)	$(18,000)	–0–	$(18,000)
20x3						
Equipment	$864,000	1,080,000	(216,000)	(64,800)	(18,000)	(46,800)
20x4						
Equipment	$691,20	1,020,000	(328,800)	(115,080)	(64,800)	(50,280)
20x5						
Equipment	$552,960	960,000	(407,040)	(142,464)	(115,080)	(27,384)

Receivable for tax recovery of $42,000 (carry-back). The 20x3 journal entry is:

Income tax expense	4,800	
Income tax receivable	42,000	
Future income tax liability		46,800

Taxable income for 20x4 is $187,200. Taxes payable on the taxable income will be ($187,200 × 35%) = $65,520. Loss carry-forward is used to offset the taxable income; therefore, there are no taxes payable in 20x4.

The journal entry, using a single entry, is as follows:

Income tax expense	50,280	
Future income tax liability		50,280
($115,080 − $64,800)		

Income tax expense is only $50,280 because of the loss carry-forward recognized in 20x4.

At the end of 20x4 the unused tax loss carry-forward is:

20x4 tax loss	$ 856,000
Carry-back to 20x2	−140,000
Carry-forward in 20x4	−187,200
Remaining carry-forward, end of 20x4	$ 528,800

In 20x5 the taxable income is $621,760. This is enough to completely absorb the remaining tax loss carry-forward.

Tax payable on $621,760 @ 35%	$217,616
Reduction of $528,800 @ 35%	185,080
Net income tax payable	$ 32,536

Future income tax liability adjustment: ($142,464 − $115,080) = $27,384

The journal entry for 20x5 will be:

Income tax expense	59,920	
Income tax payable		32,536
Future income tax liability		27,384

Assuming that probability of realization is greater than 50%, we will calculate the temporary difference and future income tax asset and liability.

	20x2	20x3	20x4	20x5
Tax basis of equipment	$1,080,000	$ 864,000	$691,200	$ 552,960
Carrying value	1,140,000	1,080,000	1,020,000	960,000
Temporary difference	60,000	(216,000)	(328,800)	(407,040)
Tax loss carry-forward		[a]716,000	528,800	
	(60,000)	500,000	200,000	(407,040)
Tax rate	30%	30%	35%	35%
Future income tax asset (liability)— balance, end of year	$ (18,000)	$ 150,000	$ 70,000	$ (142,464)

[a] 20x3 tax loss = $856,000 − $140,000 (20x2 taxable income) = $716,000

In 20x3, the income tax rate is 30%. If we combine the journal entry to reflect the carry-forward benefit:

Future income tax asset ($716,000 × 30%)	214,800	
Income tax receivable	42,000	
Future income tax liability		46,800
Income tax expense		210,000

In 20x4, $187,200 of the carry forward is utilized. The adjustment is:

Income tax expense	80,000	
Future income tax asset		80,000
($150,000 – $70,000)		

In 20x5, the remaining carry-forward is used and the future income tax goes from a debit of $70,000 to a credit of $142,464. The entry is:

Income tax expense	245,000	
Income tax payable ($621,760 – $528,800 @ 35%)		32,536
Future income tax liability ($70,000 + $142,464)		212,464

	Tax basis dr. (cr.)	Carrying value dr. (cr.)	Temporary difference	F.I.T. asset (liability) (dr. (cr.)	Beginning balance dr. (cr.)	Adjustment to F. t. T. dr. (cr.)
20x2						
Equipment	$1,080,000	$1,140,000	$(60,000)	$ (18,000)	–0–	$ (18,000)
20x3						
Equipment	864,000	1,080,000	(216,000)	$ (64,800)	(18,000)	$ (46,800)
Loss carry-forw.			716,000	214,800	–0–	214,800
				$150,000		$ 168,000
20x4						
Equipment	691,200	1,020,000	(328,800)	$(115,080)	(64,800)	$ (50,280)
Loss carry-forw			528,800	185,080	214,800	(29,720)
				$ 70,000		$ (80,000)
20x5						
Equipment	552,960	960,000	(407,040)	$(142,464)	(115,080)	$ (27,384)
Loss carry-forw			–0–	–0–	(185,080)	(185,080)
				$(142,464)		$(212,464)

9. INTRAPERIOD ALLOCATION OF TAX LOSS CARRYFORWARD BENEFITS

When the future benefits of a tax loss carryforward are recognized in the year of the loss the benefits will be given intraperiod allocation. If the benefits are recognized in a period following the loss, any income statement impacts will not be given intraperiod allocation. The delay in recognition can move the benefit from one category to another on the income statement (e.g. from extraordinary items to operating income).

10. DISCLOSURE

The CICA *Handbook,* paragraph 3465.85, recommends that income tax expense related to continuing operations be shown on the face of the income statement.

Paragraph 3465.91 adds that further disclosures relating to tax losses consist of the following:

- Current tax benefit from loss carry-backs and carry-forwards, segregated between (1) continuing operations and (2) discontinued operations and extraordinary items.
- The amount and expiry date of unused tax losses -recognized and unrecognized.

Paragraph 3465.92 states that public companies also would disclose unused tax losses "that give rise to future income tax assets."

If a company has elected to use **differential reporting** they will report on a taxes payable basis in a loss year as well as a profitable year. Only the amount of taxes actually recovered through carrybacks in a loss year will be reported as income tax recovery. When carryforwards are used to reduce taxes in following years, the reduced amount of tax actually paid is reported as income tax expense.

11. EVALUATION OF FUTURE BENEFIT ACCOUNTING

The AcSB's recommendations on accounting for the future benefit of a loss carryforward are consistent with U.S. practice. There are problems with recognition as follows:

- There has been no transaction to establish the right. The right is contingent on generating future income.
- Recognition is highly dependent on management judgement.
- When the likelihood is marginal, management may delay recognition to enhance future income.
- When the source of the loss is other than continuing operations management may delay recognition to move the loss to continuing operations.

TRUE–FALSE QUESTIONS

T F 1. A taxable operating loss may first be carried back for 3 years and then forward for up to 10 years.

T F 2. Under no circumstances should the tax benefits due to a taxable operating loss carried forward be recognized in the year of loss.

T F 3. Tax benefits due to taxable operating loss carry-back should be measured at the tax rate for the year of loss.

T F 4. The future benefits of tax loss carry-forwards should be recognized in the year of the loss if there is a greater than 60% probability that the benefits will be realized.

T F 5. Once a future income tax asset has been recorded for a tax loss carry-forward, the balance of that account must be adjusted to reflect the tax rate that is expected to be in effect when carry-forward is utilized.

T F 6. Assuming a company uses the valuation allowance method and has losses that expire the journal entry would include a debit to the valuation allowance account.

T F 7. Future benefits of loss carrybacks should be given intraperiod allocation.

T F 8. Companies that elect to use differential reporting can recognize future benefits of loss carryforwards if they are more likely that not to be realized.

MULTIPLE CHOICE QUESTIONS

___ **1.** A company, which operated profitably during its first five years, sustained a loss in the sixth year which equaled its pretax income of any four of the first 5 years of its operations. The company can choose to obtain a refund of income taxes paid by filing an amended return for:
    a. any of the first years of operations.
    b. the three years immediately preceding the loss.
    c. any years before the loss, provided the loss equals or exceeds profits of those years.
    d. the four most profitable years preceding the loss.

___ **2.** Bowen Company earned income in 20x4 and suffered a loss for tax purposes in 20x5. Bowen Co. decided to carry the loss back to 20x4 in order to realize a benefit from the loss. The journal entry would include:
    a. Dr. income tax receivable, cr. income tax expense
    b. Dr. income tax expense, cr. income tax payable.
    c. Dr. income tax expense, cr. income tax receivable.
    d. Dr. future income tax asset, cr. income tax expense.

___ **3.** Verena Inc. earned income in 20x4 and suffered a loss for tax purposes in 20x5. Assume that even after carrying back and recovering taxes previously paid, there is still some loss remaining to carry forward. The journal entry related to the recognition of any benefit from carry-forward will be recognized as follows (assume the realization is more likely than not)
    a. Dr. future income tax asset; cr. income tax expense.
    b. Dr. income tax expense; cr. future income tax asset.
    c. Dr. future income tax asset; cr. income tax payable.
    d. Dr. income tax payable; cr. future income tax asset.

___ **4.** Future income tax asset relating to unused tax losses would be recognized if it is more likely than not that the benefit will be realized. Which of the following is *not* an example of favourable evidence to support recognition?
    a. Existing sufficient taxable temporary differences that will result in taxable amounts against which the unused tax losses can be utilized.
    b. Existing contracts, or firm sales backlog income to realize the future income tax asset based on existing sales prices and cost structures.
    c. An excess of fair value over tax basis of the enterprise's net assets in an amount sufficient to realize the future income tax asset.
    d. Unsettled circumstances that will adversely affect future operations and profit levels on a continuing basis in future years.

_____ 5. A corporation is entitled to offset the loss against past and future taxable income as follows:
   a. The loss carried back 3 years and forward 7 years.
   b. The loss carried back 3 years and forward 10 years.
   c. The loss carried back 7 years and forward 3 years.
   d. The loss carried back 3 years and forward 3 years.

_____ 6. Tax planning strategies that can be implemented to realize a future income tax asset are as follows, *except* for:
   a. reducing or eliminating CCA in the year of loss and future years.
   b. increasing the CCA to maximum allowable amount in the year of loss and future years.
   c. amending prior years' tax returns to reduce or eliminate CCA
   d. recognizing taxable revenues in the carry-forward period that might ordinarily be recognized in later periods.

_____ 7. The tax rate that should be used to recognize the future benefits of a tax loss carry-forward is
   a. historic rate.
   b. current rate.
   c. enacted future rate.
   d. estimated future rate.

_____ 8. The amounts relating to income tax recoveries that should be shown on the face of the income statement are:
   a. income tax expense.
   b. effective tax rate.
   c. future income tax assets.
   d. future income tax liabilities.

SOLUTIONS TO TRUE-FALSE QUESTIONS

1. T

2. F The criterion for recognizing the future benefits is simply that "the amount recognized should be limited to the amount that is more likely than not to be realized."

3. F The tax benefits due to taxable operating loss carry-back are the income taxes actually paid in the previous 3 years. Therefore, use the tax rate at which it was originally paid.

4. F The probability is 50% not 60%.

5. T

6. T

7. T

8. F Companies that use differential reporting can only recognize loss carryforwards on the taxes payable basis.

SOLUTIONS TO MULTIPLE CHOICE QUESTIONS

1. b Can only carry back 3 years immediately preceding the loss.

2. a The loss carry-back will result in a debit to income tax receivable (current asset) and a credit recognized on the income statement as income tax expense (recovery).

3. a The carry-forward will result in an asset, debit to future income tax asset, and a credit recognized on the income statement as income tax expense.

4. d This is the only evidence that has a negative impact on the firm's ability to recognize the tax loss benefit.

5. b The Income Tax Regulations state that a tax loss can be carried back 3 years and forward 10 years.

6. b Increasing CCA deduction in the year of loss will increase the loss, and a loss is limited to 7 years' carry-forward. Not claiming CCA has the effect of increasing taxable income, against which the carry-forward can be used. After the carry-forward benefits have all been realized, the company can resume deducting full CCA to reduce its future taxable income.

7. c The future rates that are only estimated and not enacted should not be used. Only the enacted future rates should be used. If the future rates are not enacted, then we will use current rates.

8. a According to the *CICA Handbook*, paragraph 3465.85, "Income tax expense related to continuing operations should be shown on the face of the income statement."

PROBLEMS

Problem 1
PURPOSE: To illustrate accounting for tax loss carry-back.

Jack Company (JC) is a wholesaler of hiking boots. JC has been in the business since 20x2. The following information is related to the company's net income and taxable income since incorporation:

	20x2	20x3	20x4	20x5
Net income per F/S	$100,000	$180,000	$260,000	$(300,000)
Amortization expense	40,000	40,000	40,000	40,000
CCA claimed	50,000	87,500	65,626	–0–
Tax rate	30%	35%	40%	40%

Assume that there is sufficient information given above to calculate the taxable income. Assets were purchased for $400,000 at the beginning of 20x2. There have been no acquisitions or disposals since then.

Assume that the tax rate is enacted during the current year.

Required

Prepare the journal entries to record the taxes payable for each of the four years.
Assume that the company does not adjust previously taken CCA.

Problem 2

PURPOSE: To illustrate accounting for tax loss carry-forward when it is more likely
than not to be realized.

Assume the same information as in problem 1 for Jack Company (JC) except that the
loss in Year 20x5 is $900,000, not $300,000.

Required

Prepare the journal entry for Year 20x5. Assume that it is more likely than not that any
benefits will be realized and that the losses will be carried back to offset the past
taxable income. Also, assume that the company does not adjust previously taken CCA.

Problem 3

PURPOSE: To illustrate accounting for tax loss carry-forward in the absence of
likelihood that the tax benefit will be realized.

Assume the same information as in problem 1; however, also assume that it is not
likely that the benefit will be realized.

Required

Prepare the journal entry and/or the required note disclosures.

SOLUTIONS TO PROBLEMS

Problem 1

Step 1: Calculate taxable income and taxes payable—

	20x2	20x3	20x4	20x5
Net income per financial statements	$ 100,000	$ 180,000	$ 260,000	$(300,000)
Temporary difference: amortization expense	+40,000	+40,000	+40,000	+40,000
CCA	−50,000	−87,500	−65,626	−0−
Taxable income	90,000	132,500	234,374	(260,000)
Tax rate	30%	35%	40%	
Income tax payable	$ 27,000	$ 46,375	$ 93,750	

Step 2: Compare tax basis with the carrying values (financial statements) on the
balance sheets and calculate future income tax assets or future income tax liabilities.

Journal entries to record the income taxes payable for each of the first 3 years:

	20x2		20x3		20x4	
Income tax expense	30,000		63,500		106,875	
F.I.T. liability		3,000		17,125		13,125
Income taxes payable		27,000		46,375		93,750

Year 20x5—the loss year. Tax loss = $130,000.

	Tax basis dr. (cr.)	Carrying value dr. (cr.)	Temporary difference dr. (cr.)	F.I.T. asset (liability) dr. (cr.)	Beginning balance dr. (cr.)	Adjustment, current yr. dr. (cr.)
20x2						
Capital assets	$350,000	$360,000	$(10,000)	$(3,000)	–0–	$(3,000)
20x3						
Capital assets	262,500	320,000	(57,500)	(20,125)	(3,000)	(17,125)
20x4						
Capital assets	196,874	280,000	(83,126)	(33,250)	(20,125)	(13,125)
20x5						
Capital assets	196,874	240,000	(43,126)	(17,250)	(33,250)	16,000

Take the loss and carry it back 3 years to reduce the taxable income in any of those 3 previous years. Then multiply the loss by the historic tax rate to arrive at a tax refund.

Carry back to 20x2, 20x3, and part of 20x4 as follows:

Loss	$260,000				
20x2	(90,000)	×	30%	=	$27,000
20x3	(132,500)	×	35%	=	46,375
Subtotal	37,500				
20x4	(37,500)	×	40%	=	15,000
Remaining loss	–0–				$88,375 tax refund

The journal entry for Year 20x5 will be as follows:

Income tax receivable	$88,375	
Future income tax liability	16,000	
Income tax expense		104,375

There is no loss left over; the full benefit has been realized by carry-back.

Problem 2

Calculate the tax loss for year 20x5:

Net loss	$(900,000)				
Add: depreciation expense	40,000				
Tax loss	(860,000)				
20x2	90,000	×	30%	=	$27,000
20x3	132,500	×	35%	=	46,375
20x4	234,374	×	40%	=	93,750
Remaining loss	$(403,126)				$167,125 tax refund
Enacted tax rate	40%				
Future income tax asset	$ 161,250				

The journal entry to recognize the benefits assuming carry-back, and that more likely than not the future benefit will be realized, is as follows:

Income tax receivable	$167,125	
Future income tax assets (loss carry-forward)	161,250	
Future income tax liability (capital asset)	16,000	
Income tax expense		344,375

The journal entry was combined to recognize the benefit from tax loss carry-back and carry-forward, and also to adjust for changes in temporary differences.

Problem 3

The only benefit recognized in 20x5 will be the loss carry-back. However, the amount of unused loss will be recorded in the notes to the financial statements (see paragraph 3465.91)

The journal entry will be as follows:

Income tax receivable	167,125	
Future income tax liability	16,000	
Income tax expense		183,125

CASE

Downhill Ski Company (DSC) is experiencing financial difficulties. Earnings have been declining sharply for the past several years, and the company has barely maintained positive earnings for the past four years. In the current year, DSC is expected to suffer a substantial loss for the first time in 10 years. A tax loss will also be reported. The losses are expected to be significantly greater than the profits reported in the previous three years.

DSC is a small manufacturer specializing in downhill racing skis and boots. The company supplies the Canadian National Ski Team, but competition from larger manufacturers has forced it to keep its prices low even while its expenses are increasing. Also, the continued popularity of snowboarding continues to have a negative impact on sales. However, it is expected that in the next few years older snowboarders will switch back to skiing. Ted Johnson, the sales and marketing manager, has left the company to join Rossignol, a large multinational ski company. Dave Bowen, former national ski champion, has since been hired by DSC as sales and marketing manager.

The owner of DSC, Jim Wilson, is not overly concerned with the loss in the current year and has the following comments to make:

> With the hiring of Dave Bowen as sales and marketing manager, we will develop relationships with the National Ski Team and work on improving our service and involvement with sponsorship of events. This should increase our sales.

> Downhill Ski Company is developing a new ski that is not on the market yet. It will be introduced next year. This is the first new ski since our successful parabolic design six years ago. We tested the prototype of that ski and we are sure that the sales from the new product will give us solid profits for the future. We

plan to offer this ski to retail stores. We have already lined up buyers across Canada and the U.S.A. Our financial forecast for next year is to make a profit.

We have a large new piece of equipment acquired at the end of last year. This manufacturing equipment is more efficient and will save us money on maintenance and repairs, and production time.

Required

Assume that you are a consultant to the company. Determine whether DSC should recognize the benefits of the loss suffered in the current year's financial statements.

KEY POINTS IN THE CASE

This case should be written as a report to the company.

Management seems to have high expectations of the company's ability to turn around and continue to grow.

There is no problem in accounting for the tax benefits of the loss carry-backs; the taxes recovered are recognized on the income statement as a tax recovery, and the refund receivable is shown on the balance sheet as a current asset. *Recognition* and accrual basis *realization* occur in the same period because there is no uncertainty about whether the company will actually receive the benefit.

If after the carry-back there is still a carry-forward remaining, as in this case, the benefit of the carry-forward will not be realized until future years. The accounting question is whether the future tax benefit of the carry-forward can be recognized in the current year, the period of the loss. The *CICA Handbook*, paragraph 3465.24 states, "The benefits may be recognized if it is more likely than not that the benefits will be realized."

The same section provides four examples of *favourable evidence* that support recognition:

CICA

(a) *Existing sufficient taxable temporary differences which would result in taxable amounts against which the unused tax losses can be utilized; [We have no knowledge about the future income tax assets or liabilities.]*

(b) *Existing contracts or firm sales backlog that will produce more than enough taxable income to realize the future income tax asset based on existing sales prices and cost structures; [The owner says that the company has commitments from buyers; you would investigate these potential sales and establish whether they are firm sales.]*

(c) *An excess of fair value over the tax basis of the enterprise's net assets in an amount sufficient to realize the future income tax asset; [Because the new equipment was acquired last year, the fair value is probably over the tax basis of the enterprise's net assets, but we don't know to what extent or whether it is sufficient to realize the future income tax asset.]*

(d) *A strong earnings history exclusive of the loss that created the future deductible amount together with evidence indicating that the loss is an aberration rather than a continuing condition. [The past four years have not been years of strong earnings, even if there was no loss. The forecast shows strong earnings again.]*

According to paragraph 3465.27, unfavourable evidence includes the following:

- a history of tax losses expiring before they have been used; [This is not the case. This is the first loss.]
- an expectation of losses in the carry-forward period; [The owner is expecting solid profits in the future.] and
- unsettled circumstances that, if unfavourably resolved, would adversely affect future operations and profit levels on a continuing basis in future years. [The Company seems to be resolving its problems.]

ANALYSIS AND RECOMMENDATIONS

The *CICA Handbook* states that it is difficult to form a conclusion that the benefits are more likely than not. The recommendations suggest that "the weight given to the potential effect of unfavourable and favourable evidence would be commensurate with the extent to which it can be verified objectively" (3465.29).

In this case, unfavourable evidence includes the fact that there is a history of marginal profits for the last four years and the loss of the current year.

Further, there is the fact that the company's only client is the Canadian National Ski Team and that larger manufacturers are their competitors. There is also competition from snowboarding.

On the other hand, the company has big plans to expand into the retail market and is launching a new product. There are sufficient new customers to purchase the new product, such that the company is predicting to experience solid profits for the future.

DSC has a new sales and marketing manager with strong experience, and the company is expecting that its sales will improve because of the reputation and skills of Dave Bowen. We do not know the impact on the business of the loss of Ted Johnson.

The company has also purchased a new piece of equipment that is more efficient and will reduce expenses and improve production.

Management has better insight into its own company and customers, and probably is in a better position to predict the future.

In conclusion, management is able to make a strong case for profitability, but this is still a projection, and recognizing the benefit is a matter of professional judgment. Management may want to consider the following "tax-planning strategies that would be implemented to realize a future income tax asset" [3465.25(d)]:

- Reducing or eliminating CCA in the year of the loss and future years.
- Amending prior years' tax returns to reduce or eliminate CCA.
- Recognizing taxable revenues in the carry-forward period that might ordinarily be recognized in later periods.

After the above strategies are implemented, any remaining tax loss benefits should be recognized as assets in the year of loss.

Remember that once the future tax benefit of a tax loss carry-forward has been recognized as an asset, the asset is subject to review at each balance sheet date.

SELECTED SOLUTIONS FROM THE TEXTBOOK

Assignment 16-11

Requirement 1

Taxable income:	20x3	20x4	20x5	20x6
Accounting income	$10,000	$15,000	($40,000)	$10,000
Permanent difference:				
Golf club dues	3,000	4,000	3,000	4,000
Accounting income subject to tax	13,000	19,000	(37,000)	14,000
Temporary difference:				
Depreciation	6,000	6,000	6,000	6,000
CCA	(3,000)	(6,000)	(12,000)	(10,000)
Taxable income	16,000	19,000	(43,000)	10,000
Tax rate	20%	20%	30%	35%
Income tax payable	$ 3,200	$ 3,800	n/a*	$ 3,500

* Part of loss is carried back at rate of 20%; current year rate is not applicable. See Requirement 2

Requirement 2

	Taxable Amounts	Benefit
Tax loss	($43,000)	
Carryback ($16,000 + $19,000)	35,000	$7,000 (20%)
Carryforward	($ 8,000)	

The $8,000 loss carryforward would be recorded at a rate of 30% ($2,400) if recorded in 20x5. This is the enacted tax rate in 20x5. The 20x6 rate cannot be used until enacted.

This data is used further in Assignment 16-12.

Assignment 16-12

Note: Students should have completed Assignment 16-11 prior to this assignment.

Income tax receivable (1)	7,000	
Future income tax asset – LCF (2)...	2,400	
Future income tax - long term (3)...		1,500
Income tax expense (4)...		7,900

(1)   Taxable income, 20x3 & 20x4: (see solution to Assignment 16–11) $16,000 + $19,000 = $35,000. Amount paid, $3,200 + $3,800 = $7,000

(2)
Taxable loss in 20x5 (see solution to Assignment 16-11).............................	$43,000
Loss carryback to 20x3 and 20x4 ($16,000 + $19,000)....................................	(35,000)
Tax loss carryforward..	8,000
Benefit of tax loss carryforward (@ 30%)	$ 2,400

(3)

(in 000's)	Tax Basis	Accounting Basis	Temporary Difference	FIT Liability	Opening Balance	Adjustment
20x5				@ 30%		
Capital assets	$54 (a)	$57 (b)	$(3)	$(.9)	$.6 (c)	($1.5)

(a) $75,000 – ($3,000 + $6,000 + $12,000)
(b) $75,000 – ($6,000 x 3)
(c)   [($75,000 – $9,000) – ($75,000 – $12,000)] x .20

(4) $7,000 + $2,400 – $1,500

In order to record the benefit of the tax loss carryforward in 20x5, the company must be able to establish that its realization during the carryforward period is more likely than not. This is defined as a probability of more than 50%.

Assignment 16-24

Schedule of Accounting and Taxable Income
(amounts in thousands)

	20x5	20x6	20x7	20x8	20x9
Accounting income (loss)	$ 0	($980)	$ 0	$2,000	$4,000
Less: non-taxable dividends	0	(20)	(20)	0	0
	0	(1,000)	(20)	2,000	4,000
Temporary differences:					
Warranty expense	60	120	160	200	300
Warranty claims paid	(60)	(80)	(200)	(90)	(75)
Depreciation expense	600	600	600	600	600
CCA	(600)	0	(500)	(450)	(400)
Taxable income	$ 0	($ 360)	$ 40	$2,260	$4,425

Schedule of Temporary Differences
(amounts in thousands)

	Tax basis	Accounting basis	Temporary difference	Future income tax	Opening balance	Adjustment
20x5–40%						
Capital assets	$5,600	$7,600	$(2,000)	$(800)	$(800)	$0
Warranty	0	0	0	0	0	0
20x6–40%						
Capital assets	5,600	7,000	(1,400)	(560)	(800)	240
Warranty	0	(40)	40	16	0	16
20x7–40%						
Capital assets	5,100	6,400	(1,300)	(520)	(560)	40
Warranty	0	0	0	0	16	(16)
20x8–45%						
Capital assets	4,650	5,800	(1,150)	(517.5)	(520)	2.5
Warranty	0	(110)	110	49.5	0	49.5
20x9–45%						
Capital assets	4,250	5,200	(950)	(427.5)	(517.5)	90
Warranty	0	(335)	335	150.75	49.5	101.25

Journal Entries (amounts in thousands):

20x5 Entry:
  No entry
No accounting or taxable income, no adjustment of temporary differences.

20x6 Entry:

Future income tax—long term	240	
Future income tax—short term	16	
Future income tax asset - LCF ($360 x .40)	144	
Income tax expense (recovery)		400

20x7 Entries:

Future income tax—long term	40	
Future income tax—short term		16
Income tax payable ($40 x .4)		16
Income tax expense (recovery)		8
Income tax payable	16	
Future income tax asset - LCF		16

Gross LCF now $360,000 – $40,000 = $320,000; recorded at 40%, or 128,000

20x8 Entries:

Income tax expense...	965	
Future income tax —long term	2.5	
Future income tax —short term	49.5	
Income tax payable ($2,260 x .45)		1,017
Income tax payable ($320 x .45)	144	
Future income tax asset - LCF ($144 – $16)		128
Income tax expense ($320 x (.45 – .40))		16

20x9 Entry:

Income tax expense...	1,800	
Future income tax—short term	101.25	
Future income tax—long term	90	
Income tax payable ($4,425 x .45)		1,991.25

Assignment 16-33

Carryback

Of the $220,000 tax loss, $120,000 can be carried back to the preceding three years. The carryback will result in CTC's realizing a full refund of taxes paid in 20x1, 20x2, and 20x3. The total refund will be $45,600.

Carryforward

The remaining $100,000 of the 20x4 tax loss can be carried forward and applied against taxable income in the next seven (or ten) years. Since management believes that the probability of realizing the future tax benefits is greater than 50%, the future income tax benefit should be recognized in the year of the loss, 20x4. The 20x5 enacted rate of 36% can be used. A future income tax asset of $36,000 will be recognized.

Temporary differences
20x3 – 40%

	Temporary Difference		Ending Balance	
Capital assets	$95,000*	deferred	$38,000*	cr.
Pensions	55,000*	deferred	22,000*	cr.
			$60,000	cr.

20x4 – 36%

Capital assets	$85,000**	deferred	$30,600	cr.
Pensions	85,000**	deferred	30,600	cr.
			$61,200	cr.

* given
** ($95,000 - $10,000); ($55,000 - $30,000 + $60,000)

Journal entry to record income tax:

Income tax receivable..	45,600	
Future income tax—LCF	36,000	
Income tax expense...		80,400
Future income tax—long term ($61,200 – $60,000)...........		1,200

Apportionment: $80,000 x .4 = $32,000 to ex.item
                ($80,400 - $32,000) = $48,400 to ordinary income,
                but see comment on next page.

Lower portion of income statement

Income (loss) from operations before income tax and extraordinary item ..	($120,000)
Income tax (recovery)...	48,400
Income (loss) from operations before extraordinary item	(71,600)
Extraordinary loss, net of taxes ($80,000 – $32,000)	(48,000)
Net income (loss)..	($119,600)

Comment: The *CICA Handbook* requires intraperiod allocation, but is silent on exactly how the apportionment should be carried out. In the example above, the extraordinary item was credited with tax benefit at the 20x4 rate.

Proportional allocation could also be used—60% of the loss pertains to continuing operations, and therefore 60% of the total tax provision of $80,400 could be allocated to continuing operations ($48,240) and the remainder ($32,160) to the extraordinary item. Alternatively, since the extraordinary item is part of the LCF, its income tax expense could be measured at the future tax rate of 36%, resulting in a tax recovery of $28,800. Then, $51,600 is allocated to operations.

There is no objective basis for a choice between these alternatives; all of them satisfy the requirement for intraperiod allocation. However, the alternative shown (a split of $48,400 and $32,000) is common.

SOLUTIONS TO CONCEPT REVIEW QUESTIONS

Page 984

1. A tax loss may be carried back 3 years and carried forward 10 years.

2. The *tax loss* of a year refers to the taxable income of a year as determined under applicable tax law resulting in a loss. The *tax benefit* of the loss is the present and future benefit that the company will be able to realize from the tax loss through a reduction of income taxes paid to governments. Essentially, a tax benefit is equal to the tax loss multiplied by the relevant tax rate.

3. A tax loss is generally carried back and applied sequentially to taxable income of prior years, as the carry-back period is limited to the three years immediately preceding. While application of the loss to the year with the highest rate of tax may yield a larger refund, the failure to apply losses sequentially may result in the taxable income of an earlier year expiring. If the company subsequently suffers tax losses in future years, the earlier carry-back year may become statute barred (beyond the 3-year carry-back period).

Page 992

1. The basic criterion for recognizing the benefit of a tax loss carry-forward prior to its realization is that realization of the benefit must be more likely than not. An event is "more likely than not" when the probability that it will occur is greater than 50%.

2. The tax rate to be used in recognizing the future benefits of a tax loss carry-forward is the substantively enacted income tax rate.

3. The future benefits of a tax loss carry-forward should be recognized in the year that the recovery is judged to be probable (i.e., more likely than not). The future tax benefit of a tax loss carry-forward may be recognized in years subsequent to the loss year if management determines, in the periodic evaluation of the probability of realization of tax losses, that the probability of realization has increased to over 50% (more likely than not). The underlying concept is that management must evaluate the likelihood of recovery on a periodic (e.g., annual) basis.

4. Once the future benefit of a tax loss carry-forward has been recognized, the probability of realizing the benefit must be evaluated at each balance sheet date. If, in a subsequent year, it is determined that the probability of realizing the tax loss benefit has become unlikely, the asset may be reduced or written off.

Page 1005

1. When a company has unused tax losses the amount of the losses and the expiry date(s) must be disclosed. This includes both recognized and unrecognized losses.

2. It is possible to show the tax expense that relates to the current year's pre-tax income even if no tax is actually payable due to a tax loss. If the benefit of the tax loss carry-forward has been recognized in a previous period, the journal entry reflecting the application of the tax loss is as follows:

Dr. Income tax expense
      Cr. Future income tax liability
      Cr. Future income tax asset (carry-forward benefit)

The income tax expense attributable to current year income is recorded; the application of the tax loss carry-forward results in a draw-down of the previously recognized future income tax asset. This offsets the liability and results in no amount of tax payable. There is no effect on the current year tax provision as a result of the loss carry-forward.

3. If the future tax benefit of the carry-forward is recognized in the year of the loss, the tax benefit will be offset against the extraordinary item giving rise to the loss. The extraordinary item will be shown on a net-of-tax basis.

CHAPTER 17

ACCOUNTING FOR LEASES

A lease is an arrangement whereby the person or company that owns an asset (**lessor**) agrees to let another person or company (**lessee**) use the asset for a period of time at a stated amount of rent.

In accounting, we should attempt to report transactions in accordance with their economic substance rather than their legal form. Often the economic substance of a lease is that the lessor is providing the lessee with use of the asset over the bulk of the asset's useful life in return for a full repayment of the cost of the asset, plus interest. The principle of reporting *substance* over *form* leads us to account for the asset as if it were a purchase financed fully by debt.

In this chapter we look at the general substance of leases, and cover accounting by the lessee. Accounting by the lessor is examined in the appendix to this chapter.

1. DEFINITION OF A LEASE

A lease is an arrangement whereby the person or company (the lessor) that owns an asset agrees to let another person or company (the lessee) use the asset for a period of time at a stated (or determinable) amount of rent.

ASSET

Lessor — — — — — — — —> **Lessee**

(owns the asset)   **(uses the asset)**

2. WHY LEASE? THE LEASING CONTINUUM

The answer to this question varies depending on the type of lease, and certainly varies with the circumstances of the lessee.

A short-term lease that provides the lessee with temporary use of an asset is called, in accounting, an **operating lease**. The lessor bears the risk of ownership and receives rental payments.

A lease that conveys substantially all the risks and rewards of ownership from the lessor to the lessee is, in *substance,* a means of financing acquisition of the asset. This is called a **capital lease.**

3. OPERATING LEASES

An *operating lease is* one that gives the lessee the right to use the asset for only a relatively short period of its useful life. Short term is a relative phrase and must be interpreted in the context of the life of the asset. The accounting for such a lease is not complicated.

Recognition only of the lease payments:

Rental expense	xx,xxx	
Cash		xx,xxx

The *lessee* accounts for the periodic payments as normal rental expense. The *lessor* records the lease payments as rental revenue. A complication can arise when lease payments are uneven. For example there may be a large initial payment of rent free period. Extra or 'forgiven' payments are deferred and amortized over the initial term of the lease.

A lease is an operating lease when it is not a capital lease. Where possible, companies prefer to treat a lease as an operating lease because that way there is no debt on their balance sheet,

WATCH!

4. GUIDELINES FOR DEFINING CAPITAL LEASES

The basic criteria is a judgement: Do the terms of the lease transfer substantially all of the risks and benefits of ownership form the lessor to the lessee? The *CICA Handbook*, paragraph 3065.06, states that normally, a lease should be assumed to transfer substantially all of the benefits and risks of ownership to the lessee when at least one of the following conditions is present at the inception of the lease:

1. There is reasonable assurance that the lessee will obtain ownership of the leased property at the end of the lease term.
   - There is automatic transfer of the title, *or*
   - The lessee is entitled to exercise a bargain purchase option.
2. The lessee will receive substantially all of the economic benefits expected to be derived through the use of the leased property.
   - The lease term is at least 75% of the asset's economic life.
3. The lessor will be assured of recovering the investment in the leased property, plus a return on the investment, over the lease term.
   - The present value of the minimum net lease payments is at least 90% of the fair market value of the asset at the inception of the lease.

Definitions
A **bargain purchase option** exists when there is a stated or determinable price given in the lease that is sufficiently lower than the expected fair value of the leased asset at the option's exercise date that it is likely the lessee will exercise the option.

The **lease term** includes:
   - all terms prior to the exercise date of the bargain purchase option,
   - all **bargain renewal terms**, *and*
   - all renewal terms at the *lessor's* option.

Bargain renewal terms are periods for which the lessee has the option of extending the lease at lease payments that are substantially less than would be expected for an asset of that age and type.

Minimum net lease payments means all payments over the lease term (including bargain renewal terms), net of any operating or executory costs that are implicitly included in the lease payment, plus any **guaranteed residual value.**

Minimum net lease payments do not include any amounts for **contingent lease payments,** which are additional payments based on subsequent events—for example, additional rent calculated as a percentage of the lessee's gross sales revenue.

A **guaranteed residual value** is an amount the lessee agrees to assure the lessor will be able to get for the asset when selling it to a third party at the end of the lease term. Any deficiency in the sales proceeds must be provided by the lessee.

The lessee **incremental borrowing rate (IBR)** is the interest rate the lessee would have to pay if it obtained financing through the bank to buy the asset.

The **implicit lease interest rate** is the interest rate that discounts the minimum net lease payments to equal the fair value of the leased property at the beginning of the lease.

The **interest rate used for discounting the net lease payments** is the lower of (1) the lessor's interest rate implicit in the lease, if known by the lessee, *or* (2) the lessee's IBR.

In no case should the asset be recorded at higher than its fair value.

5. INFORMAL CRITERIA FOR CAPITAL LEASES

The basic issue is if, in substance, the risks and rewards have been transferred from the lessor to the lessee. A useful criteria is to look at the nature of the lessor. When the lessor is a financial institution the lease is normally a capital lease.

6. LONG-TERM LEASES PROS AND CONS

PERCEIVED PRO	RELATED CON
• off-balance sheet financing	• Higher lease payments (expense) and cash flow
• 100% financing	• Only available for some types of assets and lessees with good credit ratings
• protection against obsolescence,	• Higher lease payments (expense) and cash flow
• protection from interest rate changes	• Variable rate loans may be better as the rate will decline with a decline in the economy
• transfer of income tax benefits	• Lessee may not be able to use the CCA deduction

7. ACCOUNTING FOR CAPITAL LEASES

The general approach for a capital lease is to record the asset on the books of the lessor as if it had been purchased and financed by instalment debt. The accounting is as follows:

* Determine the present value of the lease payments.

- Record the asset at the present value (not to exceed its fair value).
- Record the lease liability at the same amount.
- Accrue interest each reporting period – debiting interest expense and crediting interest payable or lease liability account.
- Record lease payments as a debit to the lease liability account (and a credit to cash).
- Amortize the asset using the company's normal amortization policy for the type of asset. (Period not to exceed the term of the lease including bargain renewal periods).

8. CAPITAL LEASE ILLUSTRATIONS

Recognition—journal entries:

1. Record the transaction as if the asset had been purchased and financed by installment debt. The present value of the lease payments is recorded as the cost of the asset and classified as a capital asset. The offsetting credit is to a lease liability account:

Asset under capital lease   xx,xxx
      Lease liability   xx,xxx

> The present value of the minimum net lease payments attempts to measure the present value of what the lessee will pay for the asset. **WATCH!**

2. Accrue the interest for each reporting period, charged to interest expense and credited to the lease liability account.

   Interest is calculated using the amount recorded as "asset under capital lease" multiplied by the same rate used to discount the payments.

> An amortization table should be constructed to determine how much of the lease payment is interest expense and how much reduces the recorded liability. **WATCH!**

The journal entry to record the accrued interest is:

Interest expense   xx,xxx
      Lease liability   xx,xxx

3. The asset is amortized by following the company's normal amortization policy for that type of capital asset.

Amortization expense, leased asset   xx,xxx
      Accumulated amortization, asset under lease   xx,xxx

> Amortization of the asset should be done over the lease term unless there is a Bargain Purchase Option or a Title Transfer in the lease agreement. A common error made for capital leases is to miss this journal entry. **WATCH!**

4. Lease payments are debited to the lease liability account. When the cash payment is made, the entry is:

Insurance expense (if any)	xx,xxx	
Lease liability	xx,xxx	
Cash		xx,xxx

If the cash payment includes an executory cost (e.g., an amount for insurance), it must be recorded accordingly.

Your textbook has illustrations of the accounting for capital leases for the lessee, with a basic example and an extended example. You should review these examples to become familiar with the procedure. When reviewing these examples, remember that you are trying to place the financial statements for the lessee in the same position as if it had purchased the asset through debt financing.

9. NON-CAPITAL LEASES: OPERATING LEASES REVISITED

A lease is accounted for as an operating lease if it is not judged to be a capital lease.

Three common ways to avoid capitalization of a lease are:
- Base a large part of the lease payment on contingent rent.
- Insert a third party between the lessee and the lessor.
- Shorten the lease term.

10. SALE AND LEASEBACK

Frequently, companies take assets that they own, sell them, and simultaneously lease them back. The cash is then used to retire debt or for operating purposes.

The lease part must be evaluated and judged to be either a capital lease or an operating lease.

The sale portion is recorded just like any other sale, with a gain or loss.

Net proceeds − Net book value = Gain (loss)

The *CICA Handbook*, paragraph 3065.68, states:

CICA If capital lease, any profit or loss arising on the sale should be deferred and amortized in proportion to the amortization of the leased asset.

Paragraph 3065.69 states:

CICA If the lease is an operating lease, profit or loss arising on the sale should be deferred and amortized in proportion to rental payments over the lease term.

And paragraph 3065.70 states:

CICA When at the time of the sale-leaseback transaction the fair market value of the property is less than the carrying value, the difference should be recognized as a loss immediately.

Journal entries for a sale and leaseback, when the lease is a capital lease are following:

1. To record the sale:

Cash	xx,xxx	
Accumulated amortization-asset	xx,xxx	
Asset		xx,xxx
Deferred gain on sale and leaseback of asset		xx,xxx

The gain on sale will be amortized over the lease term, regardless of whether the lease qualifies as capital lease or as an operating lease.

WATCH!

2. To record the lease:

Asset under capital lease	xx,xxx	
Lease liability		xx,xxx

3. At the end of the year:

   (a) To record interest expense—

Interest expense	xx,xxx	
Lease liability		xx,xxx

   (b) To record the lease payment—

Lease liability	xx,xxx	
Cash		xx,xxx

   (c) To amortize the asset—

Amortization expense, leased asset		
Accumulated amortization, leased asset	xx,xxx	xx,xxx

   (d) To amortize the deferred gain—

Deferred gain on sale and leaseback of asset	xx,xxx	
Amortization expense, leased asset		xx,xxx

11. CASH FLOW STATEMENT

If a lease is reported as an operating lease, the payments are deducted as expenses in determining net income. The impact of the lease payments stays in the cash flow from operations.

If the lease is capitalized, the effects on the cash flow statement are as follows:
- Even though the lease is viewed as a purchase, the transaction does not show on the cash flow statement as an investing activity because it is a non-cash transaction—a lease obligation is exchanged for a leased asset.
- The amortization expense is a non-cash expense included in net income. On the cash flow statement, using the indirect method, the amortization expense is added back to net income to determine cash flow from operations.
- The portion of the payments that represents interest expense must be segregated on the cash flow statement, as part of interest expense is related to long-term obligations.
- The principal repayment portion of the lease payments is shown as a financing activity.

12. DISCLOSURE OF LEASES

Operating Leases

The *CICA Handbook,* paragraph 3065.32, states:

CICA Disclosure should be made of the future minimum lease payments, in the aggregate and for each of the five succeeding years in an operating lease.

Capital Leases

The *CICA Handbook* recommends that both the leased assets and the related lease obligations be reported separately, either on the face of the financial statements (balance sheet) *or* in the notes to the financial statements.

Paragraph 3065.21 states:

CICA *The gross amount of assets under capital leases and related accumulated amortization should be disclosed.*

Section 3065.22 states:

CICA *Obligations related to leased assets should be shown separately from other long-term obligations.*

The *current* portion of the lease liability should be shown separately.

The CICA recommends the following:
- Minimum lease payments for the next 5 years, by year and in aggregate,
- Details of capital lease obligations, including interest rates and expiry dates,
- Significant restrictions imposed on the lessee by the lease agreement,
- Amount of amortization of leased assets, *and*
- The interest expense relating to lease obligations.

13. INTERNATIONAL PERSPECTIVE

The capitalization of long-term leases has become widely accepted practice around the world, although there is some difference in the criteria used to determine if a lease is a capital lease. Based on a five country study report it is likely that there will be a significant change in the accounting leasing standards within a few years.

TRUE–FALSE QUESTIONS

T F **1.** A sufficient criterion for classification as a capital lease by a lessee is that the present value of the minimum lease payments is equal to 90% or more of the fair value of the leased asset.

T F **2.** In computing the present value of the minimum lease payments, the lessee should use the higher of its incremental borrowing rate, *or* the implicit rate used by the lessor if known to the lessee.

T F **3.** An asset classified as an operating lease should be amortized by the lessee over the period of time the lessee expects to use the asset.

T F 4. In a capital lease containing a bargain purchase option, the lessee should amortize the asset over its economic life, even if it is beyond the original lease term.

T F 5. When a residual value is guaranteed by the lessee, the guaranteed residual value should be included in the minimum lease payments to both the lessee and the lessor.

T F 6. Initial direct costs should be expensed immediately, regardless of whether the lease is a capital or an operating lease.

T F 7. In a sale-and-leaseback transaction, the seller-lessee should recognize gain or loss from the sale immediately, regardless of whether the fair value of the leased asset is less than its book value.

MULTIPLE CHOICE QUESTIONS

___ **1.** When a lease transaction is accounted for as an operating lease:
   a. the leased asset should be amortized by the lessee over the term of the lease.
   b. any advance payment by the lessee should be expensed by the lessee immediately.
   c. the lessee will record a leased asset and a related obligation at the present value of the minimum lease payments.
   d. the lessor should amortize the leased asset over its economic life.

___ **2.** When a lease is classified as a capital lease and the lease contains a bargain purchase option, the leased asset should be amortized:
   a. over the term of the lease.
   b. over the economic life of the leased asset.
   c. over the term of the lease or the economic life of the leased asset.
   d. by the lessor.

___ **3.** Of the following lease arrangements, which would most likely, be classified as an operating lease by the lessee?
   a. The present value of the minimum lease payments is $31,000, and the fair value of the leased asset is $32,000.
   b. The lease contract contains a clause to transfer the title to the leased asset from the lessor to the lessee.
   c. The lease contract allows the lessee to buy the leased asset at the market price at the end of the lease term.
   d. The economic life of the asset is 10 years, and the lease term is 8 years.

___ **4.** In accounting for a lease transaction classified as a capital lease, over the term of the lease:

   a. the asset should be amortized by the lessor in a systematic and rational manner.

   b. the lease payments by the lessee constitute a payment for lease liability plus interest.

   c. the gross sum of the lease payments equals the dollar amount that would have been paid by the lessee to purchase the property on the date of the inception of the lease.

   d. any manufacturer's or dealer's profit or loss should be amortized.

___ **5.** Which of the following conditions is not a criterion for classifying a lease as a capital lease?

   a. The present value of the minimum lease payments is at least 90% of the fair value of the leased asset.

   b. The lease transfers ownership in the leased asset to the lessee at the end of the lease term.

   c. The lessee has the option of acquiring the asset at the end of the lease term at a bargain price.

   d. The lease term is greater than 90% of the economic life of the asset.

___ **6.** In a sale-and-leaseback transaction, unless the fair (market) value of the asset at the time of sale is less than its unamortized cost:

   a. a loss from the sale should be deferred and amortized, but a gain should be recognized immediately.

   b. a gain from the sale should be deferred and amortized, but a loss should be recognized immediately.

   c. any gain or loss from the sale should be deferred and amortized over the term of the lease.

   d. any gain or loss from the sale should be recognized immediately.

___ **7.** Lessee Company leased a computer from Lessor Corporation on January 1, 20x5, for a 10-year period, the useful life of the asset. Equal rental payments of $5,000 are due on January 1 of each year. The first payment was made on January 1, 20x5. The present value of the mini-mum lease payments over the lease term discounted at 10% was $33,795. The balance in Lessee's liability account (including accrued interest) at December 31, 20x5, should be:

   a. $26,680

   b. $27,256

   c. $30,392

   d. $31,675

8. On October 1, 20x5, Minor Company signed an operating lease for a building with Major Company for 6 years, at $20,000 per year. At the inception of the lease, Minor paid $40,000, covering rent for the first two years. Minor closed its books on December 31, and correctly reported $40,000 as rent expense on its 20x5 income tax return. How much should Minor report in the 20x5 income statement as rent expense?
   a. $0
   b. $5,000
   c. $3,334
   d. $6,666

9. Tire Corporation leased a machine to Rims Company on January 1, 20x5, for a 5-year lease. The machine has an economic life of 10 years, a residual value at the end of lease term of $50,000, and a residual value at the end of economic life of zero. The lease contains a bargain purchase option that allows Rims to purchase the leased machine at the end of the lease term for $25,000. Equal lease payments of $15,000 are made on each January 1, and the first payment is made on January 1, 20x5. The applicable interest rate to both the lessee and the lessor is 12%. For the year ended December 31, 20x5, Rims should report lease liabilities as:

	Current	Long-term
a.	$15,000	$51,916
b.	$15,000	$15,916
c.	$51,746	$15,000
d.	$51,916	$15,000

10. Based on the same information as in question 9, Rims should report the following in its financial statements for the year ended December 31, 20x5:

	Interest expense	Amortization expense
a.	$3,585	$15,950
b.	$7,170	$ 7,475
c.	$7,475	$7,170
d.	$3,585	$7,475

SOLUTIONS TO TRUE–FALSE QUESTIONS

1. T

2. F The lessee should use the lower of incremental borrowing rate or implicit rate.

3. F The asset is amortized by the lessor for an operating lease.

4. T

5. T

6. F The initial direct costs are normally amortized over the life of the lease. For *operating leases*, the initial direct costs should be deferred and allocated over the lease term in proportion to rental income. For *capital leases*, the initial direct costs should be added to the net investment in the lease and amortized over the life of the lease as a yield adjustment.

7. F The gain is not recognized in income but instead is deferred over the lease term.

SOLUTIONS TO MULTIPLE CHOICE QUESTIONS

1. d An *operating lease* is a lease in which the lessor does not transfer substantially all the benefits and risks to ownership of the property (3065.03[d]). So the lessor still owns the asset.

2. b The amortization period is the lease term, defined as including bargain renewal terms and not just the initial lease term.

3. c A lease contract that allows the lessee to buy the leased asset at the market price at the end of the lease term is not a bargain purchase option. This is no indication that the lessee will buy this particular asset at the end of lease when the lessee can buy any asset at market price.

4. b This statement is what constitutes the lease payments.

5. d The criterion is that the lease term is greater than 75% of the economic life of the asset.

6. c The *CICA Handbook,* Section 3065.68, states: "any gain or loss is deferred and amortized proportionately against the lease payments over the lease term." The exception to the defer-and-amortize rule is that when the fair value of the property is less than its carrying value at the time of the transaction, the loss should be recognized immediately.

7. d Lease liability (December 31, 20x5):

= Acquisition cost − First lease payment Interest for 20x5
= \$33,795 − \$5,000 + ([\$33,795 − \$5,000] × 10%)
= \$28,795 + \$2,880
= \$31,675

8. b Rent expense for the first three months (October 1 to December 31, 20x5)

= \$20,000 × 3/12 = \$5,000.

9. a Present value of minimum lease payments:

= \$15,000 × pvad (n = 5, I = 12%) + \$25,000 × pv1 (n = 5, I = 12%)
= \$15,000 × 4.03735 + \$25,000 × .56743
= \$60,560.25 + \$14,185.75
= \$74,746

Lease Amortization Schedule (on annuity due basis)

	Periodic lease payments	Periodic interest exp. (12%)	Reduction in liability	Carrying value of liability
January 1, 20x5	—	—	—	\$74,746
January 1, 20x5	\$15,000	—	\$15,000	\$59,746
December 31, 20x5	—	\$7,170	(7,170)	\$66,916
January 1, 20x6	\$15,000	—	15,000	\$51,916

Total lease liability at Dec. 31, 20x5: \$66,916

Current lease liability: $15,000
Long-term lease liability: $66,916 − $15,000 = $51,916

10. b   Interest expense, 20x5: $7,170
        Amortization expense: $74,746/10 = $7,475

PROBLEMS

Problem 1

PURPOSE: To determine the type of lease and illustrate the accounting.

Jardine Company paid $50,000 on January 1, 20x5, to Barney Properties as an advance lease bonus to secure a 3-year lease on premises it will occupy starting from that date. Additionally, $60,000 will be paid on each December 31 throughout the term of the lease. The lease contains no specific renewal agreement. Jardine's accounting period ends December 31. Barney will maintain the property and pay taxes and other ownership costs.

Required
   a. What type of lease contract is involved? Explain.
   b. Develop an interest method amortization schedule for the advance using a 14% rate (assume an ordinary annuity).
   c. What is Jardine's total occupancy cost for 20x5 under the interest method used in your response to b? What is the total occupancy cost using the straight-line basis for 20x5?
   d. What lease-related items should Jardine's financial statements report as of December 31, 20x5, if the amortization schedule developed in b is used?

Problem 2

PURPOSE: To determine the type of lease and illustrate the accounting.

Riley Ltd. leased a crane from Domtar Leasing Ltd. on January 1, 20x5. The crane had an expected economic life of 15 years and a fair market value of $120,000. The lease had the following terms:
   • Lease payments are $25,000 per year, paid each January 1, for 5 years. These lease payments include $6,000 of expected insurance and maintenance costs.
   • At the end of the 5 years, the lease is renewable at Riley's option for $10,000 per year, including $4,000 of expected insurance and maintenance costs, for a further 7 years. The normal rental costs for a similar used crane are approximately double this amount.
   • The residual value of the leased asset will be $10,000 at the end of the lease term (the original 5 years plus the additional 7 years). The residual value is guaranteed by Riley.
   • Riley has an incremental borrowing rate of 8% and has not been told the interest implicit in the lease.
   • Riley uses straight-line amortization for this type of asset.
   • Riley has a December 31 fiscal year end.
   • The asset reverts back to the lessor at the end of any lease term.

Required

    a. Is this a capital or an operating lease for Riley? Explain.

    b. Prepare an amortization schedule showing how the lease liability reduces over time.

    c. Prepare journal entries for the first 2 years of the lease.

    d. Show how lease-related accounts will appear on Riley's balance sheet on December 31, 20x5.

Problem 3

PURPOSE: To illustrate accounting for a sale-and-leaseback capital lease for lessee.

Barr Manufacturing Ltd. owns a building it uses. It originally cost $1,800,000 and had a net book value of $1,000,000 as of January 1, 20x5. On this date, the building was sold to the Mutual Leasing Company for $1,100,000 and simultaneously leased back to Barr.

The lease has a guaranteed, 10-year term and requires payments on December 31 of each year. The payments are $195,000, and the lease allows the property to revert to the lessee at the end of the lease. Barr could have mortgaged this property under similar terms at an interest rate of 10%. Mutual Leasing will pay property taxes of $16,000 per year. These costs are included in the lease payment.
Barr will pay maintenance and operating costs. The building is being amortized straight-line over its remaining 10-year life.

Required

    a. Prepare entries to record the sale and leaseback of the building.

    b. Prepare year-end adjusting entries for 20x5.

    c. Show how lease-related amounts will be presented on the balance sheet, income statement, and cash flow statement in 20x5.

SOLUTIONS TO PROBLEMS

Problem 1

Requirement a

Because Barney maintains the property and pays the taxes, the risks and rewards of ownership are not transferred. Also, it is unlikely that a 3-year lease will be 75% of the useful life of the premises. Therefore, it is assumed that this is an operating lease with a prepayment of part of the rent, because it does not meet the criteria for a capital lease.

Requirement b

Jardine could use the straight-line method or the interest method as shown below. The differences in periodic expense in this case are not material.

Amortization schedule—Interest method:

	Periodic rent	Interest at 14%	Amortization advance rental	Unamortized balance of advance rental
January 1, 20x5				$50,000
December 31, 20x5	[a]21,537	[b]7,000	[c]14,537	[d]35,463
December 31, 20x6	21,537	4,965	16,572	18,891
December 31, 20x7	21,537	2,646	18,891	–0–

[a] $50,000/2.32163 = $21,537
[b] $50,000 × 14% = $7,000
[c] $21,537 – $7,000 = $14,537
[d] $50,000 – $14,537 = $35,463

Requirement c

Using the interest method, the total occupancy cost for 20x5 is:

$60,000 + $14,537 = $74,537

On a straight-line basis, the total occupancy cost for 20x5 is:

$60,000 + ($50,000 × 1/3) = $76,667

Requirement d

Using the amortization schedule (interest method), the income statement for 20x5 will reflect an occupancy expense of $60,000 + $14,537 = $74,537. If Jardine has an operating cycle of 1 year, prepaid rent of $16,572 should be reported as a current asset and $18,891 ($35,463 – $16,572) as a deferred charge (intangible asset).

Problem 2

Requirement a

This is a capital lease for Riley Ltd. The lease term includes the bargain renewal option and is 80% (12/15) of the asset's useful life. The present value of the minimum lease payments is 91% of fair value ($108,882[a]/$120,000).

[a]Present value:

(a)	($25,000 – $6,000)(P/AD; 8%, 5)(4.31213)	$81,930
(b)	($10,000 – $4,000)(P/AD; 8%, 7)(5.62788)(P/F; 8%, 5)(.68058)	22,981
(c)	$10,000 (P/F; 8%, 12)(.39711)	3,971
		$108,882

Requirement b

Lease Amortization Schedule—Beginning of Lease Year Payments

Lease year	Outstanding balance	Interest at 8%	January 1 payment	Inc. (dec.) balance	Ending balance
20x5	108,882	—	19,000	(19,000)	89,882
20x6	89,882	7,191	19,000	(11,809)	78,073
20x7	78,073	6,246	19,000	(12,754)	65,319
20x8	65,319	5,226	19,000	(13,774)	51,545
20x9	51,545	4,124	19,000	(14,876)	36,669
2x10	36,669	2,934	6,000	(3,066)	33,603
2x11	33,603	2,668	6,000	(3,312)	30,291
2x12	30,291	2,423	6,000	(3,577)	26,714
2x13	26,714	2,137	6,000	(3,863)	22,851
2x14	22,851	1,828	6,000	(4,172)	18,679
2x15	18,679	1,494	6,000	(4,506)	14,173
2x16	14,173	1,134	6,000	(4,866)	9,307
2x16 (residual)	9,307	693	10,000	(9,307)	[a]–0–

[a] rounding

Requirement c

January 1, 20x5

Asset under capital lease	108,882	
Lease liability		108,882

Insurance and maintenance expense	6,000	
Lease liability	19,000	
Cash		25,000

December 31, 20x5

Interest expense	7,191	
Lease liability		7,191

Amortization expense	9,074	
Accumulated amortization—asset under lease		9,074

January 1, 20x6

Insurance and maintenance expense	6,000	
Lease liability	19,000	
Cash		25,000

December 31, 20x6

Interest expense	6,246	
Lease liability		6,246

Amortization expense	9,074	
Accumulated amortization—asset under lease		9,074

Requirement d

Presentation on the December 31, 20x5, balance sheet:

Property, plant, and equipment:

Machine held under capital lease	$108,882	
Less: accumulated amortization	9,074	
	$ 99,808	

Current liabilities:

Current portion of lease liability	$ 11,809

Long-term liabilities:

Lease liability	$ 97,073
Less: current portion	11,809
	$ 85,264

Problem 3

Requirement a

Cash	1,100,000	
Accumulated amortization—building	[a]800,000	
Building		1,800,000
Deferred gain on sale and leaseback of building		100,000

[a] ($1,800,000 – $1,000,000)

Building under capital lease	1,100,000	
Lease liability		1,100,000

($195,000 – $16,000)(P/A, 10%, 10)(6.14457) = $1,099,878; rounded to $1,100,000.

This is a capital lease as it covers all the remaining useful life, PV of minimum lease payments is 100% of market value of the asset, and the asset will revert to the lessee at the end of the lease.

Requirement b

Interest expense	110,000	
Lease liability		110,000
Lease liability	179,000	
Property tax expense	16,000	
Cash		195,000
Amortization expense, leased building	110,000	
Accumulated amortization, leased building		110,000
Deferred gain on sale and leaseback	10,000	
Amortization expense, leased building		10,000

Requirement c

Balance Sheet

Capital assets

Building under capital lease	1,100,000	
Accumulated amortization	110,000	$990,000 dr.

Deferred credits (L – T)

Deferred gain on sale and leaseback		90,000 cr.

Short-term liabilities

Current portion of long-term lease liability		75,900 cr.

Long-term liabilities

Lease liability ($1,100,000 + $110,000 – $179,000)	1,031,000	
Less: current portion	[a](75,900)	955,100 cr.

[a] Current portion:

Interest, 20x6: $1,031,000 × 10%	$103,100
Payment, 20x6	179,000
Principal portion	$75,900

Income Statement

Amortization expense	$100,000
Property tax expense	16,000
Interest expense	110,000

Cash Flow Statement

Operating: add back amortization	$ 90,000
Investing: cash from sale and leaseback	1,100,000
Financing: reduction lease liability	
(20x5 payment, $179,000 – $110,000)	(69,000)

CASE

A friend of yours had been reviewing the 20x5 Annual Report for Speedware Corporation. The following are extracts from that Annual Report.

7. Finance Subsidiaries (continued)

At December 31, 20x5, receivables of $898 included $595 of notes and accounts receivable and $303,000 due under noncancelable leases, maturing as follows:

	Direct financing leases ($millions)	Total receivables
Year ended December 31:		
20x6	$159	$357
20x7	77	200
20x8	54	173
20x9	38	92
2x10	21	70
Thereafter	15	67
	364	959
Less unearned income	61	61
	$303	$898

18. Commitments

At December 31, 20x5, the future minimum lease payments under capital leases and operating leases consisted of:

	Capital leases	Operating leases
Year ended December 31:		
20x6	$ 5	$132
20x7	5	114
20x8	5	83
20x9	2	56
2x10	2	37
Thereafter	9	154
Total future minimum lease payments	28	$576
Less: imputed interest	8	
Present value of net minimum lease payments	$20	

Rental expense on operating leases for the years ended December 31, 20x5, 20x4, and 20x3, amounted to $172, $170, and $131, respectively.

Your friend has asked you the following questions about the Annual Report:

Required:
Prepare a brief memorandum answering the questions for your friend.
- **a.** Is the firm a lessee or lessor?
- **b.** Where would the liabilities appear on the balance sheet, and in what amounts?
- **c.** Does Speedware Corporation have any operating leases? How do you know? How are the payments accounted for by the firm?
- **d.** What entries would Speedware Corporation make to account for its leases during 20x6, based on those leases currently on the books? (Ignore any executory costs.)

SOLUTION TO THE CASE

The solution should be written as a memorandum to the friend.

Requirement a

Both. Note 7 discloses amounts due to Speedware Corporation as a lessor. Note 18 indicates the company's obligations as a lessee.

Requirement b

The total capital lease obligation at present value is $20 million, which is reported with the long-term liabilities. Of this amount, $5 million should be reported as a current liability since it is payable in 20x6.

Requirement c

Yes. The company has accounted for most of its leases as operating leases, as can be seen from note 18. These lease obligations do not appear on the balance sheet. The yearly rentals will be included, although they are not separately identified, among the firm's expenses. The yearly rental expenses may also be considered a cost of production and inventoried. If so, they will appear as part of the firm's cost of sales when the inventory is sold.

Requirement d

Operating leases (assuming expenses):

Rent expense	132,000,000	
Cash or payables		132,000,000

Capital leases—receivables and payables:

Cash	159,000,000	
Lease receivable		159,000,000
Lease liability	5,000,000	
Cash		5,000,000

From the information provided, it is not possible to determine the amount of interest to be earned or expensed for 20x6 with respect to the direct financing leases receivable or the capital leases payable.

SELECTED SOLUTIONS FROM THE TEXTBOOK

Assignment 17-2

Requirement 1

   i. The lease term is ten years. The second five-year lease term is a bargain renewal option, based on the information regarding market rental rates.

  ii. Guaranteed residual, none.

 iii. Unguaranteed residual exists as the value of the asset to the lessor at the end of the lease term. There is no way to calculate this amount.

  iv. Bargain purchase option, none.

  v. Bargain renewal terms, $29,500 per year for the second five-year lease term

  vi. Minimum net lease payment:

a)	($79,600 – $7,900) × 5 years	$358,500
b)	($29,500 – $2,500) × 5 years	135,000
		$493,500

 vii. Incremental borrowing rate, 10%

Requirement 2

To be a capital lease, the lease would have to meet one of three criteria, applied judgementally:

1.	Transfer of title or BPO	No
2.	Economic life vs lease term	Yes; 10/12 > 75%
3.	PV of MLP vs fair value	Yes; $368,887* > 90% of $390,000

  * PV of MLP:

a) ($79,600 – $7,900) (P/AD, 10%, 5) (4.16987) $298,980

b) ($29,500 – $2,500) (P/AD, 10%, 5) (P/F, 10%, 5)

    (4.16987) (.62092)   <u>69,907</u>

                                                  <u>$368,887</u>

Requirement 3

Beginning of fiscal year and lease term:

Asset under capital lease..	368,887	
Lease liability		368,887

Insurance expense...	7,900	
Lease liability..	71,700	
Cash...		79,600

End of fiscal year:

Interest expense	29,719	
Lease liability		29,719
($368,887 – $71,700) × .10		

Amortization expense	36,889	
Accumulated amortization		36,889
$368,887 ÷ 10		

Exercise 17-7

Requirement 1

This is a capital lease for Roscoe. They pay for the equipment and provide return to the lessor over the life of the lease:

PV of MLP = ($7,600 – $200) × (P/A, 7%, 5) (4.10020) = $30,342

$30,342 ÷ $32,500 = 93%

The lease could also be classified based on the lease term versus economic life (5/5; 100%)

Requirement 2

Lease Amortization - End of Year Payments

Year	Outstanding Balance	Interest at 7%	End of period Cash Flow	Inc/(Dec) in Balance	Ending Balance
20x1	30,342	2,124	7,400	(5,276)	25,066
20x2	25,066	1,755	7,400	(5,645)	19,421
20x3	19,421	1,360	7,400	(6,040)	13,381
20x4	13,381	937	7,400	(6,463)	6,918
20x5	6,918	484	7,400	(6,916)	(2) rounding

Requirement 3

    1 January 20x1
        Asset under capital lease.. 30,342
            Lease liability.. 30,342
    31 December 20x1
        Interest expense... 2,124
            Lease liability.. 2,124
        Insurance and maintenance expense.................................... 200
        Lease liability 7,400
            Cash 7,600
        Amortization expense ($30,342 ÷ 5)..................................... 6,068
            Accumulated amortization, asset under lease.............. 6,068
    31 December 20x2
        Interest expense... 1,755
            Lease liability.. 1,755
        Insurance and maintenance expense.................................... 200
        Lease liability 7,400
            Cash 7,600
        Amortization expense.. 6,068
            Accumulated amortization, asset under lease.............. 6,068

Requirement 4

Interest expense, 20x1	$2,124 × 6/12		$1,062
Interest expense, 20x2	$2,124 × 6/12	$1,062	
	$1,755 × 6/12	878	$1,940

Requirement 5

Implicit interest rate = 14%; $25,405 = ($7,600 − $200) (P/A, x%, 5); x = 14%

First year interest: = $3,557; ($25,405 × 14%)

Assignment 17-19

Requirement 1

The lease is a capital lease to the lessee because the term, including the three bargain renewal terms, is substantially equal to the economic life of the asset. Note, however, that practically, renewal of the lease toward the end of the vehicle's life will likely depend on its working condition and may be viewed as rather contingent at this time, 'bargain' or not. The PV of the MLP's is equal to 96% of fair value ($17,316* ÷ $18,000)

*PV:
a) ($5,800 − $1,700) (P/AD, 12%, 5) (4.03735).. $16,553
b) ($2,600 − $2,100) (P/AD, 12%, 3) (P/F, 12%, 5) (2.69005) (.56743) 763
                                                                                                                     $17,316

Requirement 2

Lease Amortization Schedule - Beginning of Lease Year Payments

Lease Year	Outstanding Balance	Interest at 12%	1 January Payment	Inc/(Dec) in Balance	Ending Balance
20x2	$17,316	$ 0	$4,100	$(4,100)	$13,216
20x3	13,216	1,586	4,100	(2,514)	10,702
20x4	10,702	1,284	4,100	(2,816)	7,886
20x5	7,886	946	4,100	(3,154)	4,732
20x6	4,732	568	4,100	(3,532)	1,200
20x7	1,200	144	500	(356)	844
20x8	844	101	500	(399)	445
20x9	445	54	500	(446)	(1) rounding
		$4,683			

Requirement 3

	20x2		*20x3*	
1 January				
Asset under capital lease	17,316			
Lease liability...........................		17,316		
Lease liability.................................	4,100		4,100	
Insurance and maintenance expense	1,700		1,700	
Cash...		5,800		5,800
31 December				
Interest expense...........................	1,586		1,284	
Lease liability........................		1,586		1,284
Amortization expense..................	2,165		2,165	
Accumulated amortization, leased asset ($17,316 ÷ 8)...		2,165		2,165

Requirement 4

Income Statement	*20x2*	*20x3*
Maintenance and insurance expense	$1,700	$1,700
Interest expense	1,586	1,284
Amortization expense	2,165	2,165

Balance Sheet		
Capital assets		
Assets under capital leases	17,316	17,316
Accumulated amortization	(2,165)	(4,330)
	15,151	12,986

Current liabilities		
Current portion of lease liability	4,100	4,100

Long-term liability
Lease liability	14,802*	11,986*
Less: current portion	4,100	4,100
	10,702	7,886

*$13,216 + $1,586; $10,702 + $1,284

CFS

Operations
Add back: amortization	2,165	2,165
Increase(decrease) in interest payable	1,586	(302)

Financing
Repayment of lease liability	(4,100)*	(2,514)**

*$17,316 − $14,802 = $(2,514); $1,586 interest and $(4,100) repayment. May also be shown as the net $(2,514) change in lease liability. Practice differs.

**$14,802 − $11,986 = ($2,816); ($302) interest ($1,586 versus $1,284) and $(2,514) repayment. May also be shown as the net ($2,816) change in lease liability.

Requirement 5

Allocation of Interest Expense to Fiscal Years

Year End	Lease Payment	Implicit Interest	Allocation (5/12: 7/12)	Interest Expense
x2	$ 0			
x3	1,586	661	$661	31 May 20x2
		925		
x4	1,284	535	1,460(1)	31 May 20x3
		749		
x5	946	394	1,143	31 May 20x4
		552		
x6	568	237	789	31 May 20x5
		331		
x7	144	60	391	31 May 20x6
		84		
x8	101	42	126	31 May 20x7
		59		
x9	54	23	82	31 May 20x8
		31		
x10	0	0	31	31 May 20x9
	$4,683	$4,683	$4,683	

(1) $925 + $535, etc.

Assignment 17-25

Requirement 1

20x2	31 March	Cash	9,000,000		
		Accumulated depreciation	3,600,000		
		Distribution facility................................		10,400,000	
		Deferred gain on sale and leaseback		2,200,000	

		Distribution facility under lease	8,706,346	
		Lease liability		8,706,346
		($875,000 × P/AD 9%,20) (9.95011)	

		Lease liability..	875,000	
		Cash...		875,000

	31 Dec.	Interest expense...	528,616	
		Lease liability		528,616

($8,706,346 − $875,000) × 9% × 9/12

New balance: $8,706,346 − $875,000 + $528,616 = $8,359,962

		Depreciation expense	217,659	
		Accumulated depreciation, leased		
		distribution facility...............................		217,659

($8,706,346 × 1/30 × 9/12)

		Deferred gain on sale and leaseback.........	55,000	
		Depreciation expense.............................		55,000

($2,200,000 × 1/30 × 9/12)

Requirement 2

20x3	31 March	Interest expense..	176,205	
		Lease liability		176,205

($8,706,346 − $875,000) × 9% × 3/12

		Lease liability..	875,000	
		Cash...		875,000

New balance: ($8,706,346 − $875,000 + $528,616 + $176,205 − $875,000) = $7,661,167

	31 Dec.	Interest expense..	517,129	
		Lease liability		517,129

($7,661,167 × 9% × 9/12)

Balance: $7,661,167 + $517,129 = $8,178,296

Depreciation expense.......................................		290,212	
Accumulated depreciation, leased			
distribution facility...............................			290,212
$8,706,346 × 1/30			
Deferred gain on sale and leaseback.........		73,333	
Depreciation expense............................			73,333
$2,200,000 × 1/30			

20x4 31 March

Interest expense..	172,376	
Lease liability		172,376
($7,661,167 × 9% × 3/12)		
Lease liability..	875,000	
Cash..		875,000

New balance : ($7,661,167 + $517,129 + $172,376 – $875,000) =
$7,475,672

Dec 31

Interest expense..	504,608	
Lease liability		504,608
($7,475,672 × .09 × 9/12)		

New balance: $7,475,672 + $504,608 = $7,980,280

Depreciation expense...................................	290,212	
Accumulated depreciation, leased		
distribution facility...............................		290,212
Deferred gain on sale and leaseback.........	73,333	
Depreciation expense............................		73,333

Requirement 3

Balance Sheet	*20x2*	*20x3*	*20x4*
Capital Assets			
Distribution facility under capital lease..	$8,706,346	$8,706,346	$8,706,346
Less: accumulated amortization..............	217,659	507,871	798,083
...	$8,488,687	$8,198,475	$7,908,263
Deferred credits			
Deferred gain on sale and leaseback.......	2,145,000	2,071,667	1,998,334
Long-term liability			
Lease liability...	8,359,962	8,178,296	7,980,280
Income Statement			
Interest expense...	528,616	693,334	676,984
Depreciation expense.................................	162,659	216,879	216,879

SOLUTIONS TO CONCEPT REVIEW QUESTIONS

Page 1036

1. The basic criterion in determining whether a lease is a capital lease is whether the terms of the lease convey substantially all of the risks and rewards of ownership from the lessor to the lessee.

2. Operating lease rental payments may be allocated to periods other than those in which the payments are made in situations where the payments are not even throughout the lease term. For example, if a lease requires a large initial payment due at the outset of the lease, the payment may be amortized over the term of the lease.

3. The three guidelines provided in the *CICA Handbook* to assist in determining whether a lease is a capital lease are as follows: (1) There is reasonable assurance that the lessee will obtain ownership of the leased property at the end of the lease term (automatic transfer of ownership or bargain purchase option). (2) The lessee will receive substantially all of the economic benefits expected to be derived through the use of the leased property (lease term is at least 75% of the asset's expected useful life) *OR* (3) The lessor will be assured of recovering the investment in the leased property (minimum lease payments are at least 90% of the fair value of the asset at the inception of the lease).

4. Bargain renewal options: Provisions allowing a lessee, at its option, to renew a lease for a rental price that is sufficiently lower than the expected fair rental price of the property that at the date the option becomes exercisable, the exercise of the option appears (at the inception of the lease) to be reasonably assured.

Incremental borrowing rate: In a lease, from the perspective of the lessee, the interest rate that would be incurred by the lessee to finance an acquisition of a similar asset with similar term and security.

Lease term: The fixed, noncancelable period of a lease plus all periods covered by bargain renewal options; all periods for which failure to renew would impose on a lessee a penalty sufficiently large that renewal appears reasonably assured; all periods covered by ordinary renewal options during which a lessee has undertaken to guarantee the lessor's debt related to the leased property; all periods covered by ordinary renewal options preceding the date on which a bargain purchase option becomes exercisable; and all periods representing renewals or extensions of a lease at the lessor's option.

5. The nature (i.e., business) of the lessor can influence the lessee's accounting for the lease by providing an indication as to whether, in substance, the risks and benefits are likely to be transferred from the lessor to the lessee. For example, if the lessor is a financing company (e.g., a bank or a nonbank lender), it is highly probable that the lease is capital in nature, as the financing company is not in the business of acquiring for resale, nor would it wish to assume the risks of owning, the leased property. Such a lessor is likely performing a financing role in a capital lease.

Page 1037

1. *Off-balance sheet financing* refers to the ability to obtain the full and unfettered use of assets without having to report the assets (and the related debt obligation) on the balance sheet (i.e., the ability to finance the in-substance purchase of an asset without reporting a liability on the balance sheet).

2. The lessor retains title to an asset under lease.

3. If the lessee is a non-profit organization, an unprofitable business, or a business subject to a rate of tax lower than the lessor, the benefit of the CCA deductions are worth more in the lessor's hands than in the lessee's (assuming the lessor is profitable/taxable). By structuring the lease as an operating lease (for tax purposes), the lessor claims the CCA deductions and realizes the benefit thereof. Since the lessor calculates its return on investment on an after-tax basis, the benefit of a reduction in the lessor's taxes may be passed on to the lessee in the form of lower lease payments. Note that a lease may be structured as a capital lease for accounting but remain an operating lease for tax purposes.

Page 1042

1. Operating and executory costs must be deducted from capital lease payments before the lease payments are capitalized, as such costs are not costs associated with acquiring the asset; rather, they are costs of using the asset. The capitalized cost represents the cost of acquiring the asset.

2. The impact of lease capitalization on the lessee's balance sheet is as follows. Total assets will increase; leased assets may be shown separately or combined with similar, acquired, assets. Accumulated amortization will also be affected as amortization is taken on the asset from period to period. The outstanding balance on the lease is shown in the liabilities section of the balance sheet. The liability will be disaggregated into current and long-term portions. Since liabilities are increased by the amount of the capitalized lease, the debt-to-equity ratio will increase.

3. The leased asset should be amortized by the lessee over the lease term (i.e., initial lease term plus bargain renewal periods).

Page 1048

1. The current portion of the lease liability is the accrued interest for the period to date plus the principal reduction during the next year.

2. When lease payments do not coincide with the company's reporting periods, the interest expense is first determined in reference to the lease period and then allocated to the fiscal year. For example, if the lease anniversary is May 1 and the fiscal year end of the company is December 31, 20x5, the interest expense is comprised of the last five months of interest expense to May 1 (based on the liability at April 30, 20x4), and the first 7 months of interest expense to December 31 (based on the liability at April 30, 20x5).

Page 1052

1. *Contingent rent* is rent that depends on specified future event—for example, a store achieving a certain level of sales.

2. A company may attempt to structure a lease so as to avoid capital lease treatment for financial reporting purposes, in order to avoid having to report a liability (i.e., attempt to achieve off-balance sheet financing).

3. The gain "realized" in a sale and leaseback transaction is not recognized currently. The gain is deferred and amortized proportionately with the lease payments over the lease term. Note that a loss is recognized immediately, as it implies that the carrying value of the asset was overstated (this reflects the principle of conservatism).

APPENDIX: ACCOUNTING FOR LEASES BY LESSORS

In the chapter, we discussed the general issue of leasing for the lessee. In general, the same distinction exists for the lessors as for the lessees. To a large extent, accounting for a lease by lessors is the opposite side of leasing transactions.

A1. CLASSIFICATION AS A CAPITAL LEASE

The *CICA Handbook*, paragraph 3065.03(a) states:

A capital lease is a lease that, from the point of view of the lessee, transfers substantially all the benefits and risks incident to ownership of property to the lessee.

CICA

The guidelines provided to lessors by the *CICA Handbook* are the same as those applied from the lessee's point of view, with two additional ones:

- Normal credit risk.
- Reasonable estimate of the amounts of any unreimbursable costs.

Both of these criteria must be met.

The definitions are the same as for lessees:
- Minimum lease term includes the bargain renewal terms and renewal terms at lessor's option.
- Minimum net lease payments include lease payments during bargain renewal terms and any guaranteed residual value.
- The **interest rate used for discounting the net lease payments** by the lessor is the *rate implicit in the lease*.

  Fair market value of asset = Net lease payment (P/A due, i, n) *or*
  = Net lease payment (P/A, i, n)

In practice, lessors use the *after-tax* implicit rate, but in our examples we use the *pretax* implicit interest rate. The after-tax accounting is rather complex, and in order to clarify the principles underlying lease accounting for lessors, we use the pretax implicit interest rate.

When a lease is classified as a capital lease to the lessor, a secondary classification must be done. The capital lease may be either a **direct-financing lease** or a **sales-type lease.**
- **Direct-financing lease.** This is a capital lease to the lessor that does not involve manufacturer's or dealer's profit. The lessor is acting purely as a financial intermediary.
- **Sales-type lease.** This is a capital lease that involves manufacturer's or dealer's profit or loss plus interest revenue from the lease.

There are also two methods of recording the capital lease: the **net basis of recording**, and the **gross basis of recording.**

A2. OPERATING LEASES

If a lease does not qualify as a capital lease, it must be reported as an operating lease.

The *CICA Handbook*, paragraphs 3065.55 and 3065.56, states the characteristics of an operating lease as follows:

CICA

- *The leased asset is shown on John Leasing Company's (lessor) balance sheet.*
- *The initial direct costs are deferred and amortized over the initial lease term proportionate to the recognition of lease income.*
- *Lease income is recognized as the lease payments become due.*
- *The asset is amortized in accordance with whatever policy management chooses.*
- *Lump sum payments are amortized over the initial lease term.*

Essentially, lease revenue is recognized on a straight-line basis, matched with amortization expense on the asset and amortization of any initial lease costs. The cost of asset held for leasing should be disclosed, as should the amount of rental revenue included on the income statement.

A3. DIRECT-FINANCING LEASES—NET BASIS

The lessor in a **direct-financing lease** purchases an asset to accommodate the leasing transaction and immediately leases it to the lessee.

At inception of the lease, the lessor will make the following entry:

Equipment (capital asset)	x,xxx	
Cash		x,xxx
Lease receivable	x,xxx	
Equipment		x,xxx

WATCH! The one difference in accounting between lessees and lessors is the subtle distinction relating to residual value. For lessees, only any residual value that is guaranteed by the lessee is included in the cash flow stream for accounting purposes. Lessors, however, will include the estimated residual value of the asset regardless of whether it is guaranteed.

The receipt of the lease payment will be recorded as a reduction of the lease receivable:

Cash	x,xxx	
Lease receivable		x,xxx

At the end of the fiscal period, the lessor will accrue the interest on the receivable:

Lease receivable	x,xxx	
Finance revenue (interest revenue)		x,xxx

Interest revenue is earned over time based on the outstanding principal balance in the lease receivable account. The amount of interest earned each year may be calculated by the amortization table.

Principal Characteristics of the Gross Basis

In practice, lessors are unlikely to use the net method. The *CICA Handbook* implicitly assumes that lessors will use the gross method.

The gross and net methods result in the same amounts in the financial statements.

Lease payments receivable[a]	xxxx	
Initial lease expense[b]	xxxx	
Insurance expense[c]	xxxx	
Cash[d]		xxxx
Unearned finance revenue[e]		xxxx

[a] Lease payments receivable: Total lease payments – Executory and operating costs + Estimated residual value.

[b] Initial lease expense: A cost to close the deal and initiate the lease. The *lessee* is not responsible for reimbursing the *lessor* for these costs.

[c] Insurance expense: The *lessor* carries the insurance on leased assets in order to be certain that the assets are properly insured. The *lessor* increased the lease payments in order to recover the estimated cost from the lessee.

[d] Cash: Capital cost + Executory and operating costs (insurance costs) + Initial direct costs.

[e] Unearned finance revenue: Lease payments receivable (net method) = Unearned finance revenue.

The first lease payment is assumed to cover the initial direct costs, plus the insurance cost for the first year of the lease. The remainder reduces the outstanding receivable balance:

Cash	xxxx	
Initial lease expense		xxxx
Insurance expense		xxxx
Lease payments receivable		xxxx

At the end of the reporting period, accrued interest must be calculated, just as under the net method.

> Interest is accrued only on the net balance of the receivable. **WATCH!**

The accrued interest is recorded as a reduction of the Unearned Finance Revenue:

Unearned finance revenue	xxxx	
Finance revenue		xxxx

When the second lease payment is received, the cash receipt is split between reimbursement for the insurance and reduction of the gross lease payments receivable:

Year 2

Cash	xxxx	
Insurance expense		xxxx
Lease payments receivable		xxxx

> The two methods are only different methods of recording, not of reporting. Thus, there is no impact on the financial statement presentation. **WATCH!**

Why Use the Gross Method?
Like almost all of the accounts shown on any company's balance sheet, the lease receivables account is a **control account.**

For the sake of good internal control, it is important that a control account be easily reconcilable to the underlying subsidiary records.

Disclosure for Lessors
The *CICA Handbook,* paragraph 3065.54, recommends only the following disclosures:
- The lessor's net investment.
- The amount of finance income.
- The lease revenue recognition policy.

The *CICA Handbook* also suggests that "it may be desirable" to disclose the following information:
- The aggregate future minimum lease payments receivable.
- The amount of unearned finance income.
- The estimated amount of unguaranteed residual values.
- Executory cost included in minimum lease payments.

A4. SALES-TYPE LEASES
Basic Nature
A *sales-type lease* occurs when the lessor sells the product and finances the sale through a capital lease. The lessor makes a profit or loss from the sale, and financing income is recognized over the lease term.

The sale component of the transaction is recorded as follows (using the gross method):

Lease payments receivable	xxx	
Unearned finance revenue		xxxx
Sales revenue		xxxx
Cost of goods sold	xxxx	
Asset inventory		xxxx

The first payment is recorded:

Cash	xxxx	
Lease payment receivable		xxxx

Interest revenues will be earned over time based on the *outstanding principal* balance in the lease payment receivable account.

The income statement for the first year will include a gross profit relating to the lease transaction, which is the profit on the sale. The balance sheet will show a net lease receivable: the gross lease payments less the unearned finance revenue updated.

In practice the sales price must often be estimated The revenue split between gross profit and interest revenue is a matter of considerable judgement.

Sales-type Leases are rare in Canada. The lessor will not be able to claim the full amount of CCA on leased assets if the CCA exceeds the lease payments received, *unless* the lessor qualifies as a lessor under the Income Tax Regulations.

WATCH!

TRUE–FALSE QUESTIONS

T F 1. Both lessors and lessees should classify lease transactions as either capital leases or operating leases; and lessors should further subclassify capital leases as sales-type or direct financing leases.

T F 2. For a lessor to classify a lease agreement as a capital lease, the collectability of the minimum lease payments must be reasonably assured or all unreimbursable costs can be estimated.

T F 3. In accounting for a capital lease, the lessor debits a leased asset account for the present value of the minimum lease payments.

T F 4. If the present value of the minimum lease payments exceeds the carrying value of the leased asset, a capital lease is characterized as a sales-type lease.

T F 5. The accounting for a capital lease by the lessee is unaffected by whether the lease is a direct financing or sales-type lease.

T F 6. When a bargain purchase option is present, the bargain purchase option price should be part of the minimum lease payments to both the lessee and the lessor.

T F 7. When an unguaranteed residual value is present, the minimum lease payments to both the lessee and the lessor should include the unguaranteed residual value.

MULTIPLE CHOICE QUESTIONS

___ **1.** For the lessor to classify a lease agreement as a capital lease, there must be no important uncertainties surrounding the amount of unreimbursable costs yet to be incurred, and:
  a. the lease agreement must transfer ownership to the lessee.
  b. the lessor must be reasonably certain about the collectability of the lease payments.
  c. the lease term and the economic life of the asset must be approximately the same.
  d. the lessee must guarantee the residual value of the leased asset.

___ **2.** The primary difference between a direct-financing lease and a sales-type lease is that:

    a. in a direct-financing lease, a third party to the transaction supplies a major portion of the financing of the leased asset.

    b. the sales-type lease involves a legal transfer of title to the asset.

    c. the lessor earns both interest income and a manufacturer's or dealer's profit with a sales-type lease.

    d. in a direct-financing lease, the asset is sold by the lessee, who immediately leases the asset back from the purchaser/lessor.

___ **3.** Shopsy Supermarket leased a piece of equipment from Dewolf Leasing Company on July 1, 20x5, for an 8-year period. Equal payments under the lease are $24,000, due on July 1 of each year. The first payment was made on July 1, 20x5. The rate of interest is 10%. The selling price of the computer is $140,800, and its cost to Dewolf is $112,000. If the lease is appropriately recorded as a sales-type lease, the amount of interest income Dewolf should record for the year ended December 31, 20x5, is:

    a. $0

    b. $5,600

    c. $5,840

    d. $6,400

___ **4.** Condido Company leased a new piece of equipment to Hoestner on January 1, 20x5 for a four-year period. Rental payments of $4,000 are due on January 1 of each year. The first payment was made January 1, 20x5. The fair value of the equipment at the inception of the lease is $14,000 and the cost of the equipment to Condido is $10,000. Condido properly classified the lease as a sales-type lease. For the year ended December 31, 20x5, what amount of profit on the sale and interest income should Condido record if applicable interest rate is 10%?

	Profit on sale	Interest income
a.	–0–	$ 995
b.	$3,947	995
c.	995	3,947
d.	3,947	–0–

___ **5.** Rent should be reported by the lessor as revenue over the lease term as it becomes receivable, according to the provisions of which of the fol-lowing leases?

	Direct financing lease	Operating lease	Sales-type lease
a.	Yes	Yes	Yes
b.	Yes	No	No
c.	No	Yes	No
d.	No	No	Yes

____ 6. The excess of the fair value of lease property at the inception of the lease over its cost or carrying amount should be considered by the lessor as:
   a. unearned income from a sales-type lease
   b. unearned income from a direct-financing lease.
   c. manufacturer's or dealer's profit from a sales-type lease.
   d. manufacturer's or dealer's profit from a direct financing lease.

____ 7. A lease is recorded as a sales-type lease by the lessor. The difference be-tween the gross investment in the lease and the net receivable should be:
   a. amortized over the period of lease as interest revenue by the interest method.
   b. amortized over the period of lease as interest revenue by the straight-line method.
   c. recognized in full as interest revenue at the lease's inception.
   d. recognized in full as manufacturer's or dealer's profit at the lease's inception.

____ 8. In a lease recorded as a sales-type lease by the lessor, interest revenue:
   a. does not arise.
   b. should be recognized over the life of the lease by the interest method.
   c. should be recognized over the life of the lease by the straight-line method.
   d. should be recognized in full as revenue at the leases inception.

____ 9. On January 1, 20x5, Mill Corporation leased a machine to Ott Corporation for a 5-year term at an annual rental of $100,000. The lease is an operating lease. At the inception of the lease, Mill received $200,000, covering the first year's rent of $100,000 and a security deposit of $100,000. This deposit will not be returned to Ott upon expiration of the lease but will instead be applied to payment of rent for the last year of the lease. Mill properly reported rental revenue of $200,000 in its 20x5 income tax return. Mill's tax rate was 30%. In Mill's December 31, 20x5, balance sheet, what portion of the $200,000 should be reported as a liability?
   a. $100,000
   b. $80,000
   c. $70,000
   d. $56,000

____ 10. Beal, Inc., intends to lease a machine from Paul Corporation. Beal's incremental borrowing rate is 14%. The prime rate of interest is 8%. Paul's implicit rate in the lease is 10%., which is known to Beal. What interest rate will be used to calculate the minimum lease payments?
   a. 8%
   b. 10%
   c. 14%
   d. 12%

SOLUTIONS TO TRUE–FALSE QUESTIONS

1. T

2. F Both criteria must be met for a capital lease.

3. F If the lease is a direct-financing lease, the lessor records the transaction as a debit to lease receivable and a credit to cash. Thus in return for spending the amount of cash on the asset (which never crosses the lessor's premises or books), the lessor has the right to receive a series of payments, the present value of which is equal to the cash spent on the asset. If the lease is a *sales-type lease*, it is viewed as two distinct transactions: **1.** The sale of the product, with recognition of a profit or loss on the sale; and **2.** The financing of the sale through a capital lease, with finance income recognized over the lease term. The journal entries at the inception of the lease will be (a) debit to lease payments receivable, credit to unearned finance revenue and credit to sales revenue; and (b) debit to cost of goods sold and credit to inventory (equipment).

4. T

5. T

6. T

7. F The unguaranteed residual is included only in the lessor's calculations. This is not the concern to the lessee. The lessor will include the estimated residual value of the asset regardless of whether it is guaranteed or unguaranteed.

SOLUTIONS TO MULTIPLE CHOICE QUESTIONS

1. b This is the second criterion that must be met for the lessor to classify a lease as a capital lease.

2. c In a sales-type lease there is a profit from the sale of the asset and also the financing revenue from the lease agreement.

3. c The lease payments receivable would have been recorded as $140,800 less the first payment of $24,000 = $116,800. The interest income is calculated on $116,800 × 10% × 6/12 = $5,840.

4. b The profit is calculated by taking the difference between the PV of the minimum lease payments discounted at 10% for n = 4. $4,000 (P/A due, 10%, 4)(3.48685) = $13,947, and the cost to the lessor = $10,000. [$13,947 – $10,000 = $3,947. The interest income = $13,947 less first payment $4,000 = $9,947 × 10% = $995.

5. c Per paragraph 3065 of the *CICA Handbook*, rent should be reported by the lessor as revenue over the lease term for an operating lease as it becomes receivable according to the lease provisions. Both direct-financing and sales-
type leases are types of capital leases. For these lease types, the lessor reports interest income over the lease term rather than rental.

6. c Per paragraph 3065.03(b) of the *CICA Handbook*, the excess of the fair value of leased property at the inception of the lease over the lessor's cost is defined as the manufacturer's or dealer's profit. Answer **a** is incorrect because the unearned income from a sales-type lease is defined as the difference between the gross investment in the lease and the net receivable. Answer **b** is incorrect because the unearned income from a direct-financing lease is defined as the excess of the gross investment over the cost (also the present value of lease payments) on the leased property. Answer **d** is incorrect because a sales-type lease involves a manufacturer's or dealer's profit while a direct financing lease does not.

7. a Per paragraph 3065.48 of the *CICA Handbook,* the difference between the gross investment in the lease and the sum of the present values of the two components of the gross investment shall be recorded as unearned income. The unearned income shall be amortized to income over the lease term so as to provide a constant periodic rate of return on the net investment in the lease. The objective of the interest method is to arrive at a level (i.e., constant) effective rate (of interest). Therefore, answers **b, c,** and **d** are incorrect.

8. b Per paragraph 3065.48 of the *CICA Handbook,* revenue is to be recognized for a sales-type lease over the lease term so as to produce a constant rate of return on the net investment in the lease. This requires the use of the interest method. Therefore, answer **b** is correct and answer **c** is incorrect. Answer **a** is incorrect because, per Section 3065, interest revenue does arise in a sales-type lease. Answer **d** is incorrect because the interest is to be earned over the life of the lease, not in full at the lease's inception.

9. a Deposits and prepayments received for services to be provided in the future are unearned revenues that should be recorded as a liability until earned. The first year's rent is recorded as rent revenue, but the $100,000 deposit is recorded as rent collected in advance (unearned rent) because Mill is required to render future services (use of the machine) to the lessee. The rate (30%) does not affect the amount of the liability to the lessee, although a separate future income tax asset may be recorded in certain circumstances.

10. b The lessor wants to either recover the fair market value of the asset it is selling or recover whatever is possible. The lessor's implicit rate in the lease is the rate of interest that the lessor charges the lessee for providing financing. The implicit rate is usually higher than the lessor's own borrowing rate so that the lessor makes a profit on the interest spread. The lessee's incremental borrowing rate does not enter into this calculation. The prime rate (8%) is never used unless it happens to be the same as the implicit rate.

PROBLEMS

Problem 1

PURPOSE: To illustrate the determination of the type of lease and the accounting for the lessor.

Barney Properties purchased a building for $500,000 on December 31, 20x4. On January 1, 20x5, Barney received a payment of $100,000 from Jardine Company as an advance to secure a 3-year lease on that building, which it (Jardine) will occupy starting from that date. Additionally, $120,000 will be due on December 31 throughout the term of the lease. The lease contains no specific renewal agreement. Barney will pay the taxes of $12,000 per year, paid every January, and other ownership costs. Barney uses the straight-line basis for amortization of its capital assets. The building's estimated useful life is 20 years with no residual value. Barney has a December 31 year end.

Required

     a. What type of lease contract is involved? Explain.

     b. Prepare the journal entries to record the purchase of the building and the inception of the lease.

     c. Prepare the journal entries on December 31, 20x5.

     d. Indicate how much revenue will be shown on the income statement for the year ended December 31, 20x5.

Problem 2

PURPOSE: To illustrate the accounting for a direct-financing lease using the gross method.

Jim's Leasing Company purchased a machine (for leasing purposes) on January 1, 20x5, for $270,000. By prior agreement, the machine was delivered to Ethan Company (lessee) under a direct-financing lease whereby Ethan made the first lease payment of $73,516 on January 1, 20x5, and agreed to make three more such annual payments.

At the end of the 4-year lease term, the machine will revert to the lessor, at which time it is expected to have a residual value of $20,000 (none of which was guaranteed by the lessee). The lessor's implicit interest rate was 10% on cost.

Required

     a. Show how the lessor computed the annual payment.

     b. Prepare a lease amortization schedule for the lessor.

     c. Give all of the entries for the lessor on the following dates:

        (i) January 1, 20x5—purchase and other transactions.

        (ii) December 31, 20x5—end of the accounting period.

        (iii) December 31, 20x8—return of the machine by the lessee at the termination of the lease. At this date, the machine has an actual market value of $14,000 (instead of the $20,000 estimated residual value).

     d. How would the lessor's entries differ at the end of the lease term if the actual market value of machine turned out to be $23,000 (instead of the estimated residual value of $20,000)?

Problem 3

PURPOSE: To illustrate the accounting for a sales-type Lease using the gross method.

On January 1, 20x5, lessor Oniz and lessee Ryan signed a 4-year lease that qualifies as a sales-type lease. The equipment cost Oniz $900,000, and the cash sale price is $1,400,000. The equipment has a 6-year estimated useful life. Estimated residual values were the following: end of Year 4, $200,000, and end of Year 6, $80,000. The lease gives Ryan an option to buy the equipment at the end of Year 4 for $150,000 cash. The lease requires four equal payments starting on January 1, 2001. Oniz's expected rate of return on the lease is 15%, of which Ryan is aware, and the incremental borrowing rate for Ryan is 16%. On December 31, 20x8, the lessee exercises the purchase option, at which time a new estimate of residual value is $175,000.

Required

   a. Compute the annual payment.
   b. Prepare a lease amortization schedule for the lessor.
   c. Give the entries for the lessor from the date of inception through the lease termination date.

SOLUTIONS TO PROBLEMS

Problem 1

Requirement a

Because Barney maintains the property and pays the taxes, the risks and rewards of ownership are not transferred. The 3-year lease is not 75% of the useful life of the premises of 20 years. Therefore, it is assumed that this is an operating lease with a prepayment of part of the rent, because it does not meet the criteria for a capital lease.

Requirement b

December 31, 20x4

Building	500,000	
Cash		500,000

January 1, 20x5

Cash	100,000	
Unearned rental revenue		100,000
Property taxes	12,000	
Cash		12,000

Requirement c

December 31, 20x5

Cash	120,000	
Rental revenue		120,000
Amortization expense, building	25,000	
Accumulated amortization, building		25,000
($500,000/20)		
Unearned rental revenue	33,333	
Rental revenue		33,333
($100,000/3)		

Requirement d

	Rental revenue	Unearned rental revenue	Taxes expense	Net rental revenue	Amort.	Charge to income
20x5	$120,000	$33,333	$12,000	$141,333	$25,000	$116,333

Problem 2

Requirement a

Cost of leased machine	$270,000
Present value of estimated residual value to be realized	
= $20,000 (PV1, 10%, 4) = (.68301)	13,660
Net investment to be recovered	$256,340
Payments = ($256,340/[PVAD, 10%, 4]) = ($256,340/3.48685)	$ 73,516

Requirement b

	Annual lease payments	Annual interest @ 10%	Net lease receivable inc. (dec.)	Balance
Jan. 1, 20x5 initial value				$270,000
Jan. 1, 20x5	$73,516		$73,516	$196,484
Dec. 31, 20x5		$19,648	(19,648)	216,132
Jan. 1, 20x6	73,516		73,516	142,616
Dec. 31, 20x6		14,262	(14,262)	156,878
Jan. 1, 20x7	73,516		73,516	83,362
Dec. 31, 20x7		8,336	(8,336)	91,698
Jan. 1, 20x8	73,516		73,516	18,182
Dec. 31, 20x8		1,818	(1,818)	20,000
	$294,064	$44,064	$250,000	$20,000

Requirement c

(i)

January 1, 20x5

Machine	270,000	
Cash		270,000
To record purchase of the machine.		
Lease receivable ($73,516 × 4) + $20,000	314,064	
Machine		270,000
Unearned interest revenue		44,064
To record the inception of the lease.		
Cash	73,516	
Lease receivable		73,516
To record the collection of the first payment, annuity-due basis.		

(ii)

December 31, 20x5

Unearned interest revenue	19,648	
Interest revenue		19,648
To accrue interest earned in 20x5.		

(iii)

December 31, 20x8

Unearned interest revenue	1,818	
Interest revenue		1,818
To record interest earned.		
Machine (residual value)	14,000	
Loss on residual value of leased asset	6,000	
Lease receivable		20,000
To record the machine at its residual value at the termination date of the lease.		

Requirement d

December 31, 20x8

Machine (residual value)	20,000	
Lease receivable		20,000

No entry will be made for the $3,000 excess of market value over the estimated residual value (unguaranteed by the lessee). Losses, but not gains, are recognized in these situations when the property reverts to the lessor.

Problem 3

Requirement a

Lessor's computation of the lease payments (annuity due); the residual value is disregarded when there is a bargain purchase option (BPO).

Sale price of the leased asset	$1,400,000
Deduct: present value of bargain purchase option—	
$150,000 (PV1, 15%, 4) = $150,000 × .57175	85,763
Net cost to recover	$1,314,237
Annual payment $1,314,237/(PVAD, 15%, 4) = $1,314,237/3.28323	$ 400,288

Requirement b

(See table, top of next page.)

Requirement c

January 1, 20x5—Inception of the lease:

Lease receivable[a]	1,751,152	
Cost of goods sold	900,000	
Sales revenue		1,400,000
Equipment		900,000
Unearned interest revenue		351,152

[a] $400,288 × 4 = $1,601,152 + $150,000 (BPO) = $1,751,152.

	Annual lease payments	Annual interest @ 15%	Lease receivable (inc.) dec.	Net lease receivable
Jan. 1, 20x5				$1,400,000
Jan. 1, 20x5	$400,288		$ 400,288	999,712
Dec. 31, 20x5		$149,957	(149,957)	1,149,669
Jan. 1, 20x6	400,288		400,288	749,381
Dec. 31, 20x6		112,407	(112,407)	861,788
Jan. 1, 20x7	400,288		400,288	461,500
Dec. 31, 20x7		69,225	(69,225)	530,725
Jan. 1, 20x8	400,288		400,288	130,437
Dec. 31, 20x8		19,563	(19,563)	BPO 150,000

January 1, 20x5 through January 1, 20x8—Receipt of payments:

Cash	400,288	
Lease receivable		400,288

December 31, 20x5 through December 31, 20x8—Recognition of interest revenue:

Unearned interest revenue	149,957	
Interest revenue		149,957

From requirement b, these amounts are:
20x6 = $112,407
20x7 = $ 69,225
20x8 = $ 19,563

December 31, 20x8—Exercise of bargain purchase option (BPO):

Cash   150,000

    Lease receivable   150,000

CASE

You have just started a position as an accounting policy analyst for a company that is thinking of entering into some leasing agreements as an alternative method of selling their equipment. Your first assignment is to review Section 3065 concerning the interest rate to be used in capitalizing leases provided below.

CICA   The discount rate used by the lessee in determining the present value of minimum lease payments would be the lower of the lessee's rate for incremental borrowing and the interest rate implicit in the lease, if practicable to determine.

Interest rate implicit in the lease is defined as the discount rate that, when applied to the minimum lease payments (excluding executory costs) and to the unguaranteed residual value of the property to the lessor, causes the present value at the start of the lease term to equal the market value of the property to the lessor at the inception of the lease. (There are some qualifications to this abstracted definition, but they are not important for present purposes.)

You are asked to write a brief memorandum that addresses each of the following comments:

Evaluate the preceding criterion in light of the following assertions by writing a short explanatory memo to a superior:

1. Asking a lessor what interest rate is inherent in a lease transaction is similar to asking a farmer what rate is implicit in the price the farmer can expect now for next fall's corn crop. There are varying degrees of risk in any operation having a distant future; the higher the farmer's future risks are thought to be, the higher the farmer will set his or her rate, and the lessor will do likewise.
2. In many cases, the assumption that a lease has an implicit interest rate represents circular reasoning, in that the market value of the leased asset itself (that is, the benchmark value used in determining the implicit rate) is determined by market forces. The value of the property stems from the payments it will command rather than from the payments stemming from the value of the property.
3. One determinant of the implicit interest rate in the lease is the residual value of the property to be leased. This is a subjective judgment that, depending on the property, can be substantially in error. Lessors will not disclose what their guess is.

Required
Provide the requested memorandum.

KEY POINTS IN THE CASE

This case should be written as a memorandum.

Requirement 1

There can be different degrees of risk in leasing different kinds of property. For example, a lessor who leases computers is more likely to experience rapid obsolescence of leased property than a lessor who leases jet aircraft. (Both these types of property are leased widely.) Risk does influence aggregate payments charged, but one of the most objectively verifiable measures of risk is the lessor's *implicit rate*, because that is the lease contract rate that the lessee actually will pay. You should examine the lessor's implicit rate and make a good faith estimate if it is not known by the lessee.

Requirement 2

The assertion that using the market value of the property as the benchmark for determining the interest rate implicit in the lease employs circular reasoning is true. If the transfer transaction involved a true installment sale rather than a lease, the sale price of the asset and the periodic installment would be known with certainty. Then the single unknown—the implicit interest rate—   could be determined using the general valuation equation below:

$$\frac{\text{Known}}{\text{Cost to buyer}} = \frac{\text{Known}}{\text{Periodic payments}} \times \frac{\text{Unknown} - [\text{Solve for } i]}{\begin{array}{c}\text{Present value of annuity}\\ \text{at interest rate I}\end{array}}$$

A lease is not a true sale; therefore, the sale price of the asset is not determined with certainty. The result is that there are two unknown values in the valuation equation. To resolve this problem, the market value of the leased asset is used as a surrogate for sale price. Then the equation can be solved for i.

The valuation equation, in mathematical form, states

Sale price = Payments (P/A, interest rate, number of periods)

Thus, for accounting purposes, value is determined by the payments the property can command. In fact, the only reason the interest rate is included in this equation is to restate the future payments in terms of current dollars, for if the payments were all paid in one lump sum at the inception of the lease—and if the lease were substantively a sale of the property the lump sum payment would determine the value of the property in any sale. Based on this reasoning, the second sentence in the assertion is true for purposes of determining accounting values. That is, value stems from payments; payments do not stem from value.

Requirement 3

Accountants and others working with similar quantifiable information must constantly deal with future uncertainties. The uncertainty cited here (future residual value) is probably easier to estimate than many others. Whether a lessor discloses expected residual values does not deceive or confuse other knowledgeable parties as to the probable residual value of the property involved. Lessors have no monopoly on the ownership of such property or on common types of information about it, because they operate in a competitive environment.

SELECTED SOLUTIONS FROM THE TEXTBOOK

Assignment 17-36 (Appendix)

Requirement 1

PV of lease payments: $100,000 (P/AD, 6%, 5) = $100,000 × 4.46511 = $446,511

Year	Outstanding balance	Interest @6%	cash payment	Incr/(Decr) in balance	31 Dec. balance
20x4	446,511	–	100,000	(100,000)	346,511
20x5	346,511	20,791	100,000	(79,209)	267,301
20x6	267,301	16,038	100,000	(83,962)	183,339
20x7	183,339	11,000	100,000	(89,000)	94,340
20x8	94,340	5,660	100,000	(94,340)	0

Requirement 2

Balance sheet:

Equipment under capital lease	$446,511
Accumulated amortization (assuming full year amortization)	(89,302)
	$357,209

Current liability for capital lease*	$100,000
Long-term liability for capital lease	$267,301

   * Payment is due the next day, including both accrued interest
     and principal payment

Income statement:

Amortization expense	$ 89,302
Interest expense (from amortization table)	$ 20,791

Cash flow statement:

Operating activities – non-cash expense add-back: amortization	$ 89,302
Investing activities	
– investment in office equipment ($100,000 – $20,791 interest)	$ 79,209
Financing activities – capital lease payment	$ 79,209

Requirement 3

Yvan Limited entries for 20x5:

2 January 20x5:

Lease liability	100,000	
Cash		100,000

31 December 20x5:

Interest expense	16,038	
Lease liability		16,038
Amortization expense	89,302	
Accumulated amortization – asset under capital lease		89,302

Requirement 4

Jeffrey Leasing Inc. entries for 20x5:

2 January 20x5:

Cash	100,000	
Lease payments receivable		100,000

31 December 20x5:

Unearned finance revenue	16,038	
Finance revenue		16,038

SOLUTIONS TO CONCEPT REVIEW QUESTIONS
Page 1066

1. The two additional guidelines for lessors in the determination of whether a lease is a capital leases are as follows: (1) The credit risk associated with the lease is normal when compared to the risk of collection of similar receivables; and (2) The amounts of any unreimbursable costs that are likely to be incurred by the lessor under the lease can be reasonably estimated.

2. The interest rate used by the lessor in accounting for a capital lease is the rate implicit in the lease. The implicit rate is the rate that discounts the cash flow stream to a net present value that is equal to the cash value of the asset. Lessors may also use the after-tax implicit rate.

3. The lessor includes the amount of the estimated residual value of the lease property in the calculation of the cash flow stream whether it is guaranteed or not.

Page 1067

1. Lessors usually use the gross method of recording leases as it allows the lease receivables account to act as a control account. Since the lease receivable account records leases at their gross value, it allows for an easier reconciliation of lease payments received and total lease payments required under a lease agreement. In short, the gross method is more conducive to effective internal controls.

2. The unearned finance revenue account is contra account to the lease receivable account. It is net against the lease receivable balance and is not shown separately.

Page 1069

1. In general, capital leases are viewed as an in-substance purchase of the asset by the lessee. A sales-type lease is a form of capital lease that, from the lessor's point of view, represents the sale of an item of inventory.

2. It may be difficult to objectively determine the sales price of the asset being "sold," as the actual price is hidden in the leasing transaction. The product sold under a (sales-type) capital lease may be subject to special discounts or deals resulting in the actual price being less than the stated list price.

3. Sales-type leases in Canada are not common in Canada. The income tax act discourages the practice.

CHAPTER 18

PENSIONS AND OTHER POST-RETIREMENT BENEFITS

Post-retirement benefits are a form of deferred compensation. Therefore in order to achieve proper matching the cost should be recognized in the periods the employees is working. Post-retirement benefits are provided in the future which creates measurement problems. The pension benefits are often far in the future which makes it difficult to measure the cost of the benefits. Also, there are several different actuarial methods for measuring and allocating the cost.

The most common form of post-retirement benefit is a pension. Other examples are life insurance and extended health care. This chapter focuses on accounting for pensions because it is the largest component of post-retirement benefits and it is subject to regulations.

Canadian accounting for post-retirement benefits is governed by Section 3461 of the *CICA Handbook*.

1. TYPES OF PENSION PLANS

There are two types of pension plans:
- A **defined contribution plan** is one that specifies the formula used to determine the amount of employer's contributions. No promise is made concerning the future benefits to be received by employees.
- A **defined benefit plan** is one that specifies either the amount of benefits to be received by employees upon retirement, or—much more likely—a formula to be used for determining these benefits.

Figuring out how much the employer should contribute to a pension plan is the task of an **actuary.** An actuary is a person who calculates statistical risks, life expectancy, pay out probabilities, etc.

Summary of the Two Types of Pension Plans

Type of Plan	Contributions	Benefits
Defined contribution	Fixed	Variable
Defined benefit	Variable	Fixed

2. PENSION VARIABLES

Contributory versus Non-contributory

In a **contributory** pension plan, the employee makes contributions to the plan, normally in addition to those made by the employer.

In a **non-contributory** pension plan, the cost of the pension is borne entirely by the employer.

Vested versus Unvested

Pension plan benefits are *vested* when the employee is entitled to receive the benefits even though he or she does not remain an employee of the company until retirement.

Trusteed

An independent *trustee* receives the pension contributions from the employer, invests the contributions, and pays the benefits to the employee.

Trustees of pension funds are financial institutions such as trust companies and banks. A pension trustee is not an individual person. In order for a company to deduct pension plan contributions from taxable income the plan must be trusted. Registration of the plan also requires it to be trusted. There is an important accounting implication of trusteeship. If the plan is trusted its assets are not controlled by the company. Therefore the plan's assets and liabilities are not recorded on the company's financial statements.

Registered

Normally, pensions are *registered* with the pension commissioner in the province of jurisdiction.

An important benefit of registration is that it enables the company to deduct the contributions from taxable income.

3. DEFINED CONTRIBUTION PLANS

Pension accounting for a *defined contribution plan* is relatively easy to deal with. The contribution is readily determinable from the terms of the pension plan. The amount of contribution is treated as an expense on the income statement. The one uncertainty if the benefits do not fully vest at the start of an individual's entry into the plan is the likelihood of the person staying until vesting occurs.

The four components of pension expense are:
- **Current service cost**—employer's required contribution for the period. This is often the only component.
- **Past service cost**—contributions by the employer to a new or amended plan. These cost are relatively uncommon. When they do occur they are normally amortized over the average length of time the employees are expected to continue working for the company.
- **Interest expense on accrued but unpaid contributions**.
- A reduction for the interest income for the year on any unallocated plan surplus.

4. DEFINED BENEFIT PLANS—ACTUARIAL METHODS
Probability Factors
In *defined benefit* plans, the future benefit is known but the annual contributions that are necessary to provide the defined future benefit must be estimated.

Many factors must be taken into consideration when estimating the current cost of the distant benefit. Some of the more important ones are:
- Investment earnings.
- Future salary increases.
- Employee turnover.
- Mortality rates.
- Life expectancy after retirement.

These estimates are made by an actuary. The first 2 are important to auditors as they have a significant impact on the accounting measurements. It is not necessary to use the same assumptions for accounting as are used for funding. For funding purposed actuaries often use conservative estimates. For accounting purposes 'best estimates' should be used.

Funding versus Accounting

Funding refers to the manner in which the employer calculates the necessary contributions to the plan. It is important to keep accounting separate from funding.

Funding Approaches

There are three basic methods for calculating the cash contributions a company must make in order to provide for the defined pension benefits:

- **Accumulated benefit methods** calculates the contributions that an employer must make in order to fund the pension to which the employee currently is entitled, based on years of service to date and on current salary. This method results in the lowest degree of projections.

- **Projected benefit method** calculates the required funding based on the years of service to date on a projected estimate of the employee's salary at the retirement date.
- **Level contribution method** projects both the final salary and the total years of service, and then allocates the cost evenly over the years of service. This method results in the highest degree of projections.

5. BASIC EXAMPLE

The three methods are illustrated in the textbook. All of the methods result in full funding over the years of service but the allocations patterns are very different. Pension calculations are highly method-sensitive; and even within methods, there can be extreme fluctuations in the results.

The AcSB addresses this issue by recommending that **best estimate assumptions** be used in performing actuarial valuations for accounting purposes.

GAAP requires that the projected benefit method be used to account for current pension costs.
Differences Between Funding and Accounting Costs
Current service cost. The annual costs for providing the pension entitlement that is earned in each year. Note that *current service cost is only one component of pension expense.*

The difference between the accounting expense and the amount of cash contributed to the pension plan accumulates in either the **deferred pension liability** (credit balance) or the **deferred pension cost** (debit balance).

Interpreting the Liability

A credit balance in the deferred pension liability account does not mean the plan is underfunded. It is an a result of the accounting treatment. The level of funding is based on the actuarial funding method used.

6. PENSION EXPENSE—LIST OF COMPONENTS

There are 10 components of pension expense. There are five continuing components that will always exist or are likely to exist and five special components that arise under special circumstances.

CONTINUING COMPONENTS		SPECIAL COMPONENTS
1. Current service cost		1. Amortization of the transitional obligation (or asset)
Plus	Minus	
2. Interest on accumulated accrued benefit obligation		2. Any change to the valuation allowance for pension plan assets
3. Amortization of past service cost from plan imitation or amendment		3. Gain or loss on the plan's settlement or curtailment
	4. Expected earnings on plan assets	4. Any expense recognized for termination benefits
5. Minus amortization of excess actuarial gain	5. Amortization of excess actuarial loss	5. Any amount recognized as a result of a temporary deviation from the plan.

7. CONTINUING COMPONENTS

1. Current service cost—the basic measurement of pension cost. Section 3461.034 recommends current service cost be measured using the projected benefit method.

2. *Plus:* Interest on the accrued benefit obligation. The accrued benefit obligation is the present value of the post-retirement benefits employees have earned to date. Section 3461.050(a) recommends the rate be based on "high-quality debt

instruments with cash flows that match the timing and amount of expected benefit payments."

3. *Minus:* Expected earnings on plan assets. The expected earnings are based on the expected long-term rate of return [*CICA* 3461.076], multiplied by the weighted average of the value of the plan assets, fair value or market-related value, at the balance sheet date. Some companies use actual rather than estimated plan earnings.

4. *Plus:* Amortization of past service cost from *plan initiation.* **Past service cost (PSC)** is the obligation resulting from employees' pension entitlement for their employment prior to the initiation of the pension plan. The cost is an incentive for current and future service and therefore retroactive adjustment is not appropriate. The past service cost is amortized on a straight-line basis over the expected period to full eligibility [*CICA* 3461.079] of employee group.

Plus: Amortization of past service cost from *plan amendments.* **Past service cost (PSC)** is the liability that arises from plan amendments to increase benefits either as the result of collective bargaining or to remedy purchasing power erosion that has occurred due to inflation. There are two options for amortization: (1) amortize on the same basis as PSC plan initiation [*CICA* 3461.079]; or (2) amortize over the period to the next expected plan amendment. [*CICA* 3461.082]

5. *Plus* (or *minus*): Amortization of *excess* actuarial loss (gain). Estimates may require adjusting as a result of two sources of error:
   a. **Experience gains or losses:** Gains or losses that arise because recent experience is different from the assumptions made.
   b. **Changes in assumptions:** Changes in the assumptions about the future that underlie the calculation of the accrued pension obligation.

   Under the 10% corridor method, a company is *required* to include amortization of actuarial gains and losses only to the extent that the accumulated amount of actuarial gains and losses exceeds 10% of the *greater* of:
   (i) the accrued obligation at the beginning of the year, or
   (ii) the value of the plan assets at the beginning of the year.

These five components are the main focus of our examples.

8. EXTENDED ILLUSTRATION

An extended illustration, covering a four-year period, is provided in the textbook on pages 1113 to 1120.

EXAMPLE

Assume the following:

		20x1	20x2	20x3
1.	Projected benefit obligation			
	a. Beginning balance	$1,500	$1,550	$1,620
	b. Ending balance	1,550	1,620	1,950
2.	Plan assets (fair value)			
	a. Beginning balance	1,000	1,190	1,350
	b. Ending balance	1,190	1,350	1,460
3.	Current service cost	180	200	240
4.	Past service cost	–0–	–0–	180
5.	Experience loss (gain)			
	a. Actual return on plan assets	120	110	160
	b. (Decrease) increase in the accrued pension obligations	(100)	–0–	130
6.	Employer's contributions	250	335	350
7.	Benefits paid to retirees	180	285	400
8.	Additional information			
	a. Interest (settlement) rate			10%
	b. Expected return rate			10%
	c. Amortization policies:			
	i. Past service cost amortized over			9 years
	ii. Experience losses or gains			10 years

Calculate the pension expense and record journal entries related to the pension plan.

Prepare a pension plan spreadsheet for the three-year period.

SOLUTION

Year 20x1:
Pension expense is the sum of the following:

Current service costs	$180
Interest @ 10% on beginning-of-year accrued obligation	150
Expected earnings on plan assets ($1,000 × 10%)	(100)
	$230

The entry to record the expense will be as follows:

Pension expense	230	
Deferred pension cost/liability		230

The entry to record the $250 cash payment to the trustee is:

Deferred pension cost/liability	250	
Cash		250

Accrued pension obligation:

Accrued obligation, beginning of 20x1	$1,500
Interest on beginning obligation, @ 10%	150
Current service cost for 20x1	180
Actuarial revaluation	(100)
Benefit payments	(180)
	$1,550

The year end value of the plan assets:

Value of plan assets, beginning of 20x1	$1,000
Actual earnings on plan assets, 20x1	120
Funding contributions, end of year	250
Benefit payments	(180)
Value of plan assets, end of 20x1	$1,190

Spreadsheet for 20x1:

	Memorandum Accounts				Statement Accounts	
				Unrecognized		
	Pension obligation	Plan assets	Actuarial G/L	PSC	Pension expense	Deferred cost (liab)
20x1						
Opening balance	$(1,500)	$1,000				$(500)
Service costs	(180)				180	
Interest	(150)				150	
Expected return			100		(100)	
Actual return		120	(120)			
Actuarial revaluation	100		(100)			
Funding contribution		250				250
Benefit payments	180	(180)				
					230	(230)
Ending balance	$(1,550)	$1,190	$(120)			$(480)

Year 20x2:

At the beginning of 20x2, there is an unamortized experience gain of $120. The corridor test must be applied to this amount to see whether any amortization is needed in 20x2. Amortization is not necessary if the unamortized actuarial gain is less than 10% of the higher of the beginning-of-year accrued obligation
and the beginning-of-year pension plan assets:

	Total	10%
Accrued pension obligation	$1,550	$155
Value of pension plan assets	$1,190	$119

The unamortized actuarial gain of $120 is below the 10% limit of $155, and therefore no amortization is necessary.

Pension expense is the sum of the following:

Current service cost	$200
Interest @ 10% on the beginning-of-year accrued obligation	$155
Expected earnings on plan assets ($1,190 × 10%)	(119)
	$236

The entry to record the expense will be as follows:

Pension expense	236	
Deferred pension cost/liability		236

The entry to record the $335 cash payment to the trustee is:

Deferred pension cost/liability	335	
Cash		335

Accrued pension obligation:	
Accrued obligation, beginning of 20x2	$1,550
Interest on beginning obligation, @ 10%	155
Current service cost for 20x2	200
Benefit payments	(285)
	$1,620

The year end value of the plan assets:

Value of plan assets, beginning of 20x2	$1,190
Actual earnings on plan assets, 20x2	110
Funding contributions, end of 20x2	335
Benefit payments, end of 20x2	(285)
	$1,350

Spreadsheet for 20x2:

	Memorandum Accounts				Statement Accounts	
			Unrecognized			
	Pension obligation	Plan assets	Actuarial G/L	PSC	Pension expense	Deferred cost (liab)
20x2						
Opening balance	$(1,550)	$1,190	$(120)			$(480)
Service cost	(200)				200	
Interest	(155)				155	
Expected return			119		(119)	
Actual return		110	(110)			
Funding contribution		335				335
Benefit payments	285	(285)				
					236	(236)
Ending balance	$(1,620)	$1,350	$(111)			$(381)

Year 20x3:

A corridor test must be applied for the unrecognized actuarial gain of $111.

	Total	10%
Accrued pension obligation	$1,620	$162
Value of pension plan assets	1,350	135

The unamortized actuarial gain is less than the 10% limit; therefore, no amortization is necessary. The calculation of pension expense is as follows:

Current service cost	$ 240
Past service cost amortization ($180/9)	20
Interest on accrued obligation, beginning of year ($1,800 × 10%)	180
Expected earnings on plan assets ($1,350 × 10%)	(135)
	$ 305

The entry to record the expense is as follows:

Pension expense	305	
Deferred pension cost/liability		305

The entry to record the $350 cash payment to the trustee is:

Deferred pension cost/liability	350	
Cash		350

Accrued pension obligation:	
Accrued obligation, beginning of 20x3	$1,620
Past service cost	180
Interest on beginning obligation, @ 10%	180
Current service cost for 20x3	240
Actuarial revaluation	130
Benefit payments	(400)
	$1,950

The year end value of the plan assets:	
Value of plan assets, beginning of 20x3	$1,350
Actual earnings on plan assets, 20x3	160
Funding contributions, end of year	350
Benefit payments	(400)
	$1,460

Spreadsheet for 20x3:

	Memorandum Accounts				Statement Accounts	
			Unrecognized			
	Pension obligation	Plan assets	Actuarial G/L	PSC	Pension expense	Deferred cost (liab)
20x3						
Opening balance	$(1,620)	$1,350	$(111)			$(381)
Past service cost	(180)			180		
Adjusted beginning balance	$(1,800)					
Service cost	(240)				240	
Interest	(180)				180	
Expected return			135		(135)	
Actual return		160	(160)			
Actuarial revaluation	(130))		130			
Funding contribution		350				350
Benefit payments	400	(400)				
Amortization of PSC				(20)	20	
					305	(305)
Ending balance	$(1,950)	$1,460	$ (6)	$160		$(336)

9. SPECIAL COMPONENTS OF PENSION EXPENSE

Transitional Amortization

When Section 3461 came into effect in 2000 companies had to make two types of accounting changes for pension accounting and post-retirement benefits other than pensions. The net amount of these changes is called the transitional balance. The change in accounting policy could be made prospectively which would require amortization of this balance.

Valuation Allowance for Pension Plan Assets

When cash paid out exceeds the accounting accrual for the obligation a deferred pension cost will be recorded as an asset. As with other assets this asset must be reviewed to ensure it is not overvalued. If it is overvalued a valuation allowance is required. The valuation allowance is charged against pension expense for the period. All increases or decreases flow through pension expense. The valuation allowance requirement is complex and controversial.

Gains and Losses on Plan Settlements and Curtailments

When a plan is ended, it is **settled.** The obligation to the pensionable group is settled by transferring assets to the trustee, and any deficiencies in funding are remedied. The plan has been **curtailed** when there is a partial settlement of a plan due to the closing down of a division or an otherwise significant restructuring or downsizing of operations, and the plan continues but has significantly fewer persons in the eligible employee group. Gains and losses from settlements or curtailments are recognized immediately. Depending on the circumstances they may be classified as discontinued operations or part of costs of restructuring.

Termination Benefits

Enhanced retirement offers are called **special termination benefits.** These costs are expensed immediately. Depending on the circumstances they may be classified as discontinued part of costs of restructuring.

Temporary Deviations From the Plan

Any amount immediately recognized as a result of a *temporary deviation* from the plan. This pertains primarily to benefits other than pension plans, such as extended health care. These costs are charged to income immediately.

10. PAYMENT OF BENEFITS

Benefit payments are the responsibility of the pension plan (trustee), not the employer.

11. CASH FLOW STATEMENT

On the cash flow statement, the adjustment from pension expense to pension cash flow is incorporated into the general adjustment for "non-cash items."

---

12. DISCLOSURE REQUIREMENTS

Disclosure on the financial statements is limited to:

- Income statements – the amount of expense
- Balance Sheet –net deferred pension cost or liability

Disclosure is important to users of the statements.

Basic disclosure should include important accounting policies and measurements.

AcSB recommends the following accounting policy disclosure:
- The amortization basis for past service costs.
- The method chosen to recognize actuarial gains and losses and the period for amortization.
- The valuation method for plan assets.

The measurement disclosures include:
- The amount of deferred pension cost or accrued pension liability on balance sheet.
- A reconciliation of the pension amounts to the balance sheet account.
- The amount of expense recognized for period, and the components of the expense.
- The actuarial present value of accrued pension benefits.
- The fair value of the pension plan assets.
- The resulting plan deficit or surplus.
- The amount of funding contributions made by the company during the period.
- The amount of contributions by employees.
- The amount of benefits paid.
- Important measurement variables.
- For public companies only, the effect of a 1% change in health care costs trends.

TRUE–FALSE QUESTIONS

T F 1. Pension expense is recognized only when pension benefits are paid to retired employees.

T F 2. A defined pension plan is a plan that specifies either the amount of benefits to be paid upon employees' retirement or a formula used for determining these benefits.

T F 3. A projected benefit obligation is the actuarial present value of all the benefits attributed to employee's service on the basis of current salary levels.

T F 4. To determine periodic pension expense, all of the five continuing components have to be amortized over the expected future service years of participating employees.

T F 5. The interest cost component of pension expense is generally calculated by multiplying the beginning balance of projected benefit obligation by the actuary's discount rate.

T F 6. The accumulated benefit method is required by GAAP to calculate pension expense.

T F 7. The difference between actual return and the expected return on plan assets may be combined with gains and losses from assumption changes for possible future amortization to pension expense.

T F 8. The employer must recognize as a liability an amount equal to the excess of projected benefit obligation over the fair value of pension plan assets.

T F 9. Past service cost is amortized over the average remaining service life of employees, beginning in the year *after* the prior service cost arises.

T F 10. In accounting for additional pension liability, if the additional pension liability exceeds the unrecognized past service cost, the excess should be reported as an unrealized pension cost.

MULTIPLE CHOICE QUESTIONS

___ 1. Which of the following is not relevant for the calculation of periodic pension expense?
a. Current year's contribution to pension plan.
b. Projected benefit obligation.
c. Pension plan assets.
d. Expected rate of return on pension plan assets.

___ 2. Which of the following is not normally a component of periodic pension expense?
a. Service cost.
b. Interest cost on accumulated benefit obligation.
c. Expected return on pension plan assets.
d. Actual return on pension plan assets.

___ 3. Which of the following is not relevant to the calculation of additional pension liability?
a. Current year's contribution to pension plan.
b. Projected benefit obligation.
c. Accrued pension expense.
d. Market-related value of pension plan assets.

___ 4. The pension expense reported by a company will be increased by interest cost when:
a. projected benefit obligation exists at the beginning of the year.
b. amounts funded are greater than pension cost accrued.
c. pension plan asset exists at the beginning of the year.

d. the plan is fully vested.

___ 5. In the computation of pension expense, which of the following components is likely to be *negative* (i.e., to reduce pension expense)?
  a. Service cost.
  b. Interest cost.
  c. Amortization of past service cost.
  d. Amortization of net asset gain.

___ 6. Costs related to a new pension plan that are necessary to "catch up" for services rendered prior to the inception of the pension plan are classified as:
  a. actuarial losses.
  b. past service costs.
  c. retroactive deferred charge.
  d. service costs.

___ 7. Current service cost for 20x5 for a pension plan whose pension benefit formula considers estimates of future compensation level is:
  a. The present value of benefits earned by employees in 20x5 based on current salary levels.
  b. The increase in accrued pension obligation for 20x5 less interest cost on the beginning balance in the accrued pension obligation.
  c. The nominal value of benefits earned by employees in 20x5 based on future salary levels.
  d. The present value of benefits earned by employees in 20x5 based on future salary levels.

___ 8. The following statements describe some aspect of accounting for defined benefit pension plans. Choose the *incorrect* statement.
  a. A gain caused by a plan settlement is reported as part of the discontinued operations section when it is the result of ceasing to operate in a distinct operation.
  b. Past service cost from plan amendments must be amortized over the expected period to full eligibility.
  c. Because several components of pension expense are derived from amortizing initial present values on a straight-line or similar basis, the true total cost of these items is not reflected in pension expense.
  d. Pension expense can be negative.

___ 9. Defined contribution plans and defined benefit plans are two common types of pension plans. Choose the *correct* statement concerning these plans.
  a. The required annual contribution to the plan is determined by a formula or contract in a defined contribution plan.
  b. Both plans provide the same retirement benefits.
  c. The retirement benefit is usually determinable well before retirement in a defined contribution plan.

      d. In both types of plans, pension expense is generally the amount funded during the year.

_____ **10.** Which of the following is never one of the five continuing components of pension expense (or part of a component)?
a. Amortization of excess actuarial gain or loss.
b. Expected return on plan assets.
c. Amount paid to the pension trustee for current service during the period.
d. Growth (interest cost) in accrued pension obligation since the beginning of the period.

SOLUTIONS TO TRUE–FALSE QUESTIONS

1. F Pension expense is a cost related to current services; therefore, it is a present cost.

2. T

3. F There are many factors in addition to current salary levels. A few of the more important ones: investment earnings, future inflation rates, future salary increases, employee turnover, mortality rates, and life expectancy after retirement.

4. F The only components that have to be amortized are past service cost from plan start-up or plan amendment and the excess actuarial loss (gain).

5. T

6. F GAAP requires the projected benefit method.

7. T

8. T

9. F Past service cost is amortized over the average remaining service life of employees, beginning in the year the past service cost arises, not the year after.

10. T

SOLUTIONS TO MULTIPLE CHOICE QUESTIONS

1. a Current year's contribution to pension plan is recorded in the memorandum accounts. The journal entry to record the cash contributed to the pension plan will accumulate in the **deferred pension liability/cost.**

2. d The difference between the actual return and the expected return is an experience gain. Experience gains and losses relate to the past. A company is required to include amortization of actuarial gains and losses only to the extent that the accumulated amount of actuarial gains and losses exceeds 10% of the greater of (1) the accrued obligation or (2) the value of the plan assets (10% corridor method).

3. b The accrued obligation is the total present value of the pension entitlements to date for the employee group. Its balance is kept in a memorandum account, not in the general ledger. Current year's contribution to pension plan is debited to the deferred pension liability/cost account. Accrued pension expense is credited to the deferred pension

---

liability/cost account. Market-related value of pension plan asset results in an experience gain or loss and may be amortized in the future.

4. a Interest cost is calculated by multiplying projected benefit obligation at the beginning of the year by the discount rate.

5. d Any gain reduces the expense, so if the net asset gain is amortized it will have a negative effect on pension expense.

6. b When a pension plan is started, employees normally are given pension entitlements for their employment prior to the initiation of the plan. This beginning obligation is known as the **past service cost (PSC).**

7. d Current service cost uses a nominal value and is based on future salary levels.

8. b Past service costs from plan amendments can be amortized over the period to the next amendment as well.

9. a All the other statements are incorrect.

10. c The funding is separate from the accounting for pension expense.

PROBLEMS

Problem 1

PURPOSE: To illustrate the use of the spreadsheet as a procedural aid in calculating pension expense and in keeping track of (1) pension plan assets, (2) the accrued pension obligation, and (3) unrecognized pension costs.

The following information has been provided for Thomas Ltd. for the year ended December 31, 20x5:

Pension benefit obligation, January 1, 20x5	$634,000
Plan assets (fair value), January 1, 20x5	430,000
Unamortized past service cost, January 1, 20x5	100,000
Deferred pension cost/liability, January 1, 20x5 (cr.)	104,000
Current service costs	29,000
Expected rate of return on assets and interest on obligations	8%
Actual return on plan assets	40,000
Amortization of past service cost	10,000
Annual contribution, at year end	65,000
Benefits paid to retirees,	34,000
Decrease in pension obligation due to changes in actuarial assumptions as of December 31, 20x5	26,000
EPFE & EARSL	20 years

Required

Prepare the spreadsheet that summarizes relevant pension data for 20x5. As part of the spreadsheet, calculate pension expense and the related balance sheet deferred cost/liability for 20x5.

Problem 2

PURPOSE: To illustrate the spreadsheet approach in a year when there is an unamortized actuarial gain/loss at the beginning of the year.

Use the information calculated in question 1 for Thomas Ltd. and the following data for year 20x6:

Current service cost	$45,000
Expected rate of return on assets and interest on obligations	8%
Actual return on plan assets	42,000
Amortization of past service cost	10,000
Annual contribution, at year end	71,000
Benefits paid to retirees	37,000
Increase in pension obligation due to changes in actuarial assumptions as of December 31, 20x6	12,000
EPFE & EARSL	20 years

Required

Prepare the spreadsheet that summarizes relevant pension data for 20x6. As part of the spreadsheet, calculate pension expense and the related balance sheet deferred cost/liability for 20x6.

Problem 3

PURPOSE: To show the disclosure requirements for pension plans.
Use the information in question 2. In Thomas Ltd's December 31, 20x6, balance sheet, income statement, and notes to financial statements, what appears in relation to the pension?

SOLUTIONS TO PROBLEMS

Problem 1

PENSION PLAN SPREADSHEET

	Memorandum Accounts				Statement Accounts	
	Pension obligation Dr. (cr.)	Value of plan assets	Unamort Actuarial G/L	PSC	Pension expense	Deferred cost (liability)
20x5						
Beginning balance	$(634,000)	$430,000		$100,000		cr. 104,000
Service cost	(29,000)				dr. 29,000	
Interest obligation	(50,720)				dr. 50,720	
Actual return		40,000	(40,000)			
Expected return			34,400			
PSC amortization					cr. 34,400	
Benefits paid	34,000	(34,000)		(10,000)	dr. 10,000	
Actuarial valuation	26,000		(26,000)			
					dr.55,320	cr.(55,320)
Funding		65,000				dr. 65,000
Ending balance	$(653,720)	$(501,000)	$(31,600)	$90,000		$94,320

Pension expense for 20x5:

Current service cost	$29,000
Interest @ 8% on beginning-of-year accrued obligation	50,720
Amortization PSC given	10,000
Expected earnings on plan assets ($430,000 × 8%)	(34,400)
	$55,320

The entries for these amounts are as follows:

Pension expense	55,320	
Deferred pension cost/liability		55,320
Deferred pension cost/liability	65,000	
Cash		65,000

The accrued pension obligation at the end of 20x5 is:

Accrued obligation, beginning of 20x5	$634,000
Interest on beginning obligation, @ 8%	50,720
Current service cost for 20x5	29,000
Benefits paid to retirees in 20x5	(34,000)
Actuarial revaluation	(26,000)
	$653,720

The year end value of the plan assets is:

Value of plan assets, beginning of 20x5	$430,000
Actual earnings on plan assets, 20x5	40,000
Funding contributions, end of year	65,000
Benefits paid to retirees	(34,000)
	$501,000

The cumulative year end unamortized actuarial gains/losses are:

Accumulated actuarial gain (from revaluation of obligations plus high return on plan assets)	$ 31,600

The accumulated actuarial gain is comprised of actuarial revaluation of $26,000 decrease in obligation plus experience gains arising from strong earnings on the plan assets: ($40,000 – $34,400 = $5,600).

There is no amortization taken on this in the year that the gain or loss arises. Amortization may begin next year but the company can choose to amortize this gain in the current year.

The memorandum accounts are not entered anywhere in the general ledger. The ending balances in the pension obligation and plan assets must be disclosed in the notes to the financial statements related to the pension plan.

Problem 2

PENSION PLAN SPREADSHEET

	Memorandum Accounts				Statement Accounts	
	Pension obligation Dr. (cr.)	Value of plan assets	Unamort. Actuarial G/L	PSC	Pension expense	Deferred cost (liability)
20x6						
Beginning balance	$(653,720)	$501,000	(31,600)	$ $90,000		cr. 94,320
Service cost	(45,000)				dr. 45,000	
Interest obligation	(52,298)				dr. 52,298	
Actual return		42,000	(42,000)			
Expected return			40,080		cr. 40,080	
PSC amortization				(10,000)	dr. 10,000	
Benefit paid	37,000	(37,000)				
Actuarial valuation	(12,000)		12,000			
					dr. 67,218	cr.(67,218)
Funding		71,000				dr. 71,000
Ending balances	$(726,018)	$577,000	$(21,520)	$ 80,000		$ (90,538)

Pension expense for 20x6:

Current service cost	$ 45,000
Interest @ 8% on beginning-of-year accrued obligation	52,298
Amortization PSC given	10,000
Expected earnings on plan assets	(40,080)
	$67,218

The entries for these amounts are as follows:

Pension expense	67,218	
Deferred pension cost/liability		67,218
Deferred pension cost/liability	71,000	
Cash		71,000

The accrued pension obligation at the end of 20x6:

Accrued obligation, beginning of 20x6	$653,720
Interest on beginning obligation @ 8%	52,298
Current service cost for 20x6	45,000
Benefits paid to retirees in 20x6	(37,000)
Actuarial valuation	12,000
	$726,018

The year end value of the plan assets is:

Value of plan assets, beginning of 20x6	$501,000
Actual earnings on plan assets, 20x6	42,000
Funding contributions, end of year	71,000
Benefits paid to retirees	(37,000)
	$577,000

The cumulative year end unamortized actuarial gains/losses are:

Accumulated actuarial gain (from revaluation of obligations plus high return on plan assets)	$21,520

The accumulated actuarial gain is comprised of a beginning balance of $31,600 *less* an actuarial revaluation of $12,000 increase in obligation and *plus* experience gains arising from strong earnings on the plan assets: $42,000 – $40,080 = $1,920.

At the beginning of 20x5, there was an unamortized actuarial gain of $31,600. A corridor test must be applied to this amount to see whether any amortization is needed for 20x6. Amortization is not necessary if the unamortized actuarial gain is less than 10% of the higher of the beginning-of-year accrued obligation and the beginning-of-year pension plan assets:

	Total	10%
Accrued pension obligation	$653,720	$65,372
Value of pension plan assets	501,000	50,100

The unamortized actuarial gain of $31,600 is well below the 10% limit of $65,372, and therefore no amortization is necessary. Remember that the company can choose to amortize this gain.

Problem 3

The only pension amount that directly affects the balance sheet is net deferred pension cost or liability that reflects the difference between the accumulated accounting expense and the accumulated funding.

There are no requirements in the *CICA Handbook's* Section 3461 to disclose either the pension expense or the prepaid/. deferred pension credit separately.

Balance sheet:
If the amount of deferred pension liability is material, it should be reported separately, because it is useful to the users of the financial statements.

Deferred pension liability		$90,538
20x5: ($104,000 + $55,320 − $65,000)	$94,320	
20x6: ($67,218 − $71,000)	(3,782)	
	$90,538	

If the amount is not material, the deferred pension liability will probably be grouped with other liabilities or other deferred credits. Other deferred credits, because of their nature, will be part of long-term liabilities.

Income statement:
If the amount is material, the pension expense should be shown separately on the income statement.

Pension expense	$67,218

If the amount is not material, the pension expense will probably be grouped with payroll costs on the income statement.

Notes to the financial statements:
The notes should disclose the net amount separately for:
- Pension plans.
- Other post-retirement benefits.

AcSB recommends the following accounting policy disclosure:

- The amortization period for past service costs.
- The method chosen to recognize actuarial gains and losses and the period for amortization.
- The valuation method for plan assets.

The measurement disclosures include:
- The amount of deferred pension cost or accrued pension liability on balance sheet.
- The amount of expense recognized for period.
- The actuarial present value of accrued pension benefits.
- The fair value of the pension plan assets.
- The resulting plan deficit or surplus.
- The amount of funding contributions made by the company during the period.
- The amount of contributions by employees.
- The amount of benefits paid.
- Important measurement variables.

CASE

You are the senior auditor for the audit of a client firm in considerable financial difficulty. In particular, debt covenants may be violated if liabilities are increased. In addition, the client's balance in retained earnings is minimal as a result of excessively high dividends and diminished earnings in the past several years.

The client firm is dominated by its CEO, a person who has worked up the corporate ladder and has served the firm for 30 years. The CEO makes most of the major decisions in the firm. This person is the firm's primary representative working with the audit staff. At present, there is no organized audit committee. The CEO is very aggressive with respect to earnings.

From the minutes, you have discovered that extreme emphasis has been placed on meeting earnings projections. Department officers have been fired for not meeting earnings goals for two successive years. The firm uses FIFO, straight-line amortization, and other accounting techniques that reduce or delay expense recognition. The firm has resisted using the installment sales method for customers with questionable credit ratings.

Per the *CICA Handbook's* Section 5135, "Auditor's Responsibility to Consider Fraud and Error," you know that part of your responsibility as an auditor is to develop an audit plan that is sensitive to audit risk. Audit risk is the probability that you may unknowingly fail to modify your audit report on financial statements that are materially misstated. Your audit plan should be designed to provide reasonable assurance that material errors and irregularities are detected.

Required

You understand that the pressures faced by this firm may create incentives for unethical and fraudulent financial reporting. What aspects of pension accounting should you inspect with special care? What pension-related variables may have been changed, and in what direction, to achieve reduced pension expense and liabilities? Include in your discussion reasons why you chose these variables.

KEY POINTS IN THE CASE

There are several factors to consider before focusing on pensions. The firm is an inherently risky audit client. There will be considerable pressure to manage earnings and the balance sheet to obtain financial results that lower the firm's perceived risk. Shareholders may be accustomed to the increased dividends. The CEO will try to meet the debt covenants however possible so that the bank loan will not be due.

In addition, the domineering personality of the CEO creates a climate in which certain ethical violations may be produced. For example, accounting and financial staff may be requested to misstate the company's financial position or earnings. Their employment may be indirectly or directly affected by their responses. There is a history of extreme preoccupation with reported earnings and this suggests that all areas of accounting have been scrutinized for ways to increase earnings. Pensions is an area fraught with variables that can be manipulated to such an effect.

One accounting ethical standard states that accountants should not actively or passively subvert the attainment of the organization's legitimate and ethical objectives. Another requires that unfavourable as well as favourable information be communicated. In the type of environment exemplified by this client, the auditor must be particularly careful. Ethical behaviour by management is of particular importance to internal control and the resulting representations in the financial statements.

In the pensions area, the following variables or factors should be examined carefully by the auditor, to the extent possible: discount rate, expected turnover, expected future compensation levels, expected retirement age, expected life expectancy, expected long-term rate of return on plan assets, and the number of years chosen to amortize unrecognized pension items. The CEO may be particularly worried about underfunded PBO, the resulting minimum liability disclosure, and the possible effect on debt covenants.

For example, slight increases in the trend of the discount rate, which may be changed yearly, can have a tremendous reducing effect on PBO. Furthermore, service cost, the primary component of pension expense, can be similarly reduced, and swamp the minor increase in interest cost.

The auditor should also discuss with the actuary any changes in underlying actuarial assumptions made recently, or whether there has been a trend in a particular direction. If changes have been made, evidence of corroboration with current events should be requested. For example, the following changes in estimates will be favoured by a CEO interested in decreasing pension expense and liabilities: increased turnover, decreased future compensation levels, increase in the general retirement age, and decrease in life expectancy.

These changes will decrease service costs and PBO through a reduction in future benefits.

Related to these changes is the practice of regular actuarial gains. If changes in the above variables have been frequent, they should be supported by frequent actuarial gains. Does the firm use shorter service periods to amortize unrecognized gains than unrecognized losses? Does the company calculate the corridor test for the minimum amortization?

In addition, the long-term expected rate of return may have been increased. This decreases pension expense. The auditor should be aware of the composition of plan assets. If a significant portion is represented by real estate and other assets that are not traded regularly, market values should be audited.

Although the actuary provides many of these values, the actuary must work together with the firm (in this case, the CEO) to derive them. It is likely that the CEO will attempt to provide information that will support his agenda. Increases and increases in expected rates of return are disclosed in the footnotes to the financial statements. Small percentage changes may not be noticed if spread over several years.

SELECTED SOLUTIONS FROM THE TEXTBOOK

Assignment 18-5

Requirement 1

To record 20x6 pension expense

Pension expense ($165,000 + $15,000 − $18,000)	162,000	
Deferred pension cost	23,000	
Cash		185,000

Requirement 2

Deferred pension cost   <u>$43,000</u>

20x5: ($170,000 − $150,000)	$20,000	
20x6: (above)	<u>23,000</u>	
	$<u>43,000</u>	

Assignment 18-15

Requirement 1

Pension expense, 20x5

Current service cost..	$ 14,000
Amortization of PSC ($20,000/10)	2,000
Interest cost ($60,000 x .08)...	4,800
Expected earnings..	(4,000)
Experience gain amortization	(267)
Gain on plan curtailment..	(18,000)
Pension expense (negative)	$(1,467)

Corridor test:

Experience gain, 1 January	$10,000
Obligation x 10% ($60,000 x 10%)....................................	(6,000)
Excess	4,000
Amortization ($4,000 / 15)	$267 (gain)

Entries:

Deferred pension cost/liability..	1,467	
Pension expense		1,467
Deferred pension cost/liability..	16,000	
Cash		16,000

Requirement 2

Pension expense, 20x5

Current service cost..	$ 14,000
Amortization of PSC ($20,000/10)	2,000
Interest cost ($60,000 x .08)...	4,800
Expected earnings..	(4,000)
Experience gain ($4,000 - $6,000)	(2,000)
Gain on plan curtailment..	(18,000)
Pension expense (negative)	$(3,200)

Note that this is equivalent to including actual return ($6,000 = $4,000 + $2,000) in pension expense.

Entries:

Deferred pension cost/liability..	3,200	
Pension expense		3,200
Deferred pension cost/liability..	16,000	
Cash		16,000

Assignment 18-18

Requirement 1

Pension expense, 20x5
Current service cost	$67,000
Past service cost ($200,000/14)	14,286
Interest, opening liability ($200,000 x .05)	10,000
Total expense	$91,286
Deferred pension cost ($99,500 - $91,286)	$8,214

Requirement 2

Pension Plan Spreadsheet

		Memorandum Accounts			Statement Accounts	
	Pension Obligation	Plan Assets	Unrecognized Actuarial G/L	PSC	Pension Expense	Deferred Cost (Liab)
20x5						
Beginning	($200,000)	0	0	200,000		
CSC	(67,000)				$67,000	
Interest	(10,000)				10,000	
PSC Amort				(14,286)	14,286	
					$91,286	($91,286)
Funding		99,500				99,500
	($277,000)	$99,500	0	$185,714		$8,214

Assignment 18-27

	Memorandum Accounts				Statement Accounts	
			Unrecognized			
	Pension Obligation	Plan Assets	Actuarial G/L	PSC	Pension Expense	Deferred Cost (Liab)
20x6 - Opening	($369,758)	$191,800	$14,920	$194,400		$31,362
CSC	(65,000)				$65,000	
Interest*	(22,185)				22,185	
PSC Amort				(10,800)	10,800	
Fund– 31 Dec**		80,000				80,000
Exp.earnings***			11,508		(11,508)	
Actual earnings		12,610	(12,610)		$86,477	(86,477)
Benefits paid	12,000	(12,000)				
Assumptions	5,000		(5,000)			
	($439,943)	$272,410	$8,818	$183,600		$24,885

Corridor test: $14,920 vs 10% of $369,758. No amortization.

* $369,758 x .06

** $65,000 + $20,000 – $5,000   *** $191,800 x .06

20x7						
Opening	($439,943)	$272,410	$8,818	$183,600		$24,885
CSC	(72,000)				$72,000	
Interest*	(26,397)				26,397	
PSC Amort				(10,800)	10,800	
Fund– 31 Dec**		92,000				92,000
Benefits paid	23,000	(23,000)				
Exp.earnings***			16,345		(16,345)	(92,852)
Actual earnings		11,440	(11,440)		$92,852	
	$(515,340)	$352,850	$13,723	$172,800		$24,033

Corridor test: $8,818 vs 10% of $439,943. No amortization.

* $439,943 x .06   *** $272,410 x .06

** $20,000 + $72,000

Requirement 2

20x6:

Pension expense	86,477	
Deferred pension cost		86,477
Deferred pension cost	80,000	
Cash		80,000

20x7:

Pension expense	92,852	
Deferred pension cost		92,852
Deferred pension cost	92,000	
Cash		92,000

SOLUTIONS TO CONCEPT REVIEW QUESTIONS

Page 1101

1. Examples of post-retirement benefits other than pensions include extended health care and dental care.

2. A *defined contribution pension plan is* one in which the employer (often the employee as well) makes agreed upon cash contributions. The pension the employee actually receives is a function of the investment success of the pension fund. A *defined benefit pension plan is* one in which the benefits received by the employee are stated in the pension (therefore, not contingent on the investment success of the pension fund). In a defined benefit plan the contributions are variable while the benefits are fixed. In a defined contribution plan the contributions are fixed while the benefits are variable.

3. A trusteeship is critical for accounting because it means the assets are beyond the control of the company and therefore neither the plan assets or liabilities are reported n the company's balance sheet.

4.If an employee's pension rights are not vested if the employment is terminated he/she has no rights to receive a pension.

5. If a plan is non-contributory only the employer makes contributions to the plan.

Page 1107

1. The actuarial method recommended by the Accounting Standards Board (AcSB) for accounting for defined benefit plans is the projected benefit method.

2. The advantage of having a pension plan registered with the regulating body is that the company can then deduct the amounts of its contributions to the pension plan for tax purposes. If a plan is unregistered, the employer (contributor) cannot deduct the contributions until the benefits are paid to the employee.

3. The *deferred pension liability* or *deferred pension cost* represents the difference between the accounting expense and the amount of cash contributed to the pension plan (funding). While these accounts may create the perception of underfunding or overfunding of the pension plan, the nature of these accounts is that they are purely the result of using different measurements for different purposes (i.e., accounting vs. funding).

Page 1113

1. The five components that are always part of the pension expense are the current service cost, interest on the accumulated accrued pension obligation. expected earnings on pension assets, amortization of past service cost from plan initiation or amendment, and the amortization of excess actuarial loss (gain).

2. Past service costs arise as the result of granting pension entitlements to employees for employment services rendered prior to the initiation of the plan or as a result of a pension plan amendment.

3. Additional accrued pension obligations arising from plan amendments may be amortized over the expected period to full eligibility (EPFE); alternatively; the company may amortize the PSC over the period to the next expected plan amendment.

4. A company is required to include amortization of actuarial gains and losses only to the extent that the accumulated amount of actuarial gains and losses exceeds 10% of the greater of (1) the accrued obligation, or (2) the value of the plan assets. The period of amortization of actuarial gains/losses exceeding this "10% corridor" is the average remaining service period (ARSP) of employee participants.

5. The amortization period may be shorter than the minimum required.

Page 1126

1. Losses or gains from plan settlements and curtailments not reported as part of the pension expense on the income statement may appear instead as part of the charge for discontinued operations (shown on the income statement as a separate line item below operating earnings). Termination benefits may also be reported as part of the restructuring charge (i.e., a nonrecurring item), as opposed to being included in the normal pension expense amount.

2. The AcSB recommends using a valuation allowance on potentially over-valued assets in order to limit the carrying value of any accrued benefit to the amount of the expected future benefit.

3. The intention of the AcSB in requiring disclosure of the effect of a 1% increase in health care costs is likely to show users the impact of a change in estimates on the reported costs.

CHAPTER 19

EARNINGS PER SHARE

Earnings per share (EPS) is one of the primary indicators of a company's financial performance, and a driving force behind common stock market prices.

The earnings per share calculation is conceptually very simple: the earnings of the company divided by the number of common shares outstanding. EPS accounting has technically complex calculations because (1) new shares may be issued during the year; (2) there may be several different classes of shares outstanding; (3) the measure of earnings used may vary; (4) convertible senior securities affect EPS if they are converted; and (5) outstanding stock options may be present.

The uses and limitations of EPS data is also discussed in this chapter.

1. APPLICABILITY OF SECTION 3500

Section 3500 of the *CICA Handbook* applies only to public companies. If other companies use EPS the recommendations of Section 3500 must be followed.

2. EPS FIGURES

The *CICA Handbook* recommends that companies report and disclose, on the income statement, basic and diluted earnings per share calculations both on:
- earnings before discontinued operations and extraordinary items, and
- net income.

Other per share income amounts and cash flow per share disclosures are not permitted.

3. BASIC EARNINGS PER SHARE

The following formula is applied to calculate the "basic" EPS:

$$\text{EPS} = \frac{\text{Net income available to common shareholders}}{\text{Weighted average number of common shares outstanding}}$$

Earnings per share is calculated in order to indicate each common shareholder's proportionate share in the company's earnings. It is not necessarily related to the amount of dividends paid out. It shows the residual net income available after preferred shareholders have been allocated their return on capital.　　**WATCH!**

Net Income Available to Common Shareholders
Net income less preferred dividends.

ATCH!

For *cumulative* preferred shares, the prescribed dividend is subtracted from net income whether it was declared or not. However, for *noncumulative* preferred shares, only those dividends actually declared during the period are subtracted in determining the EPS numerator.

There may be other adjustments – the important question is "What are the earnings available to common shareholders?"

Weighted Average Number of Shares

The denominator of the EPS calculation reflects the number of shares, on average, that were outstanding during the year.

There are three methods of calculating the weighted average number of shares. These are illustrated in the textbook on page 1176.

The method used is irrelevant since they all provide the same answer.

Stock Splits or stock Dividends

If there were **share splits** or **share dividends** during the year, the denominator is stated in equivalent share units *after* the split or dividend. All previous calculations of EPS are restated (for comparative purposes). This treatments is based on the fact that stock splits or dividends do not bring new capital into the business.

WATCH! When a share dividend, split, or reverse split occurs, the denominator of the EPS calculation must be adjusted to reflect the shares as though they have been outstanding since the beginning of the year, even if they are issued after year end.

ILLUSTRATION: Basic EPS

At the end of 20x5, the records of Helmen Corporation reflect the following:

Common shares, authorized 100,000 shares:

January 1, 20x5	Outstanding	30,000 shares
April 1, 20x5	Sold and issued	6,000 shares
June 1, 20x5	Declared stock dividends	10%
July 1, 20x5	Retired shares	(1,000) shares
August 5, 20x5	Declared stock split	2 for 1
October 1, 20x5	Sold and issued	2,000 shares

Preferred shares, $1, cumulative and nonconvertible, 50,000 shares outstanding for the whole year	$500,000
Net income before extraordinary loss	140,000
Extraordinary loss, net of tax	(20,000)
Net income	$120,000

Required

1. Identify capital structure—

The capital structure is simple because the preferred shares are nonconvertible and there are no dilutive stock rights outstanding during the period.

2. Compute earnings to common—

Earnings available to common shareholders
= Net income − Preferred dividends
= $120,000 − (50,000 × $1)
= $70,000

3. Compute weighted average outstanding common shares—

	No. of shares		Stock dividend		Stock split		WA factors		WA no of shares
January 1, 20x5	30,000	×	1.1[a]	×	2[b]	×	12/12	=	66,000
April 1, 20x5	6,000	×	1.1[a]	×	2[b]	×	9/12	=	9,900
July 7, 20x5	(1,000)			×	2[b]	×	6/12	=	(1,000)
October 1, 20x5	2,000					×	3/12	=	500
S (weighted ave. # of outstanding common shares)									75,400

[a] Retroactive adjustment for 10% stock dividends declared on 6/1/20x5.
[b] Retroactive adjustment for 2-for-1 stock split declared on 8/5/20x5.

4. Compute EPS—

$$EPS = \frac{\text{Earnings available to common shareholders}}{\text{Weighted average \# of common shares}}$$

$$= \frac{\$70,000}{75,400 \text{ shares}}$$

$$= \$.93$$

5. Present earnings per share

Earnings per share should be calculated and presented for (a) income before extraordinary items and (b) net income.

Basic EPS figures are presented as follows

Earnings per common shares:
Income before extraordinary loss ($90,000[a]/75,400)	$1.19
Extraordinary loss ($20,000/75,400 shares)	(.26)
Net income	$0.93

[a] Income before extraordinary loss to common:
= Income before extraordinary loss − Preferred dividends
= $140,000 − $50,000
= $90,000

Multiple Classes of Shares

Canadian corporations often have multiple classes of common or residual shares outstanding. A primary reason for having two or more classes of common shares is to vary the voting rights between the different classes, normally in order to prevent the controlling shareholders from losing control to hostile investors.

If sharing of dividends is unequal, more than one EPS may have to be calculated.

4. DILUTED EARNINGS PER SHARE

Diluted EPS is a "what if" number that reflects hypothetical earnings dilution if:
- Dilutive convertible senior securities outstanding at the end of the fiscal year are converted to common shares [*CICA* 3500.35], and
- All dilutive options to purchase shares that are outstanding at the end of the fiscal year are exercised [*CICA* 3500.38], and
- Dilutive convertible senior securities that actually converted during the year did so at the beginning of the fiscal year [*CICA* 3500.34], and
- shares issued because of (dilutive) share option contracts during the year were issued at the beginning of the year [*CICA* 3500.34].

Diluted EPS is a worst case scenario. If conversion of senior securities or exercise of options would increase EPS, they are called **anti-dilutive** and are excluded from the calculation.

Diluted EPS Calculation

To calculate dilutive EPS adjustments are made for:
- options that are in-the-money—exercise price is lower than the market value of common shares, and
- convertible securities—bonds and preferred shares.

Option adjustments are based on the **treasury stock method** where proceeds are assumed to be used to reacquire and retire common shares at the average market price during the period [*CICA* 3500.38]. The denominator is increased by the shares issued and decreased by shares retired.

Bonds and preferred shares are based on **if-converted method** where the numerator and denominator are adjusted to reflect if securities were converted at the beginning of the period [*CICA* 3500.35]. For bonds, the numerator is increased by the after tax interest avoided and for preferred shares increased by the dividend claim avoided. The denominator for both is increased by the shares issued.
Three technicalities to note:
- If there are a variety of conversion terms the most dilutive must be used.
- If the securities were issued during the year the assumed conversion goes to the issue date not the beginning of the year.
- If the conversion option lapsed during the year or the security was redeemed or settled during the year, the conversion is still included for the period it was outstanding.

Steps in Calculating Diluted EPS and Example

The steps are listed in Exhibit 19-2 and 19-8 in the textbook and an example is provided for diluted EPS.

Reporting Diluted EPS

Basic and diluted EPS must be reported on the income statement with equal prominence.

Diluted EPS Cascade

Adjustments are done from most to least dilutive. Options that are in-the-money are always dilutive and done first. Next are convertible securities with the lowest individual EPS effect. Remember any items that would increase EPS (anti-dilutive) are excluded.

Actual Conversions During the Period

Backdating is used to reflect actual conversions and actual options exercised at the beginning of the fiscal period. The textbook provides two examples.

5. COMPLICATING FACTORS

Convertible Securities and Options Issued During the Year

If convertible securities or options are issued during the year, the effect of the hypothetical conversion is backdated in the calculation of diluted EPS *only to the date of issue.*

Convertible Securities and Options Extinguished During the Year

Potential common shares, if dilutive, are included in the calculation of diluted EPS up to the date of redemption, settlement, or expiry.

Reference Point for Diluted EPS

In deciding if a potentially dilutive security has an individual effect that is anti-dilutive or dilutive *CICA* 3500.32 requires the use of income before discontinued operations and extraordinary items. If an item is included for EPS based on income before discontinued operations and extraordinary items, it is also always included for EPS based on net income.

Measuring Interest Expense

Most bonds are issued at or very near the market rate of interest. If a bond is offered at a significant discount or premium it complicates the EPS calculation. In EPS calculations, when making the adjustment to earnings available to common, the adjustment must be made for *interest expense* not interest paid.

Measuring the Dilutive Effect of Options

The price of options may increase or decrease based on a pre-determined schedule over time. In calculating diluted EPS, the most dilutive (lowest) price is used [*CICA* 3500.27].

Diluted EPS in a Loss Year
Diluted EPS is generally equal to basic EPS in a loss year because all potentially dilutive items are classified as anti-dilutive. This is because when a loss is reported adding anything positive to the numerator (the loss) and/or increasing the number of common shares outstanding will reduce the loss per share.

6. COMPREHENSIVE ILLUSTRATION
A comprehensive illustration of the calculation of fully dilutive EPS is presented in the textbook starting on page 1180.

WATCH! When the conversion or exercise of the option results in an increase in earnings per share, it is *not* included in the calculation of the fully diluted EPS.

7. RESTATEMENT OF EARNINGS PER SHARE INFORMATION
EPS will be recalculated if:
- There has been a retroactive change in accounting principle or error correction.
- There has been a stock dividend or stock split during the fiscal year.

8. SUBSEQUENT EVENTS
If a subsequent event would significantly change the number of common shares or potential common shares used in basis or diluted EPS, the transaction must be disclosed and described [*CICA* 3500.67].

9. DISCLOSURE PRACTICES
The *CICA Handbook*, paragraph 3500.60, recommends that basic and diluted EPS be shown either on the face of the income statement or in a note cross-referenced to the income statement. Information to disclose in a note is outlined in *CICA* 3500.58, .65, .67.

10. USING EPS
The following summarizes the usefulness of the various EPS numbers available:

Basic EPS: This is a historical amount.

Diluted EPS: If the company is successful in its financing strategy, the convertible senior securities will be converted before the due date. The fully diluted EPS suggests the long-run impact that the likely conversions will have on the earnings attributable to common shares.

11. A FINAL COMMENT
EPS calculations are complex and difficult to evaluate what the numbers mean. The emphasis on EPS may encourage transactions for the purpose of generating book profits to increase EPS.

TRUE–FALSE QUESTIONS

T F 1. The Bass Company began the calendar year accounting period with 100,000 shares of common stock outstanding, and on October 1 sold 10,000 additional shares. Its weighted average number of shares outstanding is 105,000.

T F 2. In computing the weighted average number of common shares outstanding, shares issued as *stock dividends* are weighted by the fraction of the period during which these additional shares are outstanding.

T F 3. The *CICA Handbook* for public companies requires that basic and diluted EPS be calculated.

T F 4. If a firm declares no dividends on cumulative preferred shares, no adjustment of the earnings to common is required in earnings per share calculations.

T F 5. For private corporations, reporting earnings per share is not required.

T F 6. The current dividend of cumulative preferred shares should be ignored in computing earnings per share if the company incurred a net loss for the period and no dividends were declared during the period.

T F 7. In computing basic EPS for a simple capital structure, net income is reduced by cumulative preferred dividends on nonconvertible preferred shares, whether dividends are declared or not.

T F 8. In calculating diluted EPS when making adjustments to earnings available to common, the adjustment is for interest paid.

T F 9. If the capital structure is simple, neither stock dividends nor stock splits will be considered when computing earnings per share.

T F 10. All the dilutive securities and stock rights, whether dilutive or antidilutive, should be included in fully diluted EPS.

T F 11. Options are said to be in-the-money if the exercise price is lower than the market value of common shares.

MULTIPLE CHOICE QUESTIONS

___ 1. In computing the weighted average number of shares outstanding, the number of shares should be weighted by the fraction of the period they are outstanding for each of the following, *except*:
   a. new shares of common stock sold during the period.
   b. shares reacquired and retired during the year.
   c. shares issued by a stock option plan initiated in mid-year.
   d. shares of common stock issued during the period pursuant to a stock dividend.

_____ 2. In determining basic earnings per share, dividends on nonconvertible cumulative preferred stock should be:
   a. deducted from net income whether declared or not.
   b. deducted from net income only if declared.
   c. added back to net income whether declared or not.
   d. disregarded.

_____ 3. Which of the following does not require a retroactive adjustment when calculating weighted average number of shares for the basic EPS calculation?
   a. A stock dividend.
   b. A reverse split.
   c. A stock split.
   d. A share conversion.

_____ 4. When determining earnings per share, interest expense, net of income taxes, on convertible bonds that are dilutive should be:
   a. deducted from net income from both the basic EPS and the diluted EPS calculation.
   b. not deducted from net income for basic EPS, but deducted for the diluted EPS calculation.
   c. added back to net income for both basic EPS and the diluted EPS calculation.
   d. not added back to net income for basic EPS, but added back for the diluted EPS calculation.

_____ 5. Stock options that are antidilutive generally are used in the computation of:

	Basic earnings per share	Diluted earnings per share
a.	Yes	Yes
b.	Yes	No
c.	No	No
d.	No	Yes

_____ 6. At December 31, 20x4, Rousseau Corp. had outstanding 200,000 shares of common shares and 2,000 shares of $10, no-par value nonconvertible but cumulative preferred shares. No dividends were declared on either the preferred or the common shares in 20x5. No shares were issued during the year. Net income for 20x5 was $100,000. For 20x5, basic EPS was:
   a. $.40
   b. $.50
   c. $.60
   d. $2.00

____ 7. Joseph Company's balance sheet at December 31, 20x4 included the following:

	Shares issued and outstanding
Preferred shares, no-par value noncumulative and nonconvertible	200,000
Common shares, no-par value	400,000

On October 1, 20x5, Joseph issued a 25% stock dividend on its common shares and paid $500,000 cash dividends on preferred shares. Net income for the year ended December 31, 20x5, was $2,000,000. Joseph's 20x5 basic EPS should be:

a. $3.00
b. $3.53
c. $4.00
d. $5.00

____ 8. On December 31, 20x4, Muskoka Inc. had 600,000 shares of common shares issued and outstanding. Muskoka issued a 10% stock dividend on July 1, 20x5, and on October 1, 20x5, purchased and retired 48,000 of its common shares. The number of shares Muskoka should use in computing basic earnings per share for the year ended December 31, 20x5, is:

a. 612,000
b. 618,000
c. 648,000
d. 660,000

____ 9. Epperson Co. had 100,000 common shares outstanding at the beginning of 20x5. On July 1, 20x5, it issued 6% bonds at face value of $500,000. The bonds were convertible into 20,000 common shares. Assuming net income of $185,000 and a tax rate of 40%, the diluted earnings per share for 20x5 will be (to the nearest cent):

a. $2.00
b. $1.79
c. $1.76
d. $1.85

____ 10. Basic earnings per share is $15. Including a stock option and other dilutive securities will result in an EPS of $14.75. The EPS data should be presented as:

	Basic earnings per share	Diluted earnings per share
a.	$15.00	N/A
b.	$15.00	$14.75
c.	N/A	$14.75
d.	$14.75	N/A

SOLUTIONS TO TRUE–FALSE QUESTIONS

1. F The weighted average number of shares outstanding will be calculated as follows: (100,000 shares × 12/12) = 100,000 + (10,000 shares × 3/12) = 2,500. The weighted average number of shares outstanding is 102,500 shares.

2. F Stock dividends are treated as though they have been outstanding since the beginning of the year, even if they were issued after year end.

3. T

4. F For *cumulative* preferred shares, the prescribed dividend is subtracted from net income whether they have been declared or not.

5. T

6. F For *cumulative* preferred shares, the prescribed dividend is subtracted from net income (or added to the loss), whether they have been declared or not.

7. T

8. F The adjustment is for interest expense, not interest paid.

9. F When a stock dividend or a stock split occurs, the common share equity is not changed, nor is the composition of the broad capital structure affected. However, the new EPS figures will be based on a different number of shares than were previous years' EPS.

10. F When conversion or exercise of the option would result in an antidilution of EPS, the conversion is not taken into account.

11. T

SOLUTIONS TO MULTIPLE CHOICE QUESTIONS

1. d Shares of common stock issued during the period pursuant to a stock dividend are treated as though they have been outstanding since the beginning of the year, even if they are issued after year end.

2. a For cumulative preferred shares, the prescribed dividend is subtracted from net income whether they have been declared or not.

3. d After a share conversion, the number of additional shares will part of the calculation of the weighted average number of shares. It will also be accounted for prospectively, since it also affects earnings.

4. d To calculate diluted earnings per share, we adjust the numerator by adding the after-tax interest that will be saved if the senior securities are converted. There is no adjustment to income when calculating the basic EPS. The bond interest, net of income taxes, is added back to net income when the diluted EPS is calculated.

5. c When conversion or exercise of the option is antidilutive, it is not taken into account in the computation of basic EPS *or* diluted EPS.

6. a The numerator = Net income less preferred dividends. $100,000 less (2,000 shares × $10) = $80,000. The denominator = Weighted average number of shares outstanding = 200,000 common shares. Basic EPS = $80,000/200,000 = $.40.

7. a The numerator = $2,000,000 – $500,000 = $1,500,000. When there are noncumulative preferred shares, only those dividends actually declared — in this case, paid-during the period are subtracted in determining the EPS numerator. The denominator = 400,000 shares × 1.25 = 500,000 shares. A 25% stock dividend is applied retroactively to the beginning of the year. The basic EPS = $1,500,000/ 500,000 = $3.00.

8. c

January 1, 20x5	600,000 shares × 1.10	× 12/12 =	660,000
July 1, 20x5	Stock dividend		
October 1, 20x5	(48,000) shares	× 3/12 =	(12,000)
Weighted average number of shares			648,000

9. c The numerator must be adjusted by removing the after-tax interest that will be saved if the bonds are converted. We start with net income of $185,000, and add back the bond interest. Note that the bond interest is deductible for income tax purposes, and since the net income is an after-tax amount, the interest saved must be calculated on an after-tax basis. With a tax rate of 40%, the interest saving is multiplied by 60% after-tax equivalent and calculated from July 1 to December 31 (6 months):

$$\$500,000 \times 6\% \times 6/12 \times (1.0 - .40) = \$9,000$$

The diluted earnings available to common shareholders:

$$\$185,000 + \$9,000 = \$194,000$$

The denominator is the diluted number of shares outstanding:

Common shares outstanding	100,000 shares
Additional shares issued on conversion:	
On debentures (20,000 shares × 6/12)	10,000 shares
Fully diluted number of shares o/s	110,000 shares

Diluted EPS: $194,000/110,000 = $1.76

10. b The *CICA Handbook* recommends that basic and diluted EPS be shown on the face of the income statement. When there are stock options and other dilutive securities that result in a reduction of EPS, we have diluted EPS.

PROBLEM

PURPOSE: To illustrate the calculations of EPS in a complex environment.

Jeannot Limited reported net income after income taxes of $5,400,000. The company did not report any extraordinary items in its income statement for the year ended December 31, 20x4. The following information is available:
  • As at January 1, 20x4, there were 1,300,000 common shares outstanding.

- At the beginning of the current year, 500,000 stock options, to purchase 500,000 common shares @ $10 per share, were outstanding. Fifty thousand shares were issued on August 1, 20x4, on the exercise of options. The company's average market price of shares during period was $20.
- A 10%, convertible 10-year debenture with a principal amount of $15,000,000 has been outstanding for a number of years. Interest payment dates are April 1 and October 1 each year. Each $1,000 debenture is convertible into 25 common shares. The conversion ratio would change if there was a stock split or a stock dividend, to protect the rights of the investors. On April 1, 20x4, $5,000,000 of the outstanding debentures were converted.
- For a number of years, 6% cumulative, preferred shares in the amount of $12,000,000 have been outstanding. There was no change in this during 20x4.
- Also outstanding are 8% noncumulative convertible preferred shares that were sold for $100 per share for a total cash of $9,000,000. Each preferred share is convertible into 1 share of common. Dividends totalling $3.50 per share were declared in 20x4 on these preferred shares.
- On January 31, 20x5 (before the completion of the 20x4 financial statements on February 28, 20x5), a 10%, stock dividend on common shares was declared and issued.
- On February 5, 20x5, 500,000 common shares were issued for $9,500,000 cash. The proceeds from the sale were used to finance the redemption of $9,000,000 of the 10% convertible bonds.
- The average applicable income tax rate is 40%.

Required

For the year ended December 31, 20x4, compute each of the following:
1. Basic earnings per share.
2. Diluted earnings per share.

SOLUTION TO PROBLEM

Requirement 1

Basic EPS:

Earnings available to common shareholders—

Net income	$5,400,000
Less: preferred dividends:	
$12,000,000 × 6%	(720,000)
($9,000,000/$100) × $3.50	(315,000)
	$4,365,000

Weighted average number of common shares:

	# of shares		Stock dividend		Factor	Weighted ave. # of shares
1/1/20x4	1,300,000	×	[a]1.10	×	3/12	357,500
1/4/20x4	[b]1,400,000	×	1.10	×	4/12	513,333
1/8/20x4	1,450,000	×	1.10	×	5/12	664,583
						1,535,416

[a] 10% stock dividend after the year end is treated retroactively.
[b] ($5,00,000/$1,000) × 20 = 100,000; 1,300,000 + 100,000.

Basic EPS: $4,365,000/1,535,416 = $2.84

Requirement 2
Diluted EPS:

Diluted test ratios—

OPTIONS EXERCISED
500,000 − 50,000 = 450,000 options outstanding

The options are in-the-money therefore dilutive, because the $10 is less than the $20 average market price of shares.

10% DEBENTURES

Net increase in income =
([$15,000,000 − $5,000,000] × .10 × [1 −.40])
+ ($300,000 × 10/15 × 1/10 × [1 − .40]) = $612,000

Again, we must consider these debentures as if they were converted at the beginning of the year.

Net increase in number of shares =
$10,000,000/$1,000 × 25 × 1.10   = 275,000
EPS effect of conversion: $612,000/220,000 $2.23

Since this number is less than the basic EPS, it is considered dilutive.

8% CONVERTIBLE PREFERRED SHARES

Net increase in income = Dividends declared = $315,000

(See basic EPS calculations in answer to requirement 1.)

Net increase in number of shares =
   $9,000,000/$100 × 1 × 1.10 =   99,000
EPS effect of conversion = $315,000/99,000 =   [a]$ 3.18
[a] Antidilutive.

This number is more than the basic EPS and so is considered antidilutive.

To calculate the diluted EPS—

	Earnings available to common shareholders	Weighted average # of common shares	EPS
Basic EPS (from req #1)	4,365,000	1,535,416	$2.84
Adjustment for assumed options exercised:			
Shares issued		450,000	
Shares retired		(225,000)	
Subtotal		1,760,416	$2.47
Actual conversion 10% debenture:			
Interest saved (1)	75,000		
Additional shares (2)		34,375	
Subtotal	4,440,000	1,794,791	$2.45
Potential conversion 10% debenture:			
Interest avoided	612,000		
Additional shares		275,000	
Subtotal	$5,052,000	$2,069,791	$2.44

Diluted EPS = $2.44

(1) $5,000 × .10 × (1 − .40) × 3/12 = 75,000
(2) ($5,000,000 / $1,000) × (25 × 1.10) × 3/12 = $34,375

CASE

Many people believe that earnings per share is the single most relevant number for financial statement readers. Together with earnings, it is also the most commonly reported statistic about a company's activities for the year. It is a complex calculation, as the following complaint indicates.

I really don't understand why EPS calculations have to be checked so carefully by the auditors, or made so difficult to calculate. Why can't you just take net income and divide by the common shares outstanding at year end?

This year, we skipped a preferred dividend, but had to take it off for basic EPS anyway! We also issued shares during the period on preferred shares conversion, as a stock split, and on the exercise of employee stock options. Some of these transactions were weighted to the day of issuance, but some weren't. Why did this happen? How understandable is it, if it's so complicated?

Finally, we had to disclose diluted EPS, due to some employee stock options still outstanding and a convertible bond issue. Yet none of these contingent share issues happened this year—and won't in the near future, because of terms of the issue. Why report on events that haven't happened? I thought accountants were supposed to rely on transactions!

Required
Write a brief response to the comments.

KEY POINTS IN THE CASE

EPS calculations are standardized in the *CICA Handbook,* Section 3500, and verified by independent auditors because the figures are used so extensively by investors and other interested parties to measure operating performance. EPS is the only ratio that public companies are required to provide.

Simple calculations of income divided by year end outstanding shares are inadequate for two reasons:

1. The numerator should not be net income; rather, it should be income available to common shareholders. This involves subtracting the preferred dividend entitlement.

2. The denominator should not be common shares outstanding at year end, but rather should represent the average outstanding during the period. The entity should have higher income with a higher capital investment: if this investment was only available for part of the year, the denominator should be adjusted accordingly. On the other hand, if shares issued brought in no new capital (as with a split or a dividend), then weighted-average is not appropriate.

Cumulative preferred dividends must be deducted whether declared or not, since income cannot ever be distributed to common shareholders if preferred dividends are in arrears. The preferred shares have this claim on income, declared or not. Noncumulative preferred share dividends are deducted only as declared.

In the calculation of weighted average common shares outstanding, shares issued for cash (e.g., under an options agreement) will be weight averaged to the date of sale. Shares issued on preferred share conversion are weight averaged to the day the dividend obligation on the preferred shares ceased. Since no dividends were paid this year, the common shares issued will be back-dated for EPS calculations to the date of the last dividend payment. This, again, is an effort to match the terms of the numerator and denominator. When did the company last have a charge related to preferred shares? After this date the capital was, in effect, common equity.

Shares issued in a split bring in no new equity and do not help boost income. To improve comparisons, they are backdated to the earliest reporting period, as if they had always been outstanding.

These complex computation rules are a reflection of the complexity of the under-lying transactions and business environment. Oversimplification may mislead, because using EPS as an important element in a company's goal structure can contribute to a short-term attitude on the part of management. Such an attitude can lead to decisions that are detrimental to the long-term productivity and financial health of the company. Therefore, knowledge of how EPS amounts are calculated is essential if intelligent use is to be made of the resulting figures.

Diluted EPS is another figure that is meant to improve the predictive power of financial statements. While none of the shares were issued, there are legally binding agreements in place that can be relied on to provide objective evidence. Diluted EPS provides information about the dilutive (i.e., unfavourable to current shareholders) commitments present in the existing capital structure. It is a worst-case scenario.

SELECTED SOLUTIONS FROM THE TEXTBOOK
Assignment 19-11

	Earnings available to common shareholders	Weighted average number of shares	Earnings per Share
Basic EPS:			
Net income	$366,000		
Preferred shares (30,000 x $.50)	(15,000)		
	$351,000		
Shares outstanding			
150,000 x 6/12		75,000	
450,000 x 5/12		187,500	
516,000 (1) x 1/12		43,000	
		305,500	
Basic EPS			$1.15
(1) ($600,000/$1,000 x 110) + 450,000			

Individual effect:			
Preferred shares			
Dividend avoided	15,000		
Shares issued 30,000 x 2		60,000	$0.25
Actual conversion:			
Interest avoided			
$47,250 x (1-.3)	33,075		
Shares issued			
($600,000/$1,000) x 110 x 11/12		60,500	$0.55

Diluted EPS:			
Basic EPS	$351,000	305,500	$1.15
Preferred shares			
Dividend avoided	15,000		
Shares issued 30,000 x 2		60,000	
	366,000	365,500	1.00
Actual conversion:			
Interest avoided	33,075		
Shares issued			
		60,500	
Diluted EPS	$399,075	426,000	$0.94

Assignment 19-19

	Earnings available to common shareholders	Weighted average number of shares	Earnings per Share
Basic EPS			
Net income	$600,000		
Note: preferred dividends are already deducted from net income			
	600,000		
Shares outstanding			
48,000* x 3/12		12,000	
60,000 x 9/12		45,000	
		57,000	
Basic EPS			$10.53

* Bonds: ($1,500,000 / 1,000) x 8 = 12,000; 60,000 − 12,000 = 48,000

Individual effect:			
Actual conversion, 12% debentures			
Bond interest $48,000 x (1-.4)	28,800		
Shares 12,000 x 3/12		3,000	$9.60
12% debentures outstanding			
Interest			
($624,000 - $48,000) x (1-.4)	345,600		
Shares:			
($4,500,000 / $1,000) x 8		36,000	9.60
12.4% debentures			
Interest ($450,000) x (1-.4)	$270,000		
($3,000,000 / $1,000) x 8		24,000	$11.25

The options are anti-dilutive because exercise price is greater than market value.
The individual effect of the 12% debenture items are identical and their order is irrelevant.
The 12.4% debenture is anti-dilutive.

Diluted EPS:			
Basic EPS	600,000	57,000	$10.53
Actual conversion:			
Bond interest	28,800		
Shares		3,000	
12% debentures			
Interest	345,600		
Shares		36,000	
Diluted EPS	$974,400	96,000	$10.15

Assignment 19-21

Requirement 1

Options:	Shares issued	Shares retired
Quarter 1 - 40,000 x 3/12	10,000	
(40,000 x $25)/$40) x 3/12		6,250
Quarter 2 – anti-dilutive ($25 > $15)		
Quarter 3 – anti-dilutive ($25 > $20)		
Quarter 4 - 40,000 x 3/12	10,000	
(40,000 x $25)/$35) x 3/12		7,143
	20,000	13,393

Bonds: $\dfrac{\$562,000(1 - .4)}{(\$5,000,000/\$1,000) \times 20}$ = $3.37

Preferred shares $\dfrac{300,000 \times \$1.50}{(300,000 \times 2^*)}$ = $0.75

*The most dilutive alternative is used.

Requirement 2

	Earnings available to common shareholders	Weighted average number of shares	Earnings per Share
Basic EPS:			
Earnings	$1,800,000		
Less: preferred dividends	450,000		
	1,350,000		
Shares (given)		450,000	
Basic EPS			$3.00
Diluted EPS:			
Options:			
Shares issued		20,000	
Shares retired		(13,393)	
Subtotal	1,350,000	456,607	$2.96
Preferred Shares			
Dividends (300,000 x $1.50)	450,000		
Shares (300,000 x 2)		600,000	
Bonds - Anti-dilutive; excluded			
Diluted EPS	$1,800,000	1,056,607	$1.70

Requirement 3

Basic and diluted EPS would be ($200,000 + $450,000)/ 450,000 = ($1.44).
All potentially dilutive elements are anti-dilutive in a loss year.

Assignment 19-30

	Earnings available to common shareholders	Weighted average number of shares	Earnings per Share
Basic:			
Net income	$18,000,000		
Preferred dividends			
600,000 x $.20	(__120,000)		
	$17,880,000		
Average shares			
3,300,000 x 12/12		3,300,000	
3,320,000 (1) x 0/12		0	
Basic EPS			$5.42

(1) 10,000 x 2 = 20,000 shares issued on conversion 31 December 20x6

Individual effect of:

1. Preferred shares $\frac{\$.20 \times 600,000}{600,000} = \frac{\$120,000}{600,000} = \$.20$

2. Options Shares issued: 500,000 x 9/12 = 375,000 (Dilutive in three quarters only)

    Shares retired: 243,706
    First quarter: ($53 x 500,000)/100 x 3/12 = 66,250
    Second quarter: ($53 x 500,000)/$80 x 3/12 = 82,813
    Fourth quarter: ($53 x 500,000)/$70 x 3/12 = 94,643

3. Debentures $\frac{[(\$9,000,000 \times .10) + (\$180,000^* \times 1/10)] (1 - .4)}{(9,000,000 / 100) \times 2)} = \frac{\$550,800}{180,000} = \$3.06$

    *$180,000 = $200,000 x 9/10

4. Debentures, converted

    $\frac{[(\$1,000,000 \times .10) + (\$20,000^* \times 1/10)] (1 - .4)}{(1,000,000 / 100) \times 2)} =$ $\frac{\$61,200}{20,000}$ = $3.06

    *$20,000 = $200,000 x 1/10

	Earnings available to common shareholders	Weighted average number of shares	Earnings per Share
Diluted:			
Basic, above	$17,880,000	3,300,000	$5.42
Options			
Shares issued		375,000	
Shares retired	_____	(243,706)	
	$17,880,000	3,431,294	$5.21
Preferred shares			
Dividends/Shares	120,000	600,000	
	$18,000,000	4,031,294	$4.47
Actual conversion of debentures			
Income	61,200		
Shares		20,000	
Debentures			
Interest; Shares	550,800	180,000	
Diluted EPS	$18,612,000	4,231,294	$4.40

SOLUTIONS TO CONCEPT REVIEW QUESTIONS

Page 1167

1. Public companies are required to disclose EPS, although non-public companies may do so if relevant to their shareholders or other stakeholders. The rules of Section 3500 must be followed, whether disclosure of EPS is required or voluntary.

2. The formula for basic EPS is,

$$\frac{\text{Net income available to common shareholders}}{\text{Weighted average number of common shares outstanding}}$$

3. Earnings available to common shareholders begins with net income, and so includes all elements of net income. However, returns to senior shares are also adjusted — dividends, capital charges, any gain and losses on senior share retirement — to arrive at income available to common shareholders only.

4. WACS = (2,000 x 6/12 x 2) + (2,400 x 6/12 x 2) + (4,800 x 0/12) = 4,400. The stock split is done retroactively, thus the number of shares outstanding last year will double, and EPS numbers will halve.

5. Steps in calculating EPS when there are multiple common share classes:

    1. Calculate earnings minus all dividends declared (undistributed earnings).
    2. Allocate undistributed earnings to the share classes.
    3. Determine per share amounts from step 2.
    4. Add dividends declared to step 3 amounts.

Page 1176

1. Diluted EPS reflect the potential for earnings dilution because of existing contract. It is used to provide the basis for forward predictions. Diluted EPS indicates the maximum potential decline in earnings if the company's contingent share contracts were to be exercised, if the effect is to reduce EPS as otherwise reported.

2. A dilutive element causes EPS, as otherwise calculated, to decline. An anti-dilutive element causes EPS to increase.

3. For convertible bonds, the numerator of EPS is increased by after-tax interest expense, plus the after-tax capital charge, if any. For preferred shares, dividends are added back. Dividends are only those declared on non-cumulative shares, but the entire annual dividend entitlement, declared or not, for cumulative shares.

4. Diluted EPS calculations begin with basic EPS ($5.00) and then include the most dilutive element ($1.00). If the subtotal after this $1.00 item is less than $4.50, then including the $4.50 item will increase diluted EPS. The $4.50 item would be anti-dilutive, even though its individual effect is less than basic EPS.

5. In the calculation of diluted EPS, actual conversions of senior securities are backdated to the beginning of the year, if dilutive.

6. Option contracts are dealt with using the treasury stock method. Proceeds from options issued are assumed to be used to retire shares at their market value.

Page 1180

1. The reference point for the dilution test is basic EPS, calculated before discontinued operations and extraordinary items. As items are included, the subtotal becomes the reference point.

2. Interest expense is different than interest paid when there is premium or discount amortization. Interest expense is used when considering convertible bonds in the diluted EPS calculations.

3. Diluted EPS will generally equal basic in a loss year because all potentially dilutive elements are anti-dilutive in a loss year. Adding anything positive to the numerator (the loss) and/or increasing the number of common shares outstanding will reduce the loss per share.

CHAPTER 20

RESTATEMENTS

There are circumstances when it is necessary to change previously reported financial statements – this is know as restatement. An increase in the number of restatements reduces the credibility of financial statements. Restatements are made as either the result of changes in accounting policies, or error corrections. As we will see there are limitations placed on an organization's ability to change policies. Changes in estimates do not result in restatement. The AcSB plans on releasing the final version of the new standards relating to restatements in the second quarter of 2005.

1. TYPES OF ACCOUNTING CHANGES

There are three types of accounting changes:
1. Changes in accounting policy.
    a. involuntary, to comply with new *CICA Handbook* recommendations
    b. voluntary, at the option of management or at the request of the user
2. Changes in accounting estimates.
3. Corrections of an error in previous years' financial statements.

The nature of each type of change and the appropriate accounting treatment is summarized in Exhibit 20-1 of the text.

Changes in Policy

A **change in accounting policy** is a change in the way a company accounts for a particular type of transaction or event, or for the resulting asset or liability.

There is a distinction between a change in policy and adoption of a new policy. When a policy is adopted for either transactions or events that differ in substance from those previously occurring or transactions or events that did not previously occur a new policy is adopted. The distinction is not always easy to make in practice.

New *CICA Handbook* recommendations may require a company that is constrained by GAAP to change its accounting either because (1) a previously accepted method become unacceptable, or (b) a new approach is recommended that was not previously used in practice. These changes are *involuntary*. Retroactive restatement is usually required but there are exceptions. Early adoption is also encouraged and prospective treatments is sometimes used as an incentive for early adoption.

Management may make a *voluntary* change in accounting policy only if the new policy results in

> **CICA** *a reliable and more relevant presentation in the financial statements of the effects of transactions or other events on the entity's financial position, financial performance, or cash flows.*

There is no guidance provided on how to asses relevance and relevancy is subjective therefore determining if this criteria has been met may be difficult.

Management may make a change in policy or response to a change in reporting circumstances such as:

- A change in reporting objectives, that may arise when there is a change in ownership of a company.
- A change in ways of doing business, such as a shift to higher-risk business strategies that make the prediction of future outcomes more difficult and less reliable.
- A desire to conform to common or emerging industry practice.

One of the most common reasons for changing one or more accounting policies is a change in reporting objectives.

WATCH!

For example, when the ownership of a company changes, the priority of objectives often changes, or important new objectives suddenly arise.

Reporting objectives may also change to satisfy the requirements of an important lender or other user.

Changes in Estimates

A change is estimate is a change in the *application* of an accounting policy to a specific transaction or event. Because we can never predict future outcomes with certainty, our accounting estimates often need revision.

Changes in accounting estimates can occur for several reasons:

- New reliable information is available.
- Experience has provided insight into such things as usage patterns or benefits.
- The company's economic environment has changed.
- The auditor has raised questions about the application of some of the company's accounting policies and has requested substantiation for management's estimates.
- There has been a shift in the nature of the company's business operations.

It is important, but often difficult, to distinguish between a *change in policy* and a *change in estimate*.

Consider a change in the amortization rate for a patent. If the change is due to changed *economic* circumstances, it is a change in estimate; but if it is due to different *reporting* circumstances, it is a change in policy.

WATCH!

The *CICA Handbook* suggests that when there is doubt as to whether a change is a change in policy or a change in estimate, the change should be treated as a change in estimate.

Correction of an Error

Error correction arises when management discovers that something was recorded incorrectly in one or more previous periods. Most errors are accidental. However, some errors are discovered only when fraud or deliberate misrepresentation is uncovered. A key aspect of errors is that they do not arise from a change in estimate or a change in policy. They are simply *mistakes*.

Major causes of accounting errors—
- Mathematical mistakes.
- Misapplication of accounting principles.
- Failure to recognize accruals and/or deferrals.
- Misclassification of an account.
- Intentional use of unrealistic accounting estimates (or fraud).

2. REPORTING ACCOUNTING CHANGES

There are three ways of reporting accounting changes in the financial statement:

a. **Retroactive application with restatement of prior periods.** This approach requires that financial statements issued in previous years be restated (when issued again for comparative purposes), and the beginning balance of retained earnings for the year of change be adjusted to reflect the retroactive impact of the change. The effect is to report the financial results as if the new policy has always been in effect. This makes current and future income fully comparable with results from earlier periods. Consistency and comparability are enhanced.

b. **Retroactive application without restatement.** This approach requires that the cumulative effect of the change on prior years' income be determined and included as an adjustment to opening retained earnings for the year of the change only. Prior financial statements are not restated. Since prior years' financial statements are not restated under this approach, financial statement integrity is better maintained, but the degree of comparability is reduced.

c. **Prospective application.** This approach requires neither a restatement of prior years' financial statements nor a determination of the cumulative effect of the change. The change in accounting is applied only to events and transactions occurring after the date of the change.

WATCH! In general, changes in accounting policy and error corrections are accounted for retroactively, while changes in accounting estimates are accounted for prospectively.

Retroactive restatement is normally required, An exception is permitted where this treatment is impractical.

CICA *Retroactive application of a change in accounting policy to comparative information is impractical only when:*
(a) the effect of retroactive application on prior periods is not determinable;
(b) retroactive application requires assumptions about management's intent in a prior period; or
(c) retroactive application requires significant management estimates as of a prior period.

The **correction of an accounting error** should also be accounted for *retroactively with restatement*, even if there is no adjustment necessary in the current year.

The *CICA Handbook,* paragraph 1506.27, states that changes in accounting estimates should be accounted for (a) restating the comparative amounts for the prior period(s) in which the error occurred; or (b) when the error occurred before the earliest prior period presented, restating the opening balance of retained earnings for that period; so that the financial statements are presented as if the error had never occurred.

Changes in estimates should be accounted for in the period of the change and if applicable future periods. Past periods re never changed.

A Summary of Accounting Changes and Reporting Approaches can be found in Exhibit 20–2 of the textbook.

3. RETROACTIVE APPROACH WITH RESTATEMENT

The following guidelines apply:
1. Thee cumulative impact of the change on the beginning balances of the current year must be calculated. These changes are recorded in the accounts by journal entry with the impact on prior year's income adjusted to retained earnings.
2. x The information necessary to make the change *in the current and prior periods* must be obtained from the underlying accounting records.
3. Account balances that affect the prior years' comparative financial statements, including all affected balance sheet and income statement accounts, must be recalculated using the new policy. The comparative statements must be restated.
4. Summary comparative information that is presented publicly, such as in the annual report, must be recalculated using the new policy.
5. Opening retained earnings is restated to remove the effect of the accounting change from prior earnings..

ILLUSTRATION

Medara Ltd. purchases a piece of equipment on January 1, 20x3, with a cost of $10,000, a useful life of 5 years, and an estimated salvage value of $1,000. During 20x5, Medara decided to change from the straight-line method to the double-declining balance method of amortization. The applicable income tax rate was 40%.

Note: The change was made to conform to a long-standing industry norm and was not based on new information. Therefore, the change qualifies for retroactive restatement.

Required

1. Determine the cumulative effect:
2. Record the cumulative effect.
3. Record current amortization expense based on the new method.

Requirement 1

Amortization expenses up to January 1, 20x5, using the **new method:**

DDB rate = 1/5 × 2 = .40 or 40% declining balance.

20x3   Amortization = $10,000 × 40% = $4,000
20x4   Amortization = ($10,000 − $4,000) × 40% = $2,400

Amortization using old method:	3,600	([$10,000 – $1,000] × 2/5)
Cumulative effect before tax	$2,800	
Tax effect (40%)	1,120	
Cumulative effect, net of tax	$1,680	

Requirement 2

Retained earnings, cumulative effect of accounting principle change	1,680	
Future income tax assets	1,120	
Accumulated amortization		2,800

Requirement 3

Record current amortization expense based on the new method—

Amortization expense ($6,000 – $2,400) × 40%	1,440	
Accumulated amortization		1,440

Since the effect of the double-declining balance method can be traced back to specific years, the previous years' income statements can be restated on a comparative income statement that shows the prior years.

4. RETROACTIVE APPROACH WITHOUT RESTATEMENT

The current approach applies to the changes in accounting principle for which it is possible to restate the financial statements as of the beginning of the current year, but it is *impossible to restate specific prior periods.*

The following guidelines apply to **accounting policy changes** that are reported by using the retroactive approach without restatement:

1. The cumulative impact of the change on retained earnings in prior years is computed and recorded, including the change in retained earnings.
2. The cumulative impact of the change is *reported* as an adjustment to opening retained earnings for the current year.
3. Prior financial statements included for comparative purposes remain unchanged.
4. The new policy is applied as of the beginning of the current year.

ILLUSTRATION

The management of Ontario Mops Inc. decided to change its method of costing merchandise movement from the weighted average cost method to FIFO. The change was made to conform to a long-standing industry norm and not based upon new information. However, the inventory count sheets and costs were lost for all prior years with the exception of the December 31, 20x4, inventory, the opening inventory for the current year. The January 1, 20x5, inventory under the weighted average cost method was $145,000 and under the FIFO method was $160,000. The company has a 40% tax rate.

Required
1. Determine the cumulative effect.
2. Record the cumulative effect.

Requirement 1

Opening inventory:	
FIFO	$160,000
Weighted average	145,000
Cumulative effect before tax	15,000
Tax effect (40%)	6,000
Cumulative effect, net of tax	$ 9,000

Requirement 2

Merchandise inventory	15,000	
Future income tax liabilities		6,000
Retained earnings, cumulative effect of accounting principle change		9,000

5. PROSPECTIVE APPROACH

The prospective approach is used for all **changes in accounting estimates.** It is also used for a **change in accounting policy** if allowed by a new reporting standard.

When the prospective approach is used for changes in accounting policy, the following disclosures are required:
- The fact that the change has not been applied retroactively.
- The effect of the change on current and future financial statements.

If the change is one of an accounting estimate, neither of these disclosures is required. The firm merely incorporates the new estimate in any related accounting determination.

The following guidelines apply to **changes in accounting estimates** and to applying the prospective approach to **changes in accounting policy:**

1. Prior statements shown on a comparative basis are not restated or otherwise affected.
2. The new estimate is applied as of the beginning of the current period, generally based on the book value of the relevant balance sheet account remaining at that time.
3. No entry is made for prior year effects—only the normal current-year entry, which incorporates the new estimate, is made.
4. Future years continue to use the new estimate, if applicable, until the estimate is changed again in future periods.

ILLUSTRATION

A piece of equipment with a cost of $10,000 and an estimated useful life of 10 years, without salvage value, was acquired on January 1, 20x3. During 20x5, the estimate useful life is revised from 10 years to 7 years. The straight-line method of amortization is used.

Required

1. Determine the book value of the equipment at January 1, 20x5.
2. Determine the annual amortization expense based on the new estimate for the remaining life of the equipment.
3. Record amortization expense for 20x5.

Requirement 1

Cost	$10,000
Accumulated amortization, 20x3 and 20x4,	
$10,000 × 2/10	2,000
Book value, January 1, 20x5	$ 8,000

Requirement 2

Annual amortization expense: $8,000/(7 − 2) = $1,600

WATCH! The number of years *must* also be adjusted to reflect the passage of time since the acquisition date (in our illustration, 7 years less 2 years.)

Requirement 3

Amortization expense	1,600	
Accumulated amortization		1,600

6. DISCLOSURE REQUIREMENTS

Accounting changes affect the consistency and comparability of financial statements, and therefore their reliability. The *CICA Handbook,* Section 1506, recommends specific disclosures for any types of changes or adjustments if they are material. There are disclosures required for all policy changes. In addition there specific disclosure that apply only to voluntary changes and another set of disclosures that relate to involuntary changes. For voluntary changes disclosure must include a justification of why the new policy results in information that is more relevant than the old policy.

For changes in estimates disclosure must include the nature and amount of a change in an estimate that has an effect in the current period or is expected to have an effect in the future periods.

For errors disclosure includes the fact that an error has occurred, the nature of the error, the amount of the correction for each period affected, and the fact that the results are restated.

7. ACCOUNTING RULES PRE-2005

This chapter is based on an exposure draft. The major changes from existing standards are:
1. Voluntary changes are only allowed if they result in information that is more relevant. This is a new requirement.
2. The requirement to adopt a new policy with some degree of retroactive restatement is also new. Exceptions still exist for standards that specifically allow prospective treatment.
3. Moe general disclosure is required.

8. CASH FLOW STATEMENT

A change in accounting policy may also affect the cash flow statement.

A change in accounting policy does not change cash flow but *can* affect how that cash flows are reported.

Similarly, the *correction of accounting errors* may affect the amounts shown in prior periods' cash flow statements if the error affects the amounts previously reported.

Changes in accounting *estimates* will not affect the classification of cash flows.

9. PRIOR PERIOD ADJUSTMENTS

Prior top 1996, under certain circumstances, companies were permitted to make **prior period adjustments**. Certain gains and losses were credited directly to retained earnings and did not flow through the income statement. The *CICA Handbook*, paragraph 1506.31, now states that all charges and credits must flow through the income statement. The only exceptions are for the correction of errors and for retroactively applied changes in accounting policy.

10. INTERNATIONAL PERSPECTIVE

The U.S. approach for accounting policy changes is sharply at variance with the approach used in Canada. The preferred U.S. practice for changes in accounting policy is not only to use the prospective approach instead of the retroactive approach, but also to report the cumulative impact of a policy change as a component of net income in the period in which the change is made. Retroactive treatment is prohibited, except for a short list of specific changes, and except when retroactive application is specifically required in any new standard issued by the FASB.

The International Accounting Standards Committee recommends the retroactive approach as its preferred approach.

Prospective treatment of accounting for changes in accounting estimates is generally accepted around the world.

TRUE–FALSE QUESTIONS

T F 1. The retroactive approach requires that prior years' financial statements be restated in order to enhance comparability.

T F 2. The prospective approach requires that the cumulative effect of an accounting change be reported in the current period as a separate component of income.

T F 3. When a firm changes from the weighted average method of inventory costing to the first-in, first-out method, a change in an accounting policy occurs.

T F 4. The cumulative effect of a change in accounting policy is determined by comparing the balance in retained earnings at the beginning and the end of the year of change.

T F 5. The cumulative effect of a change in accounting policy is reported net of its tax effect, as an adjustment to opening retained earnings for the current year.

T F 6. In addition to reporting the cumulative effect of a change in accounting policy as a component of current income, prior years' financial statements are restated to reflect the new accounting policy.

T F 7. When a company changes its amortization policy from DDB to straight-line based on new information, the change should be applied prospectively.

T F 8. When a previous estimate of the useful life of a building is revised in the third year of an asset's life, amortization expense for the first two years should be restated using the estimate.

T F 9. Correction of an error may be made using the prospective approach if the required information for retroactive restatement is not available.

T F 10. Changes in accounting estimates will not affect the cash flow statement.

MULTIPLE CHOICE QUESTIONS

___ **1.** Which of the following is a change in accounting policy?
   a. Correction of an error using the retroactive approach with restatement.
   b. Change from an incorrect method to a correct method.
   c. Change in the amortization method used, as a result of changed corporate reporting objectives.
   d. Change in the number of total expected service-miles for a truck amortized under the units-of-production method.

___ **2.** Which of the following is a change in accounting policy to be given retroactive treatment?
   a. Change to LIFO for a firm in its ninth year and that is unable to reconstruct LIFO opening inventory.
   b. Change in amortization method, based on new information about how assets are actually used.
   c. Change in accounting policy for construction contracts: all contracts to date have been no more than six months long, and have used completed-contract; percentage-of-completion is being used for a three-year contract.
   d. Change from full costing to the successful efforts method of accounting for natural resources to comply with industry practice.

___ **3.** The retroactive approach with no restatement is used for which of the following:
   a. Correcting errors and making estimate changes.
   b. Changing inventory cost flow assumptions (FIFO, LIFO) when only opening balances can be reconstructed.
   c. Changing to the completed-contract method of accounting for long-term contracts to conform to industry norms when prior years can be reconstructed.
   d. Correcting errors affecting prior years' income.

___ **4.** A company changed from percentage-of-completion (PC) to completed-contract (CC) for financial accounting purposes during 20x5 to conform to industry norms. Prior years' results cannot be reconstructed, but opening balances can be restated.

   a. Beginning 1 January 20x5, CC should be used for construction accounting and the difference between income under the two methods for years before 20x5 is disclosed in the 20x5 income statement.

   b. Beginning 1 January 20x5, CC should be used for construction accounting but no entry is made for the effects of the change on years before 20x5.

   c. Beginning 1 January 20x5, CC should be used for construction accounting, and the difference between income under the two methods for years before 20x5 is an adjustment to the 31 December 20x5 retained earning balance.

   d. Beginning 1 January 20x5, CC should be used for construction accounting, and the difference between income under the two methods for years before 20x5 is an adjustment to the 1 January 20x5 retained earnings balance.

___ **5.** When accounting changes or error corrections are recorded, certain disclosures are usually required. A description of the effect of the change on the financial statements of the current and prior periods is required disclosure except for:

   a. Change in accounting policy.

   b. Change in accounting estimate.

   c. Correction of an error.

   d. None of the above.

___ **6.** When a company changes its method of amortization of an asset because of a change in economic conditions, the change should be accounted for:

   a. Retroactively with restatement of prior years.

   b. Retroactively without restatement of prior years.

   c. All in the year of the change.

   d. Over the remaining service life of the asset.

___ **7.** Quick Company changed revenue recognition methods for accounting purposes and correctly computed a cumulative effect before tax of $600 (reduces income). The tax rate is 30%. The change is a temporary difference between accounting and taxable income. The entry to record the change in accounting principle includes:

   a. Credit accounts receivable $420.

   b. Debit future income tax asset $180.

   c. Debit income tax payable $420.

   d. Debit retained earnings $600.

___ 8. Fido Dog Food Company changed its method of accounting for inventory from Average Cost to FIFO in 20x5 for both tax and financial accounting purposes. Tax returns were refiled. The 20x4 ending inventory was $40,000 under Average Cost and $55,000 under FIFO. Fido discloses 20x4 and 20x5 results comparatively. The tax rate is 30%. The entry to record the change in accounting policy includes:
   a. Credit future income tax liability $4,500.
   b. Debit retained earnings $10,500.
   c. Credit income tax payable $4,500.
   d. Debit income tax receivable $4,500.

___ 9. An asset purchased 1 January 20x4, costing $10,000, with a 10-year useful life and no salvage value, was amortized under the straight-line method during its first three years. During 20x7, the total useful life was re-estimated to be 17 years. What is the amount of amortization expense in 20x8?
   a. $462
   b. $412
   c. $464
   d. $500

___ 10. Which of the following is *not* appropriate when it is discovered that a 5-year insurance premium payment 2 years ago was debited to insurance expense?
   a. A credit to prepaid insurance.
   b. A retroactive restatement of the income statement of the previous year.
   c. A retroactive restatement of the balance sheet of the previous year.
   d. A footnote explaining the impact of the error on net income and earnings per share of the current year.

___ 11. The Great Company understated its inventory by $5,000 at the end of 20x4. If the error was discovered early in 20x5 after the 20x4 books have been closed, which of the following will be appropriate to correct the error? (Ignore income tax effect.)
   a. A debit to inventory and a credit to retained earnings of $5,000.
   b. A cumulative effect of $5,000 presented on the retained earnings statement for 20x5.
   c. A deduction of $5,000 from the beginning balance of retained earnings in the statement of retained earnings for 20x5.
   d. None of the above.

___ 12. If the error described in question 11 is discovered after the 20x5 books have been closed, the discovery of the error will require: a.
   a. a debit to inventory of $5,000.
   b. a $5,000 adjustment in the 20x6 income statement.
   c. a debit to prior year adjustment.
   d. none of the above.

___ **13.** During 20x5, Yamma Company discovered that its inventories were overstated by \$10,000 and \$20,000 at the end of 20x4 and 20x5, respectively. If the 20x5 books are still open, these errors will be corrected by debiting retained earnings, effect of error, and crediting inventory at:

a. \$0

b. \$10,000

c. \$20,000

d. \$30,000

___ **14.** Assume the same data as in question 13, except that those errors were discovered after the 20x5 books were closed. These errors will be corrected by debiting retained earnings, effect of error, and crediting inventory account at:

a. \$0.

b. \$10,000.

c. \$20,000.

d. \$30,000.

SOLUTIONS TO TRUE–FALSE QUESTIONS

1. T

2. F A cumulative adjustment is not computed or reported. Prior periods' results remain unchanged.

3. T

4. F The cumulative effect of a change in accounting principle is determined by comparing the balances affected by the change between the old method and the new method.

5. T

6. F The cumulative impact of the accounting policy change on prior year's net income is recorded as an adjustment to the beginning balance of retained earnings, not as a component of current income.

7. T

8. F No entry is made for prior year effects; only the normal current year entry, which incorporates the new estimate, is made.

9. F Error correction is made on a retroactive basis, There is no reason for the information being unavailable.

10. T

SOLUTIONS TO MULTIPLE CHOICE QUESTIONS

1. c A change in method of accounting policy due to changing corporate reporting objectives is a change in accounting policy. The other examples are changes in estimates or an error.

2. d The change in accounting policy to comply with industry practice requires a retroactive adjustment.

3. b When there is a change in accounting policy where opening numbers cannot be provided a retroactive adjustment without restatement can be completed.

4. d Since prior results cannot be reconstructed but opening numbers are available, the adjustment is made to January 1 retained earnings balance instead of December 31.

5. d Disclosure is required for all changes noted..

6. d The old method was appropriate for the old circumstances. The new method is now appropriate based on new conditions, therefore, the change should be prospectively.

7. b The temporary difference changes future income taxes. ($600 x .3 = $180)

8. c ($55,000 – $40,000) x 30% = $4,500. Tax returns were refilled and more tax is owing.

9. d The book value 1 January 20x7 = $10,000 – [($10,000/10) x 3] = $7,000. The 20x8 amortization = $7,000/(17-3) = $500.

10. a The prepaid insurance should be debited to reflect the amount of insurance still not expired. The other statements are all true.

11. a The ending inventory of 20x4 is the beginning inventory of 20x5, so the debit to inventory is adjusting the beginning inventory to reflect the correct amount. The credit to retained earnings is reflecting an increase in income for 20x4. The understated ending inventory in 20x4 resulted in an understated net income.

12. d The oversight decreased ending inventory for 20x4, overstated cost of goods sold, and thereby understated net income for the year. The resulting understatement of beginning inventory in 20x5 will cause an understatement of cost of goods sold and an overstatement of net income in 20x5. If the ending inventory for 20x5 is correctly stated, the cumulative error will wash out because the overstatement of 20x5 net income will offset the understatement of 20x4 net income; retained earnings at the end of 20x5 will be correct. The error is discovered in 20x5, so no adjustment needs to be made on the books because there are no misstated accounts for 20x6.

13. b The ending inventories were overstated in 20x4 and 20x5. In 20x4 the cost of goods sold was understated by $10,000 and net income overstated by $10,000. In 20x5 the beginning inventory can still be adjusted to reflect the correct amount. The ending inventory will also be adjusted to reflect the correct amount. So the only adjustment for prior period is $10,000 debit to retained earnings.

14. c If the 20x5 books are closed, the error in 20x4 and its effects are washed out. The error (overstatement of ending inventory) in 20x5 has to be adjusted because it affected the cost of goods sold and the net income for 20x5. The adjustment is therefore a debit to retained earnings and a credit to inventory.

PROBLEMS

Problem 1

PURPOSE: To illustrate the difference in accounting approaches for change in accounting policy.

Rundle Co. has decided to change its method of accounting for inventories from weighted average to FIFO in the fiscal year ending December 31, 20x5. The change is made to conform with industry practice and the company justifies it as presenting more relevant information. The reporting for the fiscal year ends on December 31. The company's income tax rate is 40%.

From its records, the company determines the following information relating to the change:

	20x5		20x4	
	FIFO	WA	FIFO	WA
(a) Beginning inventory	$45,000	$40,000	$43,000	$35,000
(b) Ending inventory	52,000	48,000	45,000	40,000
(c) Income before extraordinary items	[a]123,000			110,000
(d) Extraordinary gains (losses), net of tax	(1,000)			4,000
(e) Retained earnings, beginning balance	156,000			82,000
(f) Dividends declared and paid	(80,000)			(40,000)

[a] Reflects FIFO policy.

Required
    a. Prepare the journal entries to account for this change in accounting policy retroactively, with restatement.

    b. Prepare the journal entries to account for this change, assuming that for some reason the information for prior years is missing.

Problem 2

PURPOSE: To illustrate the accounting approach for a change in accounting estimate.

Cyros Inc. has been amortizing equipment over a 10-year life on a straight-line basis. The equipment, which cost $224,000, was purchased on January 1, 20x1. It has an estimated residual value of $20,000. On the basis of experience since acquisition, management has decided to amortize it over a total life of 15 years instead of 10 years, with no change in the estimated residual value. The change is to be effective on January 1, 20x5. Disregard income tax considerations.

Required
Prepare the entry, or entries, to appropriately reflect the change and 20x5 amortization in the accounts for 20x5, the year of change.

Problem 3

PURPOSE: To illustrate the accounting approach to changes due to accounting error.

An examination of North's books at the beginning of 20x5 reveals the following errors:
    a. A piece of equipment acquired on January 1, 20x1, for $100,000 was charged to other expenses. The equipment should have a 5-year useful life with a salvage value of $10,000. North used the straight-line method to amortize its capital assets.

    b. The merchandise inventory at December 31, 20x4, was overstated by $8,000.

c. In January 20x4, North purchased a 2-year insurance policy costing $2,000 and debited the total amount to prepaid insurance account. No adjusting entry has been made for the insurance.

d. At the end of 20x4, North failed to accrue an interest expense of $4,000. This amount was expensed when paid in 20x5.

Required
Prepare appropriate correcting entries for the above errors, assuming that the 20x5 books are (1) open and (2) closed. Ignore income taxes.

SOLUTIONS TO PROBLEMS

Problem 1

Requirement a

Change in accounting policy (retroactive approach, with restatement)—

To make the change, Rundle must recalculate its inventory balances for the end of 20x4 in order to determine net income for 20x5, but also must recalculate its inventory balances for the beginning of 20x4 in order to restate the comparative results for 20x4.

Step 1: Determine which balances will be affected by the change.
— beginning inventory
— ending inventory
— cost of goods sold
— income tax expense
— future income tax
— retained earnings

The income statement, balance sheet, and retained earnings statement will require restatement for 20x4.

Step 2: Calculate the cumulative effect on balances up to January 1, 20x4.

Impact to January 1, 20x4
The change in the beginning inventory for 20x4 reflects the cumulative impact of the change in policy on previous years' cost of goods sold, which flows through to net income and thus to retained earnings, to that date:

$43,000 (FIFO) − $35,000 (WA) = $8,000

After income tax, assuming a 40% tax rate, the impact on accumulated earnings is:

(1 − 40%) × $8,000 = $4,800

Step 3: Calculate the specific impact on the accounts for the year 20x4, for comparative restatement purposes.

The effect on 20x4 net income is as follows:
- FIFO has a higher beginning inventory, increasing cost of goods sold and lowering pretax net income of $8,000.
- FIFO also has a higher ending inventory, lowering cost of the goods sold and increasing pretax net income by $5,000.
  - The net effect of the changes in the beginning and ending inventories is to decrease 20x4 income before tax by $3,000: $5,000 increase due to the impact on ending inventory minus the $8,000 decrease caused by the change in beginning inventory.
  - The income tax rate is 40%. Assuming that the inventory method for income tax purposes is not changed retroactively, the offset for the increase in income tax expense is the current future income tax account on the balance sheet.

The changes to the 20x4 statements can be summarized as follows:

Income statement
Cost of goods sold increases by	$3,000	(debit)
Income tax expense increases by	$1,200	(credit)
Net income increases by	$1,800	(debit)

Balance sheet
Inventory (ending) increases by	$5,000	(debit)
Current future income taxes changes by	$2,000	(credit)
Retained earnings increases by	$3,000	(credit)

The changes in the income statement reflect the impact of the accounting policy change only for 20x4, The change in the balance sheet; however, reflects the cumulative impact of the changes up to the end of 20x4:

WATCH!

Impact on retained earnings prior to the beginning of 20x4	$4,800 credit
Impact on net income and retained earnings for 20x4	1,800 debit
Total change in retained earnings	$3,000 credit

Step 4: Record the impact of the change.

The journal entry to record the effects of the change in policy is as follows:

Inventory	5,000	
Future income tax, current		2,000
Retained earnings		3,000

Requirement b

The prior years' results are not restated because it is not possible to reconstruct the income effect on prior-year results.

Step 1: Determine the cumulative effect.

Opening inventory
FIFO	$45,000
Weighted average	40,000
Cumulative effect before tax	5,000
Tax effect (40%)	2,000
Cumulative effect, net of tax	$ 3,000

Step 2: Record the cumulative effect.

Inventory	5,000	
Future income tax, current		2,000
Retained earnings		3,000

This example assumes that the company continues to use the weighted average method of inventory costing for tax purposes. Therefore, the tax impact of the prior years' earnings under the FIFO method is credited to the future income tax account.

WATCH! The non-restatement approach is used when the available information cannot be obtained.

Problem 2

Step 1: Calculate the book value of the equipment on January 1, 20x5.

Original cost	$224,000
Accumulated amortization at December 31, 20x4[a]	81,600
Book value, January 1, 20x5	$142,400

[a] ([$224,000 − $20,000]/10 years) × 4 years = $81,600

Step 2: Calculate the annual amortization.

The book value of $142,400 at the beginning of 20x5 is the basis on which amortization for 20x5 and future years will be based. The equipment is 4 years old at the beginning of 20x5, which leaves 11 years of useful life remaining
under the revised estimate. As well, the previous residual value of $20,000 remains the same. Annual amortization beginning in 20x5 will be:

($142,400 − $20,000)/11 = $11,127

Step 3: Prepare the journal entry to record the amortization expense for 20x5.

Amortization expense	11,127	
Accumulated amortization		11,127

Problem 3

Requirement a(1)

Step 1: Determine the cumulative effect up to January 1, 20x4.

Cost of equipment	$100,000
Accumulated amortization	54,000
Retained earnings understated	$46,000

Step 2: Prepare the journal entry.

Equipment	100,000	
Accumulated amortization		54,000
Retained earnings, error correction		46,000

Step 3: Record current amortization expense (20x4).

Amortization expense	18,000	
Accumulated amortization		18,000

Requirement a(2)

Step 1: Determine the cumulative effect up to January 1, 20x5.

Cost of equipment	$100,000
Accumulated amortization	72,000
Retained earnings understated	$28,000

Step 2: Prepare the journal entry.

Equipment	100,000	
Accumulated amortization		72,000
Retained earnings		28,000

Step 3: No entry.

Requirement b(1)

Step 1: Determine cumulative effect up to January 1, 20x4.

Beginning inventory overstated	$8,000

Step 2: Prepare adjusting entry.

Retained earnings, error correction	8,000	
Inventory (closed to COGS)		8,000

Requirement b(2)

Step 1: Determine cumulative effect up to January 1, 20x5.

Beginning inventory overstated	–0–

Step 2: No entry necessary (washed out).

Requirement c(1)

Step 1: Determine cumulative effect up to January 1, 20x4.

Prepaid insurance overstated	$1,000

Step 2: Prepare the adjusting entry:

Retained earnings, error correction	1,000	
Prepaid insurance		1,000

Step 3: Record the current insurance expense (20x5).

Insurance expense	1,000	
Prepaid insurance		1,000

Requirement c(2)

Step 1: Determine cumulative effect up to January 1, 20x5.

Prepaid insurance overstated	$2,000

Step 2: Prepare the adjusting entry.

Retained earnings, error corrections	2,000	
Prepaid insurance		2,000

Step 3: No entry.

Requirement d(1)

Step 1: Determine cumulative effect up to January 1, 20x4.

Retained earnings overstated	$4,000

Step 2: Prepare the adjusting entry.

Retained earnings, error correction	4,000	
Interest expense		4,000

Requirement d(2)

Step 1: Determine cumulative effect up to January 1, 20x5.

Retained earnings overstated	–0–

Step 2: No entry.

CASE

You are the accountant for Slater Floors Ltd., and you are preparing adjustments prior to the presentation of year end financial statements. Quinn Johnston, the bookkeeper, has a habit of recording items in a suspense account if he is unsure about proper classification. For the year 20x5, your analysis of the suspense accounts shows the following:

	Debit	Credit	Balance
March 31	$270,000		dr. $270,000
April 22	170,000		440,000
June 16	710,000		1,150,000
November 2		$430,000	dr. 720,000

The entry on March 31 for $270,000 represents a write-down of inventory. The items had been purchased two years ago, and the market price steadily declined this year. The colour was now not popular. This adjustment reduced inventory to the "lower of cost or market." Quinn is inclined to believe that the $270,000 should be recorded as a retroactive adjustment, since it relates to an event (purchase of inventory) that happened two years ago.

The debit on April 22 is a payment made to Canada Customs and Revenue Agency as a result of a tax audit that covered the years 20x0–20x4. Quinn believes this amount should be part of income tax expense on the income statement, along with all the other payments to Canada Customs and Revenue Agency.

The entry on June 16 represents the cost to rebuild and repair capital assets damaged by a flash flood. Some of the older employees at the plant remember the last time it happened, 199x, but the damage was not as extensive then. Quinn has concluded that he should set up the $710,000 as an asset, to be amortized over the expected life of the capital facilities.

Finally, the $430,000 credit of November 2 arose from the discovery of a mistake in the 20x4 calculation of the pension liability. Quinn was checking a document and noticed a $430,000 error in addition, which resulted in a reduction to the pension liability. Since the increase in the liability was debited to pension expense, Quinn reasons that the credit must also be an element of current pension expense.

Required
Comment on the proper classification for each of these items. Prepare a compound journal entry to reallocate the suspense account. Ignore the impact of income taxes.

KEY POINTS IN THE CASE
Quinn is not correct in any of his tentative conclusions.

Inventory write-down. The write-down of inventory to its lower of cost or market value is not a retroactive adjustment. Only the correction of error and retroactively applied changes in accounting policy are recorded as a retroactive adjustment. Any loss must be shown on the income statement, as an element of operating income. It may be classified as an unusual item, if in fact it is infrequent. The critical event is not the purchase of inventory, but rather the decline in market value, a current year event. Further, due to its nature as a normal business risk, and it was the result of a management decision the item does not qualify as an extraordinary item.

Income tax assessment. The payment of a tax reassessment must flow through the income statement. The amount should be shown separately from the income tax expense. It does not qualify for retroactive adjustment because it is not a correction, or an error, or a retroactively applied change in accounting policy. So Quinn was not totally wrong in wanting to put it on the income statement.

Flood damage. Quinn is not entitled to set up a repair cost as an asset, since the repairs do not impart any benefit to future periods. The cost of the assets already reflected in the balance sheet reflects those future benefits; the assets have not been made more useful by the repairs.

However, the $710,000 does not have to be treated as an ordinary repair expense. This cost qualifies as an extraordinary item on the income statement, due largely to the infrequent nature of flooding. Extraordinary items are shown separately, net of tax, after the calculation of "net income before extraordinary item."

Error in pension calculation. The correction of an error must be shown in the financial statements as a retroactive correction to opening retained earnings, since it does indeed relate to a prior year.

In this case, the error can clearly be traced to 20x4, and as a result, the 20x4 income was understated. In order to correctly reflect this in the financial statements, retained earnings, not current income, must be adjusted.

Compound journal entry—

Unusual expense, income tax expense	170,000	
Cost of goods sold—inventory	270,000	
Extraordinary item—flood damage	710,000	
Retained earnings, error correction		430,000
Suspense account		720,000
To close suspense account and reallocate elements.		

SELECTED SOLUTIONS FROM THE TEXTBOOK
Assignment 20-7

Requirement 1

Gunnard Company
Income Statement - Successful Efforts
For the Years Ended 31 December

	20x5	20x4
Revenues	$7,100,000	$4,400,000
Expenses:		
Resource exploration costs	4,700,000	3,200,000
Amortization	200,000	40,000
Other	2,050,000	720,000
Total	6,950,000	3,960,000
NI before tax	150,000	440,000
Income tax expense (30%)	45,000	132,000
Net income	$105,000	$308,000

Requirement 2

Resource exploration costs to be capitalized	$(3,200,000)
Additional amortization expense, 20x4 ($240,000 – $40,000)	200,000
Net effect on 20x4 income, pre-tax	$(3,000,000)
Additional resource exploration costs, asset, 20x4 ($3,200,000 – $200,000)	$3,000,000

Journal entry:

Resource exploration costs (see above)...	3,000,000	
Future income tax liability ($3,000,000 x .3).........................		900,000
Retained earnings, ($3,000,000 x .7)		2,100,000
Cumulative effect of accounting change		

Amortization expense, 20x5	850,000	
Resource exploration costs...		850,000

This assumes that the $4,700,000 resource development costs incurred in 20x5, that would have been expensed under SE, have been correctly capitalized. If not, the following entry is needed:

Resource exploration costs (asset)	4,700,000	
Resource exploration expense		4,700,000

Requirement 3

Gunnard Company
Income Statement - Full Costing
For the Years Ended 31 December

	20x5	20x4
Revenues	$7,100,000	$4,400,000
Expenses:		
Exploration cost amortization	850,000	240,000
Other...	2,050,000	720,000
Total	2,900,000	960,000
NI before tax	4,200,000	3,440,000
Income tax expense (30%)..	1,260,000	1,032,000
Net income..	$2,940,000	$2,408,000

In 20x5, the Company changed from SE to FC for accounting for resource exploration costs. The change increased 20x4 net income by $2,100,000 and 20x5 income by $2,835,000*. The 20x4 comparative statements are restated to reflect the change.

* Reduced resource exploration costs...	$(4,700,000)
Increased amortization expense ($850,000 – $200,000).................................	650,000
Net effect on income...	(4,050,000)
After-tax effect (1 – .3)	$(2,835,000)

Requirement 4

Gunnard Company
Retained Earnings Statement
For the Years Ended 31 December

	20x5	20x4
Opening retained earnings, as previously reported..............	$ 308,000	$ --
Cumulative effect of accounting policy change, net of income tax of $900,000...	2,100,000	--
Opening retained earnings, as restated..................................	2,408,000	--
Net income	2,940,000	2,408,000
Closing retained earnings	$5,348,000	$2,408,000

Requirement 5

Under successful efforts, expenditures for exploration costs would be an outflow under the operations section. Under FC, such costs would be an investing outflow. Using the indirect method to present the operations section, the amortization would be a non-cash expense add-back.

The change in policy is not disclosed on the CFS.

Assignment 20-8

Requirement 1

This is a change in estimate; therefore, the prospective approach should be used. Revision of accounting estimates are normal and expected; therefore, their effects should be allocated to the current and future periods.

	20x1	20x1–20x4	20x5
Analysis:			
Cost	$24,000		$24,000
Amortization to date		($1,800 x 4 yrs.)	(7,200)
Residual value..	(6,000)		(6,000)
To be depreciated.......................................	$18,000		$10,800
Annual depreciation (SL):			
Ten year life—per year	$ 1,800		
Life (14 – 4 yrs)—per year			$ 1,080

Requirement 2

No correction or adjusting entry is necessary at the date of change because (under the prospective approach) the unamortized balance is amortized over the remaining life. To record amortization at year-end, 20x5

Amortization expense [$10,800 ÷ (14 – 4 years)].........................	1,080	
Accumulated amortization, equipment		1,080

Requirement 3

Comparative balance sheet, 31 December:

	20x5	20x4
Equipment...	$24,000	$24,000
Accumulated amortization	(8,280)*	(7,200)
Net book value...	$15,720	$16,800

*$7,200 + $1,080 = $8,280

Comparative income statement for year:

	20x5	20x4
Income prior to amortization and tax..	$52,800	$49,800
Amortization expense	(1,080)	(1,800)
Net income before tax..	$51,720	$48,000

No note disclosure is required because the change is very ordinary. However, if the company wishes to make disclosures:

Note X: Change in accounting estimate—Effective in 20x5, the company revised the estimated life on equipment. In 20x5, this change in estimated useful life caused net income to be higher than under the prior basis by $720.

Assignment 20-24

Requirement 1

This is a change in accounting principle, from completed-contract to percentage-of-completion. It should be applied retroactively with restatement.

Requirement 2

Construction in progress inventory ($195 – $180).............................. 15,000		
Future income tax liability (1)..		6,000
Retained earnings: cumulative effect of change in accounting		
principles (1)...		9,000

(1) CC Income, 20x3—20x6 ($60,000 + $120,000)		$180,000
PC Income, 20x3—20x6 ($40,000 + $65,000 + $50,000 +		
$40,000)..		195,000
Increase in NI...		15,000
Tax effect (40%)		6,000
Impact on retained earnings...		$ 9,000

Requirement 3

KLB Corporation
Retained Earnings Statement
For the Year Ended 31 December 20x7

	20x7	20x6
Opening retained earnings, 1 January	$440,000	$320,000
Cumulative effect of a change in accounting principle (2)	9,000	57,000
Opening retained earnings, as restated	449,000	377,000
Net income (1)	160,000	92,000
Dividends	(20,000)	(20,000)
Closing retained earnings, 31 December	$589,000	$449,000

(1) CC income, 20x6	$120,000
PC income, 20x6	40,000
Decrease in income	80,000
Tax effect (40%)	32,000
Change in 20x6 income	48,000
20x6 income, as reported	140,000
Revised 20x6 income	$ 92,000

(2) Cumulative effect (increase)	$ 9,000
20x6 effect (see #1) (decrease)	48,000
	$57,000

Proof: CC income 20x3—20x5	$ 60,000
PC income, 20x3—20x5 ($40,000 + $65,000 + $50,000)	155,000
Increase in income	95,000
After tax (1 − .4)	$ 57,000

Requirement 4

KLB Corporation
Retained Earnings Statement
For the Year Ended 31 December 20x7

	20x7	20x6
Opening retained earnings, 1 January, as previously reported	$440,000	$320,000
Cumulative effect of a change in accounting principles	9,000	—
Opening retained earnings, as restated	449,000	320,000
Net income	160,000	140,000
Dividends	(20,000)	(20,000)
Closing retained earnings, 31 December	$589,000	$440,000

Requirement 5

If it were impossible to restate any opening balances, the change would be made in 20X8. Information could then be gathered to restate closing 20X7 (opening 20X8) balances and the change could be accounted for retroactively with no restatement in 20X8.

Assignment 20-28

Case A:

1. Change in accounting "estimate"—prospective basis. Amortization policies are "principles" and some will automatically respond that this is a change in principle. However, amortization methods must be reviewed regularly and changes applied prospectively if based on a different pattern of expected benefit. Thus, the classification is a change in estimate.

2. a)   Amortization expense 5,500
         Accumulated amortization 5,500
         $60,000 – $5,000 = $55,000/10 = $5,500

    b)   No entry is required for a prospective change.

         c)   Amortization expense.. 7,600
              Accumulated amortization 7,600
         Net book value = $60,000 – ($5,500 x 4) = $38,000
         $38,000 x .2 = $7,600

3. 20x4 balances reflect straight-line amortization and are not changed.

Case B:

1. Change in accounting principle to conform to industry practice—retroactive approach with no restatement. No restatement is possible because prior opening balances cannot be restated. Report the effect of the accounting change as an adjustment to the beginning balance of retained earnings.

2. Entry to record the effect of the change:

    1 January 20x5:
    Inventory ($17,000 – $12,000) 5,000
        Retained earnings, accounting change 5,000

3. a)   The effect of the change is reported on the 20x5 comparative statement of retained earnings as an adjustment to the beginning balance of 20x5 retained earnings.

    b)   On the 20x5 comparative statements, the 20x4 income statement amounts are unchanged, and are reported on the LIFO basis, as data is not available to retroactively restate balances.

Case C:

1. This is a change in estimate; the prospective approach is used. Revision of accounting estimates are normal and expected; therefore, their effects should be apportioned to the current and future periods.

2. a) 31 December 20x4, adjusting entry (based on the prior estimates):
    Amortization expense, patent 1,000
    Patent.. 1,000
    $17,000 ÷ 17 yrs = $1,000.

    b) No entry is made to record the cumulative effect of the change in estimate.

    c) 31 December 20x5, adjusting entry (based on the new estimates and the unamortized balance):

    Amortization expense, patent 1,625
    Patent.. 1,625

    Computation:
    Patent cost $17,000
    Amortization to date ($17,000 x 4/17 yrs.) .... (4,000)
    Residual value .... (____0)
    Unamortized balance.. $13,000

    Amortization each year:
    [$13,000 ÷ (12 − 4) = 8 yrs.] .... $ 1,625

3. The 20x4 financial statement amounts as originally reported in 20x4 are reported in the 20x5 comparative financial statements.

SOLUTIONS TO CONCEPT REVIEW QUESTIONS

Page 1219

1. The three types of accounting changes are changes in accounting estimates, the changes in accounting policies, and the correction of accounting errors.

2. If a company discovers that there are more uncollectible accounts from the prior year than it had previously provided as expense, this represents a change in an estimate. The assessment of doubtful accounts is an accounting estimate made by management. Therefore, the accounting change required to reflect the new assessment of doubtful accounts is a revision in the estimate.

3. If a company is uncertain as to whether an accounting change is a change in policy or a change in estimate, the *CICA Handbook* suggests that the item be treated as a change in estimate.

Page 1222

1. The three different ways in which changes can be accounted for are:
- Retroactive application with restatement of prior periods.
- Retroactive application without restatement of prior periods.
- Prospective application.

2. The preferred method of reporting a change in accounting policy is retroactive application of the change in policy with a restatement of prior periods. The reason is that prior period restatement provides readers of financial statements with comparative data for the current period.

3. Correction of errors of prior years should be done retroactive with restatement.

Page 1230

1. The future income tax account should be debited. If the accumulated amortization decreased the accounting basis of the asset increased. The temporary difference would increase therefore the future tax liability would be debited.

2. The cumulative adjustment to opening retained earnings is $10,500 ($105,000 - $120,000) x (1 - 30%)]

3. Opening retained earnings decrease (Assets decrease so to balance equity decreases.)

Page 1233

1. There is a recovery of $10,000 this year. [($200,000 x 15%) - $40,000}
2. The amortization expense for the current year is $40,000 calculated as follows:

Cost	$500,000
Accumulated amortization, 3 years,	
$10,000 x 3/5	300,000
Book value, January 1, 20x5	$ 200,000

Remaining revised useful life 8-3 = 5 years

Amortization current year $200,000 ÷ 5 = $40,000

Page 1237

1. For a voluntary change in accounting policy, the additional disclosure required is justification of why the new policy provides more relevant information than the old policy.

2. While a change in accounting policy cannot change cash flows, a retroactive application of the policy can affect the individual components shown on the cash flow statement. Retroactive application of the change in policy will result in adjusting the net income and other amounts related to the accounting change on the cash flow statement. The net cash flow will be unaffected, but the amounts that are used to derive the net cash flow from operations will be altered as the result of the change in policy.

3. Under U.S. rules the cumulative effect of a change in accounting policy is normally reported as a component of net income in the period in which the change is made. There is a short list of specific changes that require retroactive restatement.

CHAPTER 21

FINANCIAL STATEMENT ANALYSIS

Financial statement analysis is an organized approach for extracting information from the financial statements that is relevant to the particular decision the analyst is making.

Financial statement analysis is a broad and complex field. This chapter focuses on analysis of the statements themselves. One of the most important first steps is to decide on the *decision focus* of the analysis. If the accounting policies used by the company are not appropriate to the focus the statements must be recast before the analysis can begin.

Ratios are useless unless they can be compared to historical trends or averages or comparable ratios of companies in the same industry. Comparable is a key word for ratio comparison. To be comparable the companies must have similar accounting policies. Ratio analysis is misleading if inappropriate comparisons are made.

The first appendix to this chapter summarizes the procedures to prepare a cash flow statement and includes a comprehensive example. The second appendix illustrates financial statement restatement and analysis.

1. OVERVIEW OF STATEMENT ANALYSIS

Clarify the Decision Focus

The starting point is to be clear about what decision is to be made as a result of the financial statement analysis. Possible decisions include:

- Equity investment decisions.
- Lending decisions.
- Contractual decisions, such as accepting employment, negotiating collective agreements, or entering into a joint venture.
- Regulatory decisions, including the need for rate or price increases or the impact of past regulatory decisions.

Each of these decisions will require a somewhat different approach to the analysis and a different set of principles. This is why it is crucial to know the nature of the decision in question.

Examine the Auditor's Report

Another important step in analyzing financial statements is to read the accompanying auditor's report. A public company must be audited and if listed on the stock exchange must have a "clean" or unqualified opinion. A private company may use one or more accounting policies that do not comply with the *CICA Handbook* and have a qualified opinion. This may not be a cause of concern if done to meet the needs of the primary stakeholders. An adverse or reservation of opinion are very serious and means the auditor is in serious disagreement about the suitability of the accounting policies or believes the financial statements are misleading.

If a private company does not have an audit, a professional accountant may be retained for a **review engagement.** Here, an audit is not performed but the accountant does review the financial statements for general consistency with GAAP and for reasonableness of presentation.

You must remember that a review engagement provides no assurance that the company's internal control policies and procedures are operating properly; nor does it ensure that there is external evidence to support the amounts presented on the financial statements.

Examine Accounting Policies

A company's **footnotes, statement of accounting policies,** and **supplementary schedules** must also be analysed. Exhibit 21-1 in the textbook shows some of the accounting policy decisions and accounting estimates that management must select.

Focus of the Analyst

An analyst has to figure out which reporting objectives are implicit in the financial statements. If the implicit objectives do not correspond to the user's objectives, adjustments to the financial statements will probably be needed before they can be of maximum use.

Most of the clues to the implicit reporting objectives can be found in the notes to the financial statements.

Often, the accounting policy note gives only the broadest possible explanation of an accounting policy, but more information can be found in the other notes.

Other accounting and operating policies relate to the balance sheet, and the analyst must examine those as well. Further clues may be gleaned from the cash flow statement. Finally, the income statement must be examined for nonrecurring items.

Recast the Financial Statements

Users must often revise the financial statements to suit their needs before applying other analytical approaches.

WATCH! In recasting the statement to reflect accounting policies, it is important to remember to adjust for both sides of transactions.

For example, when a non-recurring gain is removed from the income statement, the balance of the non-recurring gain must be subtracted from retained earnings and must not simply be ignored.

Seek Comparative Information

Comparative financial statements present financial information for the current period and one or more past periods, in a way that facilitates comparison across several reporting periods.

There are two basis for comparison: **cross-sectional** and **longitudinal.**

Cross-sectional comparisons analyze a company in relation to other companies in the same year. Caution must be exercised to ensure that similar measurements are being used. For example if different accounting polices are used then the comparison will not be valid unless adjustment is made.

Longitudinal comparisons look at a company over time, comparing this year's performance with earlier years. Comparison may also be made to other companies or general economic trends.

Apply Analytical Techniques
Once the statements have been adjusted to suit the needs of the analyst, the statements may be subject to numerical analysis, or "number crunching." The basic tools of numerical analysis are **ratios.**

There are two common types of ratios:
- **Vertical analysis or common-size analysis ratios.** These are cross-sectional ratios in which the components of one year's individual financial statements are computed as a percentage of a base amount, using (for example) total assets as the base for the balance sheet and total sales as the base for the income statement.
- **Horizontal analysis or trend analysis ratios.** Here, longitudinal ratios for a single financial statement component are computed, with a base year's amount set at 100 and other years' amounts recomputed relative to this base amount.

2. RATIO ANALYSIS
Ratio analysis is the term applied to a large family of ratios that compare the proportional relationship between two different account's amounts in a single year's financial statements.

Depending on the characteristics they are attempting to capture and the specific user needs they are intended to satisfy, financial ratios can be classified under the following four categories:
- profitability ratios
- solvency ratios (including debt service ratios and leverage ratios)
- liquidity ratios
- efficiency (activity) ratios

It is important for analysts to focus on the ratios that have primary meaning for the decision at hand.

Profitability Ratios
These ratios are intended to measure various aspects of a firm's profit-making activities. Profitability is assessed as some form of *return on investment*. The analyst has to view the investment from an appropriate viewpoint. Profitability ratios will always

include information from the income statement and the balance sheet. Focusing on the income statement only is inadequate.

A common shareholder will be interested in **return on equity**. A bond holder will be interested in the return on long-term capital, sometimes called **capital employed** or **total capitalization.**

The numerator of any profitability ratio will reflect a return *over time* since it is derived from the income statement. The denominator will reflect balance sheet values at a *point in time*. Therefore, to make the numerator and denominator consistent, the denominator should be calculated as an *average* over the year. The common approach is to average the numbers at the beginning and end of the year.

(1) *Return on long-term capital, before taxes:*

$$\frac{\text{Net income + Interest expense on long term debt + Income tax expense}}{\text{Average long-term debt + average total owners' equity}}$$

(2) *Return on long-term capital, after taxes:*

$$\frac{\text{Net income + (interest expense on long-term debt} \times [1 - t])}{\text{Average long-term debt + average total owners' equity}}$$

ATCH! These ratios are useful for comparing to interest rates to test for leverage effect. That is, if a company can earn a rate of return on its assets that is higher than the rate it has to pay on debt, the shareholders will benefit because the surplus return will flow through to benefit the shareholders it the form of higher earnings per share.

(3) *Return on total assets, before taxes:*

$$\frac{\text{Net income + total interest expense + income tax expense}}{\text{Average total assets}}$$

(4) *Return on total assets, after taxes:*

$$\frac{\text{Net income + (total interest expense} \times [1 - t])}{\text{Average total assets}}$$

A common shareholder, a preferred shareholder, and a bond holder will all be interested in the underlying return on total assets.

These ratios indicate the overall return that the company is earning on its asset investment.

WATCH!

(5) *Return on common shareholders' equity:*

$$\frac{\text{Net income} - \text{preferred dividends}}{\text{Average total shareholders' equity} - \text{preferred share equity}}$$

This ratio shows the historical after-tax return to shareholders for the period.

(6) *Return on gross assets:*

$$\frac{(\text{EBIT} + \text{Amortization})}{\text{Average total assets (net)} + \text{accumulated amortization}}$$

This ratio indicates the return on invested capital without including amortization.

(7) *Operating margin:*

$$\frac{\text{Net income} + \text{interest} + \text{income tax (EBIT)}}{\text{Total revenue}}$$

This ratio indicates the profit margin (before taxes) earned on each dollar sales.

Profitability ratios can be useful, but must be treated with caution. The analyst's eyes must be wide open to the substantial variability that is unavoidably introduced by accounting measurements.

WATCH!

In considering profitability rations the following points must be noted:
- The ratios must have a measure on investment in the denominator and a measure of profitability in the numerator.
- The denominator and the numerator must be logically consistent.
- Accounting policies and estimates affect the denominator and the numerator.
- Adjustment may be required to the denominator and/or the numerator for accounting policies and off-balance sheet financing and investment.

Exhibit 21-5, in the text, provides a summary of profitability ratios.

Efficiency Ratios
These ratios provide information about how efficiently the firm is using its assets. They are also known as turnover ratios.

(1) *Accounts receivable turnover:*

$$\frac{\text{Sales revenue (on account)}}{\text{Average trade accounts receivable}}$$

This ratio indicates how quickly a firm is able to collect the accounts receivable.

To calculate the average trade accounts receivable, you take the opening balance and ending balance of accounts receivable and divide by two.

WATCH!

(2) *Average collection period of accounts receivable:*

$$\frac{365 \text{ (days)}}{\text{Accounts receivable turnover}}$$

This ratio shows the average number of days to collect trade accounts receivable.

WATCH! The accounts receivable turnover ratio is difficult to interpret. The accounts receivable shown on the balance sheet may not be typical throughout the year. The accounts receivable turnover ratio can be used by an external analyst only as a very rough indication of collection period.

(3) *Inventory turnover:*

$$\frac{\text{Cost of goods sold}}{\text{Average inventory}}$$

This ratio indicates how quickly inventory typically is sold. A high inventory turnover is not necessarily good and a low turnover is not necessarily bad. The goal is to maintain optimum not minimum inventory. .

(4) *Asset turnover:*

$$\frac{\text{Total revenue}}{\text{Average total assets}}$$

Asset turnover is a major component of return on assets. The higher this ration is the more efficient a company is at using its assets.

WATCH! Asset turnover is a component of return on assets. Operating margin multiplied by asset turnover equals return on assets:

$$\frac{\text{EBIT}}{\text{Revenue}} \times \frac{\text{Revenue}}{\text{Assets}} = \frac{\text{EBIT}}{\text{Assets}}$$

Exhibit 21-6, in the text, provides a summary of efficiency ratios.

Solvency Ratios

Solvency ratios assess the ability of a company to make the interest and principal payments on its long-term obligations. They can be further classified as follows:

- **Leverage ratios**, which measure the relative amount of the company's financing that was obtained through debt.
- **Debt service ratios**, which test the ability of the company to generate sufficient cash flow from operations to pay the debt interest or debt interest plus principal payments.

The concept of leverage is that if a company can earn a rate of return on its assets that is higher than the rate it has to pay on debt, the shareholders will benefit because the surplus return will flow through to benefit the shareholders in the form of higher earnings per share. If a company earns *less* on its investment than the rate of interest, the shareholders' interest will suffer; this is known as *negative leverage*.

Leverage increases the volatility of the residual earnings to shareholders, because fluctuations in earnings will be amplified when the constant of interest expense is deducted.

Leverage ratios
(1) *Debt-to-equity ratio*—

$$\frac{\text{Total long-term debt}}{\text{Total owners' equity}}$$

or,

$$\frac{\text{Total liabilities, current + long-term}}{\text{Total owners' equity}}$$

This is the most basic measure of leverage. When the ratio is computed for assessing solvency, all monetary obligations are normally included.

This ratio indicates the relative proportions by which "permanent" investment is financed through debt versus owners' equity.

Variants to the basic debt-to-equity ratio use some measure of *invested capital* as the denominator, which includes both debt and equity:
- debt-to-total capitalization
- debt-to-capital employed
- debt-to-total assets

(2) *Debt-to-total capitalization:*

$$\frac{\text{Long-term debt}}{\text{Long-term debt + owners' equity}}$$

This ratio indicates the proportion of long-term capital that is financed through debt.

(3) *Debt-to-capital employed:*

$$\frac{\text{Long-term debt + current liabilities}}{\text{Long-term debt + current liabilities} - \text{current assets + owners' equity}}$$

This ratio indicates the proportion of total capital that is financed through debt.

(4) Debt-to-total assets:

$$\frac{\text{Long-term + current liabilities}}{\text{Total assets}}$$

This ratio indicates the proportion by which the assets are financed through debt.

The debt-to-equity ratio and its variants are measures of **financial risk.**

Debt service ratios

These ratios test a company's ability to generate sufficient cash flow from operations to pay the debt interest or the debt interest plus principal payments.

(1) Times interest earned ratio:

$$\frac{\text{Net income + interest expense + taxes}}{\text{Interest expense}}$$

This is the ratio of interest expense to earnings before interest and taxes (EBIT). This ratio is believed to indicate the relative amount by which earnings can decrease before there is not enough net income to pay the interest.

(2) Times debt service earned:

$$\frac{\text{Cash flow from operations + interest expense + tax expense}}{\text{Interest expense + [(projected annual principal payments and capital lease payments)} \div (1 - t)]}$$

This ratio looks at the amount of interest that must be paid plus the amount of principal payments that must be paid.

This ratio indicates the ability of a company to service its debt, including leases, from its pretax operating cash flow.

WATCH! Long-term creditors are primarily concerned with a firm's long-term solvency and stability.

Exhibit 21-7, in the text, provides a summary of solvency ratios.

Liquidity Ratios

The general objective of liquidity ratios is to test a company's ability to meet its short-term financial obligations.

(1) Current ratio:

$$\frac{\text{Current assets}}{\text{Current liabilities}}$$

The current ratio is only one measure of a company's ability to meet short-term obligations and must be interpreted **carefully.** In general, a high current ratio indicates a strong liquidity position.

A common rule of thumb is that current assets should be twice the current liabilities; the ratio should be 2 : 1.

WATCH!

If the current ratio is used as a measure of liquidity, the components of current assets must be "liquid"—that is, realizable in the short run. Prepaid expenses are not convertible into cash. Inventories are not readily salable. Current liabilities may include unearned revenue.

(2) *Quick ratio or acid-test ratio:*

$$\frac{\text{Monetary current assets}}{\text{Monetary current liabilities}}$$

This ratio is intended to overcome the deficiencies of the current ratio by excluding inventories and other non-monetary current assets and current liabilities.

A ratio of less than 1 : 1 is generally considered to be undesirable.

WATCH!

(3) *Defensive-interval ratio:*

$$\frac{\text{Monetary current assets}}{\text{Projected daily operating expenditures}}$$

This is an alternative ratio that tests the number of days that the company could operate if the cash inflow were cut off, such as by a strike or by an emergency shutdown.

It is difficult to decide what should be in the numerator and in the denominator. The numerator should be restricted to monetary current assets. The denominator would include only those cash expenses that will continue in the event of a shut-down.

WATCH!

Exhibit 21-8, in the text, provides a summary of liquidity ratios.

Consolidated Statements

When a company under analysis is a public company, *only* the **consolidated** financial statements will be available to most external users.

An investor who is considering purchasing the shares of a corporation usually will want to see statements that show the full resources under control of the corporation, including those held by subsidiaries. The prospective investor is investing in the *economic entity*, and the consolidated statements are the appropriate basis of analysis.

A creditor or lender is in a different position. A creditor or lender holds an obligation only of the *separate legal entity*, not of the corporate group. Lenders may demand cross-company guarantees of debt, but trade creditors usually can-not. Lenders should use unconsolidated statements for their primary analysis.

Multi-industry Corporations

Many corporations engage in several lines of business. Since industry comparisons are a common aspect of financial statement analysis, the inability to slot many corporations into a specific industry classification may appear to create a problem for the analyst. In fact, this should not be a concern to the analyst.

The *rate of return on investment* should not vary by industry. An investor should expect the same return on investment at a given level of risk no mater what industry or industries a company is in.

Solvency is also a function of risk and return, so regardless of the industry, solvency ratios will help analysts evaluate a company's ability to meet its long-term obligations and to service its debt.

Liquidity analysis depends on an assessment of risk. In a volatile or rapidly expanding company, no level of the quick ratio can give much assurance about the ability of the company to pay its creditors in the short run. If the company becomes short of cash in mid-year, it almost certainly will delay paying its creditors and may collapse.

WATCH! The key is *risk*; the analyst needs to be able to evaluate the risks to the company and its ability to survive downturns and to benefit from upturns in its fortunes.

Public companies are required to provide **segment reporting** as supplementary information in their annual financial statements. Segmented reporting gives the analyst a better idea of the company's exposure to the risks inherent in different industries and in different parts of the world.

WATCH! There is no point in computing masses of ratios; it is more important to identify one or two key ratios in each category that are relevant to the analyst's decision needs and to concentrate on those. Ratios indicate potential problems that must be further analyzed.

WATCH! Given the many estimates and approximations underlying both the numerator and the denominator of all ratios, it doesn't make sense to calculate them to more than two significant digits; computing to three or more digits gives ratios an appearance of precision that is wholly unwarranted.

3. OTHER ANALYTICAL TECHNIQUES

Other, more sophisticated analytical techniques that can be applied to the amounts in the financial statements, or to the ratios, include the following:

- *Time series analysis.* The purpose of time series analysis is to predict the future values of the ratios.
- *Residual analysis.* This is a time series analysis based on the differences between computed ratios and industry averages. It may help to discover why a company is doing better or worse than other companies over s period of time.
- *Statistical multivariate ratio analysis.* In this approach, ratios are not analyzed not one by one; rather, they are fitted into a statistical model in an attempt to predict a certain outcome, such as impending bankruptcy.

TRUE-FALSE QUESTIONS

T F 1. A summary of significant accounting policies is an integral part of financial statements.

T F 2. When calculating profitability ratios an average of the balance sheet amounts must be calculated for the denominator.

T F 3. An unqualified audit opinion is provided for private companies if they use one or more accounting policies that do not comply with the *CICA Handbook* to meet their shareholders' needs.

T F 4. A "clean" audit opinion is required by public companies listed in the stock exchange.

T F 5. Vertical analysis refers to the analytical technique of comparing accounting numbers over a period of years.

T F 6. When using ratio analysis as a means of comparing one company with another, it is important to consider the accounting policies and methods employed by the two companies.

T F 7. The current ratio generally is more useful than the acid test ratio in assessing short-run liquidity (solvency), due to its more narrow definition of liquid assets.

T F 8. In the calculation of the acid test ratio, marketable securities and prepaid expenses are both excluded from current assets before dividing by current liabilities.

T F 9. The receivable turnover ratio indicates how quickly accounts receivable are collected on average.

T F 10. If number of times of inventory turnover is high relative to industry standards, the risk of "stockout" is higher than the industry average.

MULTIPLE CHOICE QUESTIONS

___ 1. Which of the following would probably not be found in a summary of significant accounting policies:
a. That long-term equity investment is carried at cost.
b. That FIFO is used in inventory valuation.
c. That accelerated amortization is used for financial accounting purposes.
d. That an operating asset is disposed of for a gain.

___ 2. Public companies listed on the stock exchange must have:
a. unqualified audit opinion
b. qualified audit opinion
c. adverse opinion
d. denial of opinion

___ 3. Private companies may use one or more accounting policies that do not comply with the *CICA Handbook* and have the following types of opinion?
a. unqualified audit opinion
b. qualified audit opinion
c. adverse opinion
d. denial of opinion

___ 4. The following type of engagement is often provided for private companies:
a. notice to reader
b. review engagement
c. assurance engagement
d. review of internal controls

___ 5. The ratio that best provides an indication of the balance between resources provided by creditors and resources provided by owners is:
a. times interest earned.
b. the debt : equity ratio.
c. profit margin.
d. inventory turnover ratio.

___ 6. If average inventories increased from $70,000 to $80,000 during the year just ended, which of the following statements is true?
a. The acid test ratio decreased.
b. The current ratio decreased.
c. The acid test ratio increased.
d. Inventories have no effect on the acid test ratio.

___ 7. For a firm with a current ratio of 2 to 1, which of the following transactions will most likely cause an increase in this ratio?
   a. The declaration of a cash dividend.
   b. The sale of common shares.
   c. The collection of accounts receivable.
   d. The payment of a 30-day note payable.

___ 8. A very high receivable turnover ratio relative to the industry average indicates:
   a. the declaration of a cash dividend.
   b. that the firm's credit policy may be overly restrictive.
   c. that the firm's management utilizes its assets efficiently.
   d. a sluggish inventory.

___ 9. The ratio least likely to be of concern to those interested in projecting a firm's future profitability is:
   a. the current ratio.
   b. profit margin.
   c. investment turnover.
   d. rate of return on investment.

___ 10. For multi-industry corporations, segment analysis is most useful in
   a. evaluating profitability analysis.
   b. evaluating the risk of the company.
   c. assessing liquidity.
   d. recasting the company's financial statements.

SOLUTIONS TO TRUE-FALSE QUESTIONS.

1. T

2. T

3. F A qualified report is provided if one or more accounting policies do not comply with *CICA Handbook*.

4. T

5. F Vertical analysis refers to cross-sectional ratios, in which the components of one year's individual financial statements are computed as a percentage of a base amount, using total assets as the base for the balance sheet and total sales as the base for the income statement. Horizontal analysis is the analytical technique of comparing accounting numbers over a period of years.

6. T

7. F On the contrary, the acid test ratio overcomes the deficiencies of the current ratio by excluding non-monetary items.

8. F Not only prepaid expenses are excluded from current assets, but also inventory and other non-monetary current assets. Non-monetary current liabilities are also excluded from the calculation.

9. T

10. T

SOLUTIONS TO MULTIPLE CHOICE QUESTIONS

1. d The result of disposing of an asset is not an **accounting objective.** That long-term equity investment is carried at cost, that FIFO is used in inventory valuation, and that accelerated amortization is used for financial accounting purposes, are all **significant accounting objectives.**

2. a Public companies are required to have a "clean" or unqualified audit opinion.

3. b Where private companies use one or more accounting policies that do not comply with the *CICA Handbook* they would have a qualified audit opinion.

4. b A review engagement is often provided for a private company instead of an audit.

5. b The debt-to-equity ratio indicates the percentage of debt (resources provided by creditors) compared to the equity (resources provided by owners).

6. d Inventories are excluded from the calculation of the acid test ratio. The other three statements are wrong. The current ratio would increase.

7. b The sale of common shares will increase cash (current asset) and increase common shares (equity account). The declaration of a cash dividend will increase liabilities (which decrease the current ratio) and decrease retained earnings. The collections of accounts receivable will increase cash (current asset) and decrease accounts receivable (current asset). The payment of a 30-day note payable will decrease cash (current asset) and decrease current liability.

8. b This ratio indicates a low amount of accounts receivable, which in turn indicates a restrictive credit policy.

9. a The current ratio indicates the ability to pay liabilities with current assets. The other ratios (profit margin, investment turnover, and rate of return on investment) are all profitability ratios.

10. b Analyzing risk is more dependant on multi-segment analysis than the other items listed.

PROBLEMS

Problem 1

PURPOSE: To illustrate the computation and evaluation of selected ratios.

Below are data from the financial statements of PAM Manufacturing
Corporation for a 3-year period:

	20x3	20x4	20x5
Total assets	$2,100,000	$2,110,000	$1,990,000
Total current assets	510,000	550,000	600,000
Monetary current assets	210,000	190,000	180,000
Total current liabilities	400,000	300,000	310,000
Operational assets (net)	1,320,000	1,350,000	1,402,000
Total liabilities (of which $900,000 is long-term each year)	1,200,000	1,300,000	1,100,000
Common shares, no-par (10,000 shares, 11,000 in 2005)	500,000	500,000	600,000
Retained earnings	400,000	310,000	290,000
Sales revenues (net)	5,200,000	6,000,000	8,000,000
Net income—after tax	40,000	80,000	50,000
Interest expense, pretax	24,000	28,000	20,000
Income tax (rate 40%)	26,000	53,000	33,000

Required

    a. Based on the above data, compute the following ratios to measure liquidity position for each year:

        (1) Current ratio.

        (2) Quick ratio.

        Evaluate the current position. What additional information do you need to adequately evaluate the current position? Explain.

    b. Based on the above data, compute the following ratios to measure solvency:

        (1) Debt-to-equity (total liabilities).

        (2) Debt-to-total assets (total liabilities).

        (3) Times interest earned.

        Evaluate solvency. What additional information do you need to adequately evaluate solvency? Explain.

    c. Based on the above data, compute the following ratios to measure profitability and leverage:

        (1) Operating margin.

        (2) Return on assets (after tax)

        (3) Return on common shareholders' equity.

        Evaluate profitability and financial leverage.

Problem 2

PURPOSE: To illustrate the reconstruction of financial statements, given a few key ratios.

Hindra Select, the president of Select Products Corporation, has accumulated some data about her major competitor, Xena Products Corporation. She has consulted you in the hope you can reconstruct Xena's financial statements and a few key ratios from this information.

She has reason to believe that Xena maintains the following relationships between the data on its financial statements:

Gross profit rate on net sales	35%
Net profit rate on net sales	8%
Rate of selling expenses to net sales	25%
Accounts receivable turnover	10
Inventory turnover	5
Quick ratio	1.1 : 1
Current ratio	2.5 : 1
Quick asset composition:	
10% cash,	
20% marketable securities,	
70% accounts receivable	
Asset turnover	2
Ratio of total assets to intangible assets	20 : 1
Ratio of accumulated amortization to cost of capital assets	1 : 3
Ratio of accounts receivable to accounts payable	2 : 1
Ratio of working capital to shareholders' equity	1 : 1.5
Ratio of total liabilities to shareholders' equity	1.5 : 1

Hindra also tells you the following:
- Xena's 20x5 net income was $150,000 and earnings per share, $7.40.
- Share capital authorized, issued, and outstanding: common shares issued at $12; $2 preferred shares issued at $100 per share.
- Preferred dividends paid in 20x5, $2,000.
- Number of times interest earned in 20x5, 14.
- The amounts of the following were the same at December 31, 20x5, and at January 1, 20x5: inventory, accounts receivable, 8% bonds payable (due 20x8), and total shareholders' equity.
- All purchases and sales were "on account."
- There is no income tax.

Required
Hindra has specifically asked for a condensed balance sheet and condensed income statement, and has also asked you to calculate the rate of return on common shareholders' equity.

SOLUTIONS TO PROBLEMS

Problem 1

Requirement a

(See calculations at top of next page.)

	20x3	20x4	20x5
(1) Current ratio	$\dfrac{510,000}{400,000} = 1.28$	$\dfrac{550,000}{300,000} = 1.83$	$\dfrac{600,000}{310,000} = 1.94$
(2) Quick ratio	$\dfrac{210,000}{400,000} = .53$	$\dfrac{190,000}{300,000} = .63$	$\dfrac{180,000}{310,000} = .58$

Evaluation

In this situation, the current ratio has increased. This is usually viewed as favourable, although the ratio should not climb too high. At the same time, the quick ratio is fluctuating and has increased a little over year 20x3. This indicates that the increase is due to a decrease (small) in non-monetary current assets such as inventory. The inventory investment policy should be investigated further, because the quick ratio is still too low.

Requirement b

	20x3	20x4	20x5
(1) Debt-to-equity	$\dfrac{1,200,000}{900,000} = 1.33$	$\dfrac{1,300,000}{810,000} = 1.60$	$\dfrac{1,100,000}{890,000} = 1.24$
(2) Debt-to-total assets	$\dfrac{1,200,000}{2,100,000} = 57\%$	$\dfrac{1,300,000}{2,110,000} = 62\%$	$\dfrac{1,100,000}{1,990,000} = 55\%$
(2) Times interest earned	$\dfrac{90,000^a}{24,000} = 3.8$	$\dfrac{161,000^b}{28,000} = 5.8$	$\dfrac{103,000^c}{20,000} = 5.2$

[a] $40,000 + $24,000 + $26,000 = $90,000
[a] $80,000 + $28,000 + $53,000 = $161,000
[a] $50,000 + $20,000 + $33,000 = $103,000

Evaluation

The debt-to-equity ratio and debt-to-total assets reflect the same relationship, but in different ways. Both reflect a shift of the proportion of total assets provided by creditors versus owners. In short, total debt increased first, then decreased further as a percentage, and total owners' equity increased.

This change means that leverage (trading on the equity) declined. To assess the advisability of reducing leverage, we must evaluate the return on total assets and owners' equity (this is done in requirement c).

Times interest earned increased over the period, as income is lower in 20x5 but interest expense is also lower. This is still a thin margin of safety for lenders, but it has improved.

Requirement c

(See calculations at the top of the next page.)

Evaluation

The operating margin has decreased, which is unfavourable because a lower percentage of each dollar of sales is reflected in income. As a measure of profitability, however, profit margin is deficient because it does not consider the amount of assets employed to generate earnings.

	20x3	20x4	20x5
(1) Operating margin	$\dfrac{90,000}{5,200,000}=1.7\%$	$\dfrac{161,000}{6,000,000}=2.7\%$	$\dfrac{103,000}{8,000,000}=1.3\%$
(2) Return on assets (after tax)[a]	$\dfrac{40,000}{2,100,000}=1.9\%$	$\dfrac{80,000}{2,110,000}=3.8\%$	$\dfrac{50,000}{1,990,000}=2.5\%$
(2) Return on common equity	$\dfrac{40,000}{900,000}=4.4\%$	$\dfrac{80,000}{810,000}=9.8\%$	$\dfrac{50,000}{890,000}=5.6\%$

[a] Data not available to compute average.

Both return on assets and return on equity have increased significantly in 20x4 and decreased in 20x5, but not as low as 20x3. The variability in these two ratios—low in 20x3, higher in 20x4, then lower in 20x5—strongly suggests the need for further investigation and action.

Leverage is positive in all years, as ROE is higher than ROA. As with the other indicators, however, leverage is lower in 20x5, likely because ROA has declined significantly.

Problem 2

Reconstruction of financial statements—
(See tables on next page and footnoted computations.)

Rate of return on common shareholders' equity—

$$\frac{\$150,000 - \$2,000}{\$548,057 - \$100,000} = 33\%$$

CASE

Federated Furniture Company manufactures wood furniture and wood products of all types. More than 85 percent of the company's sales come from central Canada, although a market for custom furniture and wood products designed and produced by Federated is growing nationally and even internationally.

Janice Porter, the founder and president of Federated, recently received a call from Jim Kane, vice president of the Eastern Ontario region of the Corporate Bank of Canada. Kane told Porter that a deficiency report, generated by the bank's computerized system, had been filed because of Federated's deteriorating financial position. The bank requires quarterly financial statements from each of its major loan customers. Information from such statements is fed into the computer, which then calculates key ratios for each customer and charts trends in these ratios. The system also compares the statistics for each company with the average ratios of other firms in the same industry and against any protective covenants in the loan agreements. If any ratio is significantly worse than the industry average, reflects a marked adverse trend, or fails to meet contractual requirements, the computer highlights the deficiency.

(*continued on page 293*)

XENA PRODUCTS CORPORATION
Condensed Balance Sheet
December 31, 20x5

Current assets				
Cash	$ 26,786	(6)		
Marketable securities	53,571	(7)		
Accounts receivable	187,500	(5)		
Inventory	243,750	(8)		
Prepaid expenses	96,270	(11)		
Total current assets			$608,877	(10)
Capital assets				
Property, plant, and equipment	424,122	(15)		
Less: accumulated amortization	(141,374)	(16)		
Total capital assets			282,748	(14)
Intangible assets			46,785	(13)
Total assets			$937,500	(12)
Current liabilities				
Accounts payable	$ 93,750	(17)		
Miscellaneous expenses payable	149,756	(18)		
Total current liabilities			$243,506	(9)
Long-term liabilities				
8% bonds payable—due 20x8			145,937	(21)
Total liabilities			389,443	(20)
Shareholders' equity				
2% preferred, 1,000 (24) shares authorized, issued, and outstanding	100,000	(25)		
Common, 20,000 (22) shares authorized, issued, and outstanding	240,000	(23)		
Retained earnings	208,057	(26)		
Total shareholders' equity			548,057	(19)
Total liabilities and shareholders' equity			$937,500	(27)

XENA PRODUCTS CORPORATION
Condensed Income Statement
for the Year Ended December 31, 20x5

Net sales			$1,875,000	(1)
Less cost of goods sold			1,218,750	(3)
Gross profit on sales			656,250	(2)
Expenses				
Selling expenses	$468,750	(4)		
Administrative expenses	25,825	(29)		
Interest expense	11,675	(28)	506,250	
Net income			$150,000	

(1) Sales: Net income/Net profit rate, or $150,000/.08 = $1,875,000.

---

(2) Gross profit: Sales × Gross profit rate, or $1,875,000 × .35 = $656,250.

(3) Cost of goods sold: Sales − Gross profit, $1,875,000 − $656,250 = $1,218,750.

(4) Selling expenses: Sales × Selling expense rate, or $1,875,000 × .25 = $468,750.

(5) Accounts receivable: Sales/Accounts receivable turnover, or $1,875,000/10 = $187,500.

(6) Cash: Quick assets − Accounts receivable/percentage of quick assets in cash, or $187,500/.70 = $267,857; Quick assets × Percentage of quick assets in marketable securities, or $267,857 × .10 = $26,786.

(7) Marketable securities: Quick assets × Percentage of quick assets in marketable securities, or $267,857 × .20 = $53,571.

(8) Inventory: Cost of goods sold/Inventory turnover, or $1,218,750/5 = $243,750.

(9) Current liabilities : Quick assets/Quick ratio, $267,857/1.1 = $243,506.

(10) Current assets: Current liabilities × Current ratio, or $243,506 × 2.5 = $608,877.

(11) Prepaid expenses: Current assets − (cash, securities, receivables, and inventory), or $608,877 − ($26,786 + $53,571 + $187,500 + $243,750) = $96,270.

(12) Total assets: Sales/Asset turnover, or $1,875,000/2 = $937,500.

(13) Intangible assets: Total assets/Ratio of total assets to intangibles, or $937,500/20 = $46,875.

(14) Capital assets (net): Total assets − (current assets and intangibles), or $937,500 − ($608,877 + $46,875) = $282,748.

(15) Property, plant, and equipment: Ratio of accumulated amortization to Cost, 1:3 or 1/3; Ratio of book value of asset to Cost, 2:3 or 2/3; or $282,748/(2/3) = $424,122.

(16) Accumulated amortization: Property, plant, and equipment × Ratio of accumulated amortization to Cost, 1:3 or 1/3, or $424,122 × 1/3 = $141,374.

(17) Accounts payable: Accounts receivable/ratio of accounts receivable to accounts payable, or $187,500/2 = $93,750.

(18) Miscellaneous expenses payable: Total current liabilities − Accounts payable, or $243,506 − $93,750 = $149,756.

(19) Total shareholders' equity: Working capital × Ratio of working capital to Total shareholders' equity, or ($608,877 − $243,506) × 1.5 = $548,057.

(20) Total liabilities: Total assets − Total shareholders' equity, or $937,500 − $548,057 = $389,443.

(21) 8% bonds payable—due 2005: Total liabilities − Current liabilities or, $389,443 − $243,506 = $145,937.

(22) Common shares: Net income − Preferred dividends, divided by earnings per share = ($150,000 − $2,000)/7.40 = 20,000 shares.

(23) Common shares: Commons shares × Issue price, or 20,000 × $12 = $240,000.

(24) Preferred shares: Preferred dividends paid/dividend, or $2,000/$2 = 1,000 shares.

(25) Preferred shares: Preferred shares × Issue price = 1,000 × $100 = $100,000.

(26) Retained earnings: Total shareholders' equity − Preferred and common shares. $548,057 − $240,000 − $100,000 = $208,057.

(27) Total liabilities and equity: Total assets; $937,500.

(28) Interest expense : Bonds payable × Interest rate, $145,937 × .08 = $11,675.

(29) Administrative expenses: Total expenses − Gross profit − Net income − Other expenses, or $656,250 − $150,000 = $506,250 − $468,750 − $11,675 = $25,825.

The latest deficiency report on Federated revealed a number of adverse trends and several potentially serious problems (see Tables 1 through 6 for Federated's historical financial statements). Particularly disturbing were the 20x5 current, quick, and debt ratios, all of which failed to meet the contractual limits of 2.0%, 1.0%, and 55% percent, respectively. Technically, the bank had a legal right to call the loans it had extended to Federated for immediate repayment, and if the loans were not repaid within 10 days, to force the company into bankruptcy.

Jim Kane hoped to avoid calling the loans if at all possible, as he knew that this would back Federated into a corner from which it might not be able to emerge. Still, he knew that the bank's senior loan committee examined bank loan portfolios very strictly and demanded early identification of potential repayment problems.

If Federated's loan is to escape being reclassified as a "problem loan," the senior loan committee will require strong and convincing evidence that the company's present difficulties are only temporary. Therefore, it must be shown that appropriate actions to overcome the problems have been taken and that the chances of reversing the adverse trends are realistically good. Jim Kane now has the task of collecting the necessary information, evaluating its implications, and preparing a recommendation for action.

After Jim Kane's telephone call, and the subsequent receipt of a copy of the bank's financial analysis of Federated, Janice Porter began to realize just how difficult her company's financial position had become. As she started to reflect on what could be done to correct the problems, it dawned on her that the company was in even more trouble than the bank imagined. Porter had recently signed a contract for a plant expansion that would require an additional $5,000,000 of capital during the first quarter of 20x6, and she had planned to obtain this money with a short-term loan from the bank, to be repaid from profits expected in the last half of 20x6 as a result of the expansion. In her view, once the new production facility went on line, the company would be able to increase output in several segments of the furniture market. It might have been possible to cut back on the expansion plans and to retrench, but because of the signed construction contracts and the cancellation charges that would be imposed if the plans were cancelled, Porter correctly regarded the $5,000,000 of new capital as essential for Federated's very survival.

Assume that Janice Porter has hired you as a consultant to verify the bank's evaluation of the company's financial situation. The following questions are designed to help you focus on the issues, but they are not meant to be a complete and exhaustive list of all the relevant points.

Required

1. Complete the 20x5 columns of Tables 1 through 6. To be consistent with the financial community, assume that the year has 360 days.
2. Based on the information in the case and on the results of your calculations in question 1, prepare a list of Federated's strengths and weaknesses.
3. Based on your analysis to this point, does it appear that the bank should be willing to lend the requested money to Federated? Explain.

TABLE 1
Historical Balance Sheets
for the Years Ended December 31
(thousands of dollars)

	20x3	20x4	20x5
Assets			
Cash and marketable securities	$ 5,340	$ 4,195	$ 4,097
Accounts receivable	18,092	19,560	X
Inventory	23,093	34,895	47,089
Current assets	$46,525	$58,650	$73,770
Property, plant, and equipment	15,347	22,568	25,873
Less: accumulated amortization	(2,398)	(4,783)	(6,349)
Net capital assets	$12,949	$17,785	$19,524
Total assets	$59,474	$76,435	$93,294
Liabilities and equity			
Short-term bank loans	$ 3,295	$ 5,309	$19,456
Accounts payable	5,689	11,230	21,389
Accruals	3,564	4,329	7,483
Current liabilities	$12,548	$20,868	$48,328
Long-term bank loans	6,345	9,478	9,478
Mortgage	2,764	2,609	2,347
Long-term debt	$ 9,109	$12,087	$11,825
Total liabilities	$21,657	$32,955	$60,153
Common shares	$24,097	$24,097	$24,097
Retained earnings	13,720	19,383	9,044
Total equity	$37,817	$43,480	$33,141
Total liabilities and equities	$59,474	$76,435	$93,294

Notes:

a. 3,400,000 shares of common shares were outstanding throughout the period 20x3–20x5.

b. Market price of shares: 20x3–$17.80; 20x4–$8.99; 20x5–$2.97.

c. Assume that all changes in interest-bearing loans and gross capital assets occur at the start of the relevant years.

d. The mortgage loan is secured by a first-mortgage bond on property, plant, and equipment.

TABLE 2
Historical Income Statements
for Years Ended December 31
(thousands of dollars)

	20x3	20x4	20x5
Net sales	$190,560	$192,345	$186,991
Cost of goods sold	145,689	158,987	172,234
Gross profit	44,871	33,358	14,757
Administrative and selling expenses	12,367	16,039	18,489
Amortization	1,345	2,385	1,566
Miscellaneous expenses	1,234	4,387	6,386
Total operating expenses	14,946	22,811	26,441
EBIT	29,925	10,547	(11,684)
Interest on short-term loans	330	531	1,946
Interest on long-term loans	635	948	948
Interest on mortgage	243	221	192
Before-tax earnings	28,717	8,847	(14,770)
Taxes	8,615	2,654	4,431
Net income	$20,102	$6,193	$(10,339)
Dividends on shares	9,200	530	–0–
Additions to retained earnings	$10,902	$5,663	$(10,339)

Note:
a. Earnings per share (EPS): 20x3–$5.91; 20x4–$1.82; 20x5–$(3.04).

TABLE 3
Common Size Balance Sheets
for the Years Ended December 31
(amounts in percentage of total assets)

	20x3	20x4	20x5
Assets			
Cash and marketable securities	8.98	5.49	4.39
Accounts receivable	30.42	25.59	X
Inventory	38.83	45.65	50.47
Current assets	78.23	76.73	X
Property, plant, and equipment	25.80	29.52	X
Less: accumulated amortization	(4.03)	(6.25)	(6.80)
Net capital assets	21.77	23.27	20.93
Total assets	100.00	100.00	100.00
Liabilities and equity			
Short-term bank loans	5.54	6.95	20.85
Accounts payable	9.57	14.69	22.93
Accruals	5.99	5.66	8.02
Current liabilities	21.10	27.30	51.80
Long-term bank loans	10.67	12.40	X
Mortgage	4.65	3.41	2.52
Long-term debt	15.32	15.81	X
Total liabilities	36.42	43.11	64.48
Common shares	40.52	31.53	25.83
Retained earnings	23.06	25.36	X
Total equity	63.58	56.89	35.52
Total liabilities and equities	100.00	100.00	100.00

TABLE 4
Common Size Income Statements
for the Years Ended December 31
(amounts in percentage of net sales)

	20x3	20x4	20x5
Net sales	100.00	100.00	100.00
Cost of goods sold	76.45	82.66	X
Gross profit	23.55	17.34	7.89
Administrative and selling expenses	6.49	8.34	9.89
Amortization	0.71	1.24	X
Miscellaneous expenses	0.65	2.28	3.42
Total operating expenses	7.85	11.86	14.15
EBIT	15.70	5.48	(6.26)
Interest on short-term loans	0.17	0.28	X
Interest on long-term loans	0.33	0.49	X
Interest on mortgage	0.13	0.11	0.10
Before-tax earnings	15.07	4.60	(7.91)
Taxes	4.52	1.38	X
Net income	10.55	$ 3.22	(5.55)
Dividends on shares	4.83	0.28	-0-
Additions to retained earnings	5.72	2.94	(5.55)

TABLE 5
Statements of Cash Flow
for the Years Ended December 31
(amounts in percentage of total assets)

	20x4	20x5
Cash flow from operations		
Net income	$ 6,193	$(10,339)
Plus: noncash charges:		
Amortization	2,385	1,566
Plus/minus:		
Increase in accounts receivable	(1,468)	X
Increase in inventories	(11,802)	(12,194)
Increase in accounts payable	5,541	10,159
Increase in accruals	765	3,154
Net cash flow from operations	$ 1,614	X
Cash flow from investing activities		
Investment in capital assets	$(7,221)	$(3,305)
Cash flow from financing activities		
Increase in short-term loans	$2,014	$14,147
Increase in long-term loans	3,133	X
Repayment of mortgage	(155)	(262)
Dividends	(530)	-0-
Net cash flow from financing activities	$4,462	$13,885
Change in cash	(1,145)	X
Opening cash	5,340	4,195
Closing cash	$4,195	X

TABLE 6
Historical Ratio Analysis
for Years Ended December 31

	20x3	20x4	20x5
Liquidity Ratios			
Current ratio	3.71	2.81	X
Quick ratio	2.61	1.44	0.65
Solvency ratios			
Debt-to-total assets ratio	36.41%	43.11%	X
Times interest earned ratio	24.77	6.20	(3.78)
Efficiency ratios			
Inventory turnover	6.31	4.56	X
Capital assets turnover	14.72	10.82	9.58
Total assets turnover	3.20	2.52	2.00
Accounts receivable turnover	10.53	9.83	X
Average collection period of accounts receivable	34.2	36.6	X
Profitability ratios			
Profit margin	10.54%	3.21%	(5.53%)
Operating margin	15.70%	5.48%	(6.24%)
Return on total assets	33.8%	8.1%	(11.1%)
Return on shareholders' equity	53.16%	14.24%	(31.2%)

KEY POINTS IN THE CASE

Requirement 1

The missing information from Table 1 through Table 6—

Table 1:

Accounts receivable (20x5) = Current assets – Cash and marketable securities – Inventory = $73.770 – $4.097 – $47,089 = $22,584.

Table 3:

Accounts receivable (20x5) = A/R divided by Total assets = $22,584/$93,294 = 24.21

Current assets = Cash and marketable securities + Accounts receivable + Inventory = 4.39 + 24.21 + 50.47 = 79.07

Property, plant, and equipment = Land, buildings, plant, and equipment/ Total assets = $25,873/$93,294 = 27.73

Long-term bank loans = Long-term loan/Total assets = $9,478/$93,294 = 10.16

Long-term debt = Long-term loan + Mortgage = 10.16 + 2.52 = 12.68

Retained earnings = Retained earnings/Total assets = $9,044/$93,294 = 9.69

Table 4:
Cost of goods sold (2003) = Cost of goods sold/Sales = \$172,234/\$186,991 = 92.11
Amortization = Amortization expense/Sales = \$1,566/\$186,991 = 0.84
Interest on short-term loans = Interest/Sales = \$1,946/\$186,991 = 1.04
Interest on long-term loans = Interest/Sales = \$948/\$186,991 = 0.51
Taxes = Taxes/Sales = \$4,431/\$186,991 = 2.36

Table 5:
Increase in accounts receivable = \$22,584 – \$19,560 = (\$3,024)
Net cash flow from operations = \$(10,339) + \$1,566 + (\$3,024) + \$(12,194) + 10.159
    + 3,154 = \$(10,678)
Increase in long-term loans = 0
Change in cash = \$4,097 – \$4,195 = \$(98)
Closing cash = \$4,097

Table 6:
Current ratio (20x5) = Current assets/Current liabilities = \$73,770/\$48,328 = 1.53
Debt-to-total asset ratio = Total liabilities/Total assets = \$60,153/\$93,294 = 64.48%
Accounts receivable turnover = Sales divided by accounts receivable =
    \$186,991/\$22,584 = 8.28
Average collection period = 360 days/Accounts receivable
Turnover = 360/8.28 = 43.38 days

Requirement 2

Liquidity
The current and quick ratios are below industry averages and declining. The current and quick ratios are also below the contractual limits of 2.0 and 1.0, respectively.

From the common size financial statements, as well as from the statement of cash flows, we see that the more than proportionate increase in current liabilities and inventories, relative to other current assets, caused the decline in Federated's liquidity.

The increase in current assets was financed with short-term funds in 20x5. If the current asset increase is permanent in nature, permanent capital should be used.

Solvency
The rising debt ratio in 20x5 exceeds the 50% industry average and the 55% contractual limit. A large increase in short-term loans, combined with a decrease in retained earnings because of loss, notwithstanding a small reduction of mortgage debt, resulted in a higher debt ratio. The debt structure is also changing, from long-term to short-term maturity. This means that Federated is subject to higher risk.

Times interest earned ratio is negative. The safety margin does not exist in 20x5.

Efficiency

Inventory—Inventory turnover falling significantly. This suggests that the company is carrying excess inventory.

Capital assets—Capital assets turnover is declining but still at a fairly high level. This is the only strength in Federated's performance. In 20x5, Federated had a negative cash flow from operations. The investment in capital assets was financed with short-term funds—not a recommended practice.

Total assets—This ratio is declining. On the common size balance sheet you can see that there are only small changes in the percentages of current assets and fixed assets. In 20x5 the sales have declined and the total assets have increased.

Accounts receivable—The accounts receivable turnover is declining and the collection period is increasing, which suggests that there are problems with the collection of accounts receivable. The increase in receivables along with the decrease in sales shows that Federated is weak in collection policies and in credit-granting policies.

Profitability—All profitability ratios calculated for 20x5 are negative. There was a loss.

Profit margin—Reasons for loss could be lower sales, or higher costs, or both.

Operating margin—Higher loss because of the taxes saved from a loss.

Return on total assets—The net loss and the increase in assets, particularly in current assets, makes this ratio worse.

Return on shareholders' equity—This ratio has declined sharply even if the company used more debt.

Requirement 3

Based on the above analysis, it appears that the bank has no option but to call the loan and not lend additional credit. Before taking such action, the bank will want to meet with the company and discuss the situation and what, if any, actions could be taken to save this company. If this fails, the company will be forced into bankruptcy. Before forcing the company into bankruptcy, the bank will also analyze how the bankruptcy will affect the bank's interests.

Requirement 1

Bryant Company
Comparative Balance Sheet
31 December 20x4 and 20x5
(Vertical Percentage Analysis)

	20x4		20x5	
	Amount	Percent	Amount	Percent
Assets				
Current assets:				
Cash	$ 60,000	7	$ 80,000	8
Accounts receivable (net)	120,000	14	116,000	12
Inventory (FIFO, LCM)	144,000	17	192,000	19
Prepaid expenses	8,000	1	4,000	0
Total current assets	332,000	39	392,000	39
Funds and investments (at cost)	60,000	7	88,000	9
Capital assets	560,000	65	664,000	65
Accumulated depreciation	(104,000)	(12)	(196,000)	(19)
Intangible assets	12,000	1	60,000	6
Total assets	$860,000	100	$1,008,000	100
Liabilities				
Current liabilities:				
Accounts payable...........................	$160,000	19	$100,000	10
Other current liabilities.................	40,000	5	40,000	4
Total current liabilities	200,000	24	140,000	14
Long-term mortgage payable..........	200,000	23	172,000	17
Total liabilities	400,000	47	312,000	31
Shareholders' Equity				
Contributed capital:				
Common shares, no-par.................	340,000	39	520,000	52
Retained earnings	120,000	14	176,000	17
Total shareholders' equity	460,000	53	696,000	69
Total liabilities and shareholders' equity...	$860,000	100	$1,008,000	100

Requirement 2

Bryant Company
Comparative Balance Sheet
31 December 20x4 and 20x5
(Horizontal Analysis)

	20x4	20x5
Assets		
Current assets:		
Cash..	100%	133
Accounts receivable (net).............	100	97
Inventory (FIFO, LCM)	100	133
Prepaid expenses...........................	100	50
Funds and investments (at cost).....	100	147
Capital assets..................................	100	119
Accumulated depreciation...........	100	188
Intangible assets	100	500
Total assets	100	117
Liabilities		
Current liabilities		
Accounts payable..........................	100	63
Other current liabilities	100	100
Long-term mortgage payable.........	100	86
Total liabilities........................	100	78
Shareholders' Equity		
Contributed capital:		
Common shares, no-par...............	100	153
Retained earnings............................	100	147
Total shareholders' equity	100	151
Total liabilities and shareholders'		
equity	100	117

Assignment 21-12

(a) Ratios that measure profitability

Return on long-term capital	$$\frac{\text{Income + Interest exp.,}}{\text{long-term capital, net of tax}}$$ $$\overline{\text{Average LT Debt + Equity}}$$	$$\frac{\$28 + (\$4(1-.40))}{\$167}$$ $= .18$ (or 18%)	Return on long-term capital investment, excluding current liabilities.
Return on assets (after tax)	$$\frac{\text{Income +}}{\text{Interest exp. net of tax}}$$ $$\overline{\text{Average total assets}}$$	$$\frac{\$28 + (\$4(1-.40))}{\$185}$$ $= .16$ (or 16%)	Rate of return earned on all assets employed
Return on common owners' equity	$$\frac{\text{Income} - \text{Pref dividends}}{\text{Average common owners' equity}}$$	$$\frac{\$28}{\$124} =$$ $.23$ (or 23%)	Rate of return earned on assets provided by owners
Operating margin	$$\frac{\text{Income + interest + income tax}}{\text{Total revenue}}$$	$$\frac{\$28 + \$4 + \$20}{\$157}$$ $= .33$ (or 33%)	Profit margin earned on each dollar of sales
Return on gross assets	$$\frac{\text{EBIT + Depreciation}}{\text{Average total assets (net) +}}$$ $$\overline{\text{Average accumulated}}$$ $$\text{depreciation}$$	$$\frac{\$28 + \$4 + \$20 + \$8}{((\$184 + \$29) + (\$186 + \$37)) / 2}$$ $= .28$ (or 28%)	Return on invested capital exclusive of return of capital (depreciation)

(b) Ratios that measure efficiency:

1.	Asset turnover	$\dfrac{\text{Total revenue}}{\text{Total assets (average)}}$	$\dfrac{\$157}{\$185}$ = .85 times	Efficiency of asset utilization
2.	Accounts receivable turnover	$\dfrac{\text{Credit sales}}{\text{Average trade receivables}}$	$\dfrac{\$51}{\$21}$ = 2.4 times	Efficiency of collection of accounts receivable
3.	Average collection period of accounts receivable	$\dfrac{\text{365 (days)}}{\text{Receivable turnover}}$	$\dfrac{365}{2.4}$ = 152 days	Average number of days to collect receivables
4.	Inventory turnover	$\dfrac{\text{Cost of goods sold}}{\text{Average inventory}}$	$\dfrac{\$70}{\$34}$ = 2.1 times	Number of times average inventory was sold

(c) Ratios that measure solvency:

1. Debt:equity	$\dfrac{\text{Total liabilities}}{\text{Total owners' equity}}$	$\dfrac{\$57}{\$129} = .44$ (or 44%)	Compares resources provided by creditors versus owners
2. Debt: total capitalization	$\dfrac{\text{Long-term debt}}{\text{Long-term debt + owners' equity}}$	$\dfrac{\$45}{\$45 + \$129} = .26$ (or 26%)	Proportion of long-term capital financed by debt
3. Debt: capital employed	$\dfrac{\text{Long-term debt + current}}{\text{Long-term debt + current liabilities} - \text{(liquid) current assets} + \text{equity}}$	$\dfrac{\$45 + \$12}{\$45 + \$12 - (\$20 + \$4 + \$19) + \$129} = .40$ (or 40%)	Debt burden with liquid current assets netted out.
4. Debt: total assets	$\dfrac{\text{Total liabilities}}{\text{Total assets}}$	$\dfrac{\$57}{\$186} = .31$ (or 31%)	Proportion of resources provided by creditors
5. Times-interest-earned	$\dfrac{\text{Income + interest + tax}}{\text{Interest expense}}$	$\dfrac{\$28 + \$20 + \$4}{\$4} = 13$	Income available to cover interest
6. Times-debt-service-earned	$\dfrac{\text{Cash flow from ops + interest + tax}}{\text{Interest + debt service costs}}$	$\dfrac{\$22 + \$20 + \$4}{\$4} = 11.5$	Ability to co. to service debt charges

(d) Ratios that measure liquidity:

1.	Current ratio	$\dfrac{\text{Current assets}}{\text{Current liabilities}}$	$\dfrac{\$83}{\$12} = 6.9$	Short-term liquidity; adequacy of working capital
2.	Quick ratio	$\dfrac{\text{Monetary current assets}}{\text{Monetary current liabilities}}$	$\dfrac{\$83 - \$37 - \$3}{\$12} = 3.58$	Severe test of liquidity; sudden cash demands
3.	Defensive—interval ratio	$\dfrac{\text{Monetary short-term assets}}{\text{Projected daily operational expenditures}}$	$\dfrac{\$43}{(\$70 + \$20 + \$7 + \$4)/365} = 155$	The maximum days of operations with present liquid assets

Assignment 21-27

Requirement 1

Alfa Company
Cash Flow Statement
for the year ended 31 December 20x4

Cash from operating activities		
Net income		$39,000
Plus: non-operating items		
Loss on sale of investments	5,000	
Amortization...	<u>28,000</u>	<u>33,000</u>
		72,000
Plus/minus		
Changes in non-cash working capital[1]		<u>(50,800)</u>
Cash from operating activities...		$21,200
Cash for investing activities		
Sale of short-term investments		8,000
Sale of equipment...		5,000
Sale of long-term investments		32,000
Purchase of equipment...		<u>(43,000)</u>
		2,000
Cash for financing		
Repurchased shares...		(17,000)
Repaid bond		(40,000)
Dividends		<u>(21,000)</u>
		<u>(78,000)</u>
Change in cash...		(54,800)
Opening cash		(26,000)[2]
Closing cash...		$(80,800)[3]

[1] A/R, ($38,400), inventories, ($44,400), wages payable, $2,000,
income tax payable, $30,000

[2] $44,000– $70,000

[3] $5,200 – $86,000

Requirement 2

Profitability ratios

Return on long-term capital, before tax $\dfrac{\$69,000 + \$16,600}{(\$200,000 + \$19,000 + \$279,100 + \$1,900 + \$167,000) + (\$240,000 + \$30,000 + \$277,000 + \$3,000 + \$162,000)/2}$ = <u>12.4%</u>

Return on long-term capital, after tax	$\dfrac{\$39,000 + \$16,600 (.5)}{\begin{array}{c}(\$200,000 + \$19,000 + \$279,100 + \$1,900 \\ + \$167,000) + (\$240,000 + \$30,000 \\ + \$277,000 + \$3,000 + \$162,000)/2\end{array}}$	=	6.9%
Return on assets (before tax)	$\dfrac{\$69,000 + \$16,600}{(\$905,000 + \$896,000)/2}$	=	9.5%
Return on assets (after tax)	$\dfrac{\$39,000 + \$16,600 (1-.5)}{(\$905,000 + \$896,000)/2}$	=	5.3%
Return on common shareholders' equity	$\dfrac{\$39,000}{\begin{array}{c}(\$279,100 + \$1,900 + \$167,000 + \\ \$277,000 + \$3,000 + \$162,000)/2\end{array}}$	=	8.8%
Return on gross assets, before tax	n/a		
Operating Margin	$\dfrac{\$69,000 + \$16,600}{\$1,265,600}$	=	6.8%

Efficiency ratios

Asset turnover	$\dfrac{\$1,265,600}{(\$905,000 + \$896,000)/2}$	=	1.4
Accounts receivable turnover	$\dfrac{\$1,260,000}{(\$230,400 + \$192,000)/2}$	=	6
Average collection period of A/R	$\dfrac{365}{6}$	=	61 days
Inventory turnover	$\dfrac{\$948,000}{(\$360,400 + \$316,000)/2}$	=	2.8

Solvency

Debt: equity (total liabilities)	$\dfrac{\$905,000 - \$279,100 - \$1,900 - \$167,000}{\$279,100 + \$1,900 + \$167,000}$	=	1.02
Debt: total capitalization	$\dfrac{\$200,000 + \$19,000}{\begin{array}{c}\$200,000 + \$19,000 + \$279,100 + \$1,900 \\ + \$167,000\end{array}}$	=	.33
Debt: capital employed	$\dfrac{\$905,000 - \$279,100 - \$1,900 - \$167,000}{\$905,000 - (\$5,200 + \$8,000 + \$230,400)}$	=	.69

| Debt: total assets | $\dfrac{(\$905,000 - \$279,100 - \$1,900 - \$167,000)}{\$905,000}$ | = | .50 |

| Times-interest-earned | $\dfrac{\$16,600 + \$69,000}{\$16,600}$ | = | 5.2 |

Times-debt-service-earned   n/a

Liquidity

| Current ratio | $\dfrac{\$5,200 + \$8,000 + \$230,400 + \$360,400}{\$86,000 + \$90,000 + \$26,000 + \$30,000 + \$6,000}$ | = | 2.5 |

| Quick ratio | $\dfrac{\$5,200 + \$8,000 + \$230,400}{\$86,000 + \$90,000 + \$26,000 + \$30,000 + \$6,000}$ | = | 1.02 |

| Defensive-interval ratio days | $\dfrac{\$5,200 + \$8,000 + \$230,400}{(\$948,000 + \$16,600 + \$75,000 + \$124,000)*/365}$ | = | 76 |

* A variety of assumptions regarding which expenses to include in the denominator are
   supportable. For example, should cost of goods sold or interest be included?

Requirement 3

Net cash position declined over the period, as bank loans increased to finance equipment purchases and debt and equity retirement. All the cash generated by operations was distributed as dividends. Thus, investment by shareholders declined over the year.

Return figures are respectable but not spectacular. ROA is less than ROE, indicating positive leverage. Turnover, again, is respectable but not spectacular. Receivables take about 60 days to collect, and inventory turns over less than 3 times a year. Both these could likely be improved.

The company is financed about 50/50 with debt and equity. This is not especially risky. Times interest earned is only 5, which is not a wide margin for lenders.

Short-term liquidity appears acceptable but, as the CFS illustrated, has declined over the period.

Trends and industry norms should be gathered and evaluated for a more meaningful analysis, and budgets and projections should be obtained to help assess future prospects.

Assignment 21-29

CFS Limited
Partial Cash Flow Statement
For the year ended 31 December 20x5

Financing activities

Retirement of bonds payable	$(2,040,000)
Issued convertible bonds ($3,000,000 - $60,000 + $210,000)	3,150,000
Issued preferred shares	120,000
Retirement of common shares...	(410,000)
Issuance of common shares under warrants contract...............................	1,150,000
Issued common shares	795,000
Payment of dividends ($8,950,000 - $86,000 retirement + $1,450,000 NI = $10,314,000 versus $9,754,000).........................	(560,000)

$2,205,000

Common shares:

Opening balance (500,000 x $13.60)	$6,800,000
Retirement (20,000 x $13.60)	(272,000)
Cash issuance; Warrants (100,000 x $11.50)	1,150,000
Warrants	205,000
Issued for cash (plug)	795,000
Closing balance	$8,678,000

Assignment 21-31

Requirement 1

a. Basic EPS: ($770 - $40^1)/((380,000 x 1/12) + 420,000 x 11/12) = $1.75

  ^{1} Preferred shares are cumulative

b. Diluted EPS: ($770 + $98(1-.4)/416,667* + 40,000^1 + 50,000^2 + $8,000^3= $1.61

  * From basic calculation
  ^{1} Pref. shares $40/40=$1; dilutive
  ^{2} $98(1-.4)/50=$1.17; dilutive
  ^{3} Options: 40,000 shares issued and (40,000 x $16)/$20 = 32,000 retired

c. Debt: equity: ($2,190 + $833 + $619)/($500 + $166 + $2,150 + $2,461) = .69
  Note: future income tax might be classified differently: assumptions must be stated!

d. Inventory turnover : $7,619/(($2,575 + $2,110)/2 = <u>3.25</u>

e. Quick: ($1,720 + $1,150 + $450)/$2,190 = <u>1.52</u>

f. Return on assets: (after tax) ($770 + $98(1-.4))/($8,919 + $7,401)/2) = <u>10.2%</u>

g. Return on common shareholders' equity: ($770 - $40[1]) / $4,180[2] = <u>17.4%</u>

   [1] Preferred shares are cumulative.
   [2] (($2,150 + $2,461 + $166) + ($1,700 + $1,716 + $166))/2 = $4,180

h. Accounts receivable turnover: $10,450/(($1,150 + $1,170)/2) = <u>9</u>

i. Asset turnover: $10,450/ (($8,919 + $7,401)/2 = <u>1.28</u>

j. Return on long-term capital, after tax:
    ($770 + $98(1-.4))/(($8,919 - $2,190) + ($7,401 - $1,900)/2) = <u>13.6%</u>

k. Operating margin: ($770 + $98 + $513)/$10,450 = <u>13.2%</u>

Requirement 2

Pension assets

	20x4	20x5	20x6
Opening assets	$ 0	$ 118,800	$ 245,600
Investment revenue (actual)	0	7,000	15,000
Contributions - CSC	45,000	46,000	41,000
- PSC	<u>73,800</u>	<u>73,800</u>	<u>73,800</u>
Closing assets	$ 118,800	$ 245,600	$375,400

Pension obligations

	20x4	20x5	20x6
Opening balance $73,800 x (P/A 6%,20)	$846,480	$942,269	$1,044,805
Interest (@6%)	50,789	56,536	62,688
CSC	<u>45,000</u>	<u>46,000</u>	<u>41,000</u>
Ending balance	$942,269	$1,044,805	$1,148,493

Pension expense

	20x4	20x5	20x6
Current service cost	$45,000	$46,000	$41,000
PSC amortization ($846,480/25)	33,859	33,859	33,859
Interest cost	50,789	56,536	62,688
Expected earnings	0	(7,128)[1]	(14,736)[1]
	<u>$129,648</u>	<u>$129,267</u>	<u>$122,811</u>

[1] $118,800 x .06; $245,600 x .06

Requirement 3

This is an error, fixed retroactively.

	20x4	20x5	20x6
Pension expense, as calculated	$129,648	$129,267	$122,811
Pension payments expensed -CSC	(45,000)	(46,000)	(41,000)
-PSC	(73,800)	(73,800)	(73,800)
Decrease to income	10,848	9,467	8,011
Tax (40%)	4,339	3,787	3,204
Net decrease to income	$6,509	$5,680	$4,807

Retained earnings ($6,509 + $5,680)..................…....	12,189	
Pension expense (20x6)................................…	8,011	
Future income tax ($4,339 + $3,787 + $3,204)……....	11,330	
Income tax expense (20x6).......................…..		3,204
Accrued pension liability.........................…..		28,326
($10,848 + $9,467 + $8,011)		

Davison Limited
Retained Earnings Statement
For the year ended 31 December 20x8

Opening retained earnings, as previously reported	$1,716
Less: error correction, net tax of $8	(12)
Opening retained earnings as restated	$1,704
Net income ($770 - $4.807)	765
Less: dividends	(25)
Increase in retained earnings	740
Closing retained earnings	$2,444

Requirement 4

The lease term includes the renewal term. (Bargain; fair value of $29,000 for three payments of $6,000.)
The lease is a capital lease; the lease term covers all the expected life of the present value of minimum lease payments:

1. ($41,400-$2,000) x (P/AD 10%, 3) (2.73554)	$107,780
2. ($6,000) (P/AD 10%, 3) (2.73554) (P/F 10%, 3) (.75131)	12,331
	$120,111

Leased asset...120,111
      Lease liability...............................   120,111

Lease liability..   39,400
Prepaid insurance..................................   2,000
      Operating expenses....................   41,400

No amortization or interest is recorded as the lease was entered into on 31 December 20x6.

SOLUTIONS TO CONCEPT REVIEW QUESTIONS

Page 1280

1. In analyzing financing statements, it is important understand the decision to be made, as different decisions will require different approaches and different sets of priorities with respect to financial information. For example, a trade creditor will be concerned primarily with short-run liquidity, while a prospective equity investor may be concerned with long-run profitability.

2. An analyst may be able to find out the accounting policies of a company in the notes to the financial statements. Implicit clues to the policies of a company may also be found in the individual statements. For example. a comparison of the cash flow statement to the income statement may reveal revenue and expense recognition strategies.

3. Analysts may seek to recast financial statements before performing an analysis in order to (insofar as a reasonable amount of information exists to allow) revise the financial statements to suit their needs. Examples: the income statement may be revised to remove non-recurring items; and necessary recurring investments may be reclassified from the investing section to the operating section of the cash flow statement.

4. *Vertical analysis* involves a cross-sectional analysis of ratios in which the components of one year's individual financial statements are computed as a percentage of a base amount. This involves comparing various components of one year's statements to a reference amount of the same period. For example, items of the income statement are computed as a percentage of revenue. *Horizontal analysis* refers to the longitudinal analysis of a single financial statement component compared with a base year's amount. Such analysis compares the changes in a specific financial statement account over several periods. For example, revenues over several years may be computed relative to a base year to measure relative growth or decline.

Page 1295

1. The essential relationship between the numerator and the denominator in any profitability ratio is that of measuring a return on invested capital. Thus, a profitability ratio will consist of a numerator from the income statement (measuring return) and a denominator from the balance sheet (measuring invested capital). It is critical that the numerator and the denominator be logically consistent.

2. While a high turnover ratio is often presumed to be better than a low ratio, because it implies that less investment is needed to generate sales, it may not necessarily be a positive indicator. Consider: a high turnover of inventory may be the result of carrying very low levels of inventory. The risk of low levels of inventory is that products may not be available when customers demand them so that potential sales are lost. Therefore, the low level of invested capital is achieved with the opportunity cost of lost sales.

3. Some analysts prefer to use debt service ratios as opposed to "times interest earned" because they relate to a company's ability to service its full debt load, including interest and principal. The times interest earned ratio implicitly assumes that the debt can be refinanced; therefore the principal repayment may be deferred and the company may only be required to service its interest obligation. However, the "times debt service earned" ratio will measure a company's ability to repay its principal borrowings as well.

4. A creditor or lender should be wary of basing lending decisions on consolidated financial statements, as such statements aggregate the financial results of all entities under common control (the economic entity). The lender's recourse lies only with the legal entity to which it has extended credit; consolidated statements show economic entity information and therefore do not indicate what assets may be available as security or collateral.